THE VINE

Green or blue, fruit of the wall, growing,
dividing heaven and earth.
Through the years
it becomes stronger, more green,
native to stone, avid body
of tangled tips that touch,
carrying the same juice, a brief plant
and also a forrest;
they are the years
that knot and break,
they are the days
of hue of fire,
they are the wind
that through autumn
touches the world,
the dark
roots of death
and the offspring
of shadow lifting itself in the vine.

(translated by margaret randall)

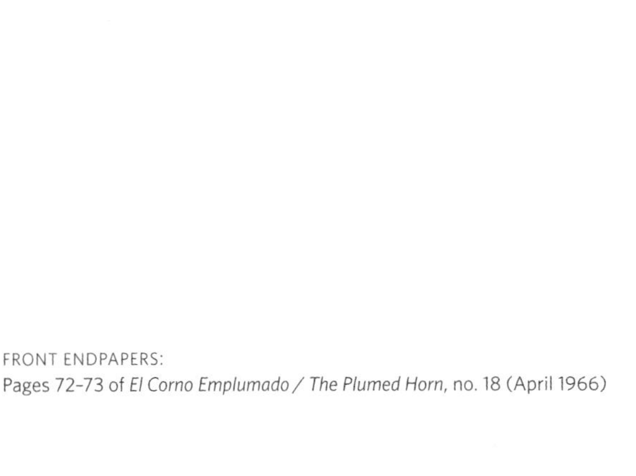

FRONT ENDPAPERS:
Pages 72–73 of *El Corno Emplumado / The Plumed Horn*, no. 18 (April 1966)

much wider than a line

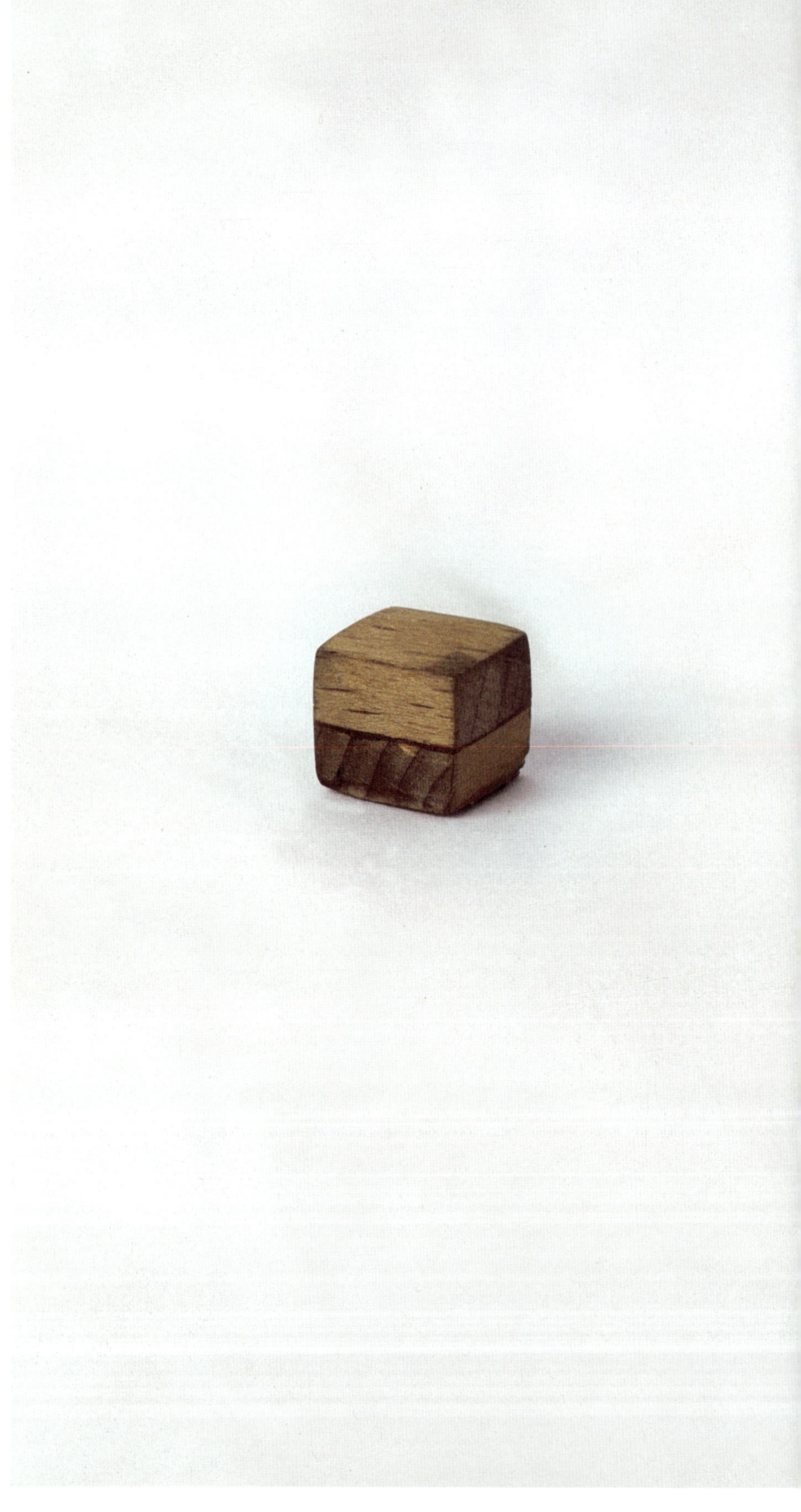

much wider than a line

CURATORIAL TEAM

Rocío Aranda-Alvarado
Kathleen Ash-Milby
Pip Day
Pablo León de la Barra
Kiki Mazzucchelli

SITElines TEAM

Irene Hofmann
Candice Hopkins
Brandee Caoba
Joanne Lefrak

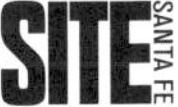

OPPOSITE:
Cildo Meireles, *The Southern Cross*, 1969–70

FOLLOWING SPREAD:
David Lamelas, *The Desert People*, 1974

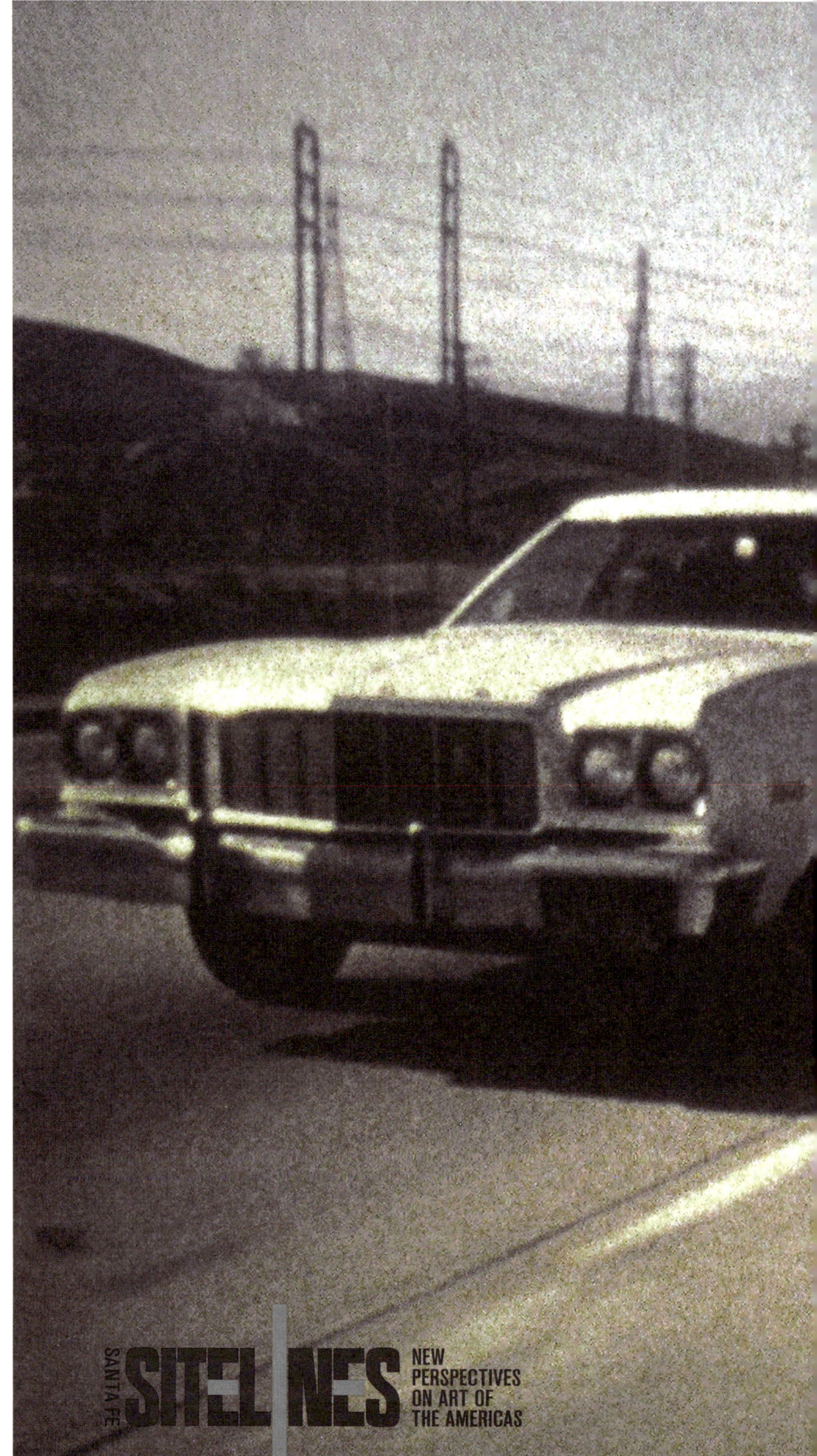

SANTA FE SITELINES
NEW PERSPECTIVES ON ART OF THE AMERICAS

This catalogue accompanies the exhibition

much wider than a line

SITE Santa Fe, July 16, 2016 – January 8, 2017

Significant support provided by

The Andy Warhol Foundation for the Visual Arts

Canada Council for the Arts | Conseil des arts du Canada

CELEBRATING 50 YEARS

National Endowment for the Arts

Participants in the Exhibition

Xenobia Bailey | USA

Francisca Benitez | CHL | USA

Lina Bo Bardi | IT | BRA

Anna Boghiguian | EGY | CAN

Margarita Cabrera | MEX | USA

Mariana Castillo Deball | MEX

Raven Chacon | USA

Benvenuto Chavajay | GTM

William Cordova | PER | USA

Jonathas de Andrade | BRA

Lewis deSoto | USA

Aaron Dysart | USA

Carla Fernández | MEX

Miguel Gandert | USA

Jeffrey Gibson | USA

Jorge González | PRI

Pablo Helguera | MEX | USA

Maria Hupfield | CAN | USA

Graciela Iturbide | MEX

Sonya Kelliher-Combs | USA

Zacharias Kunuk | CAN

David Lamelas | ARG | USA

Cildo Meireles | BRA

Marta Minujín | ARG

Paulo Nazareth | BRA

Margaret Randall | USA

Abel Rodríguez | COL

Rometti Costales | FRA | BLR | MEX

Conrad Skinner | USA

Tanya Tagaq | CAN

Javier Téllez | VEN | USA

Juana Valdes | CUB | USA

Pierre Verger | FRA | BRA

Erika Verzutti | BRA

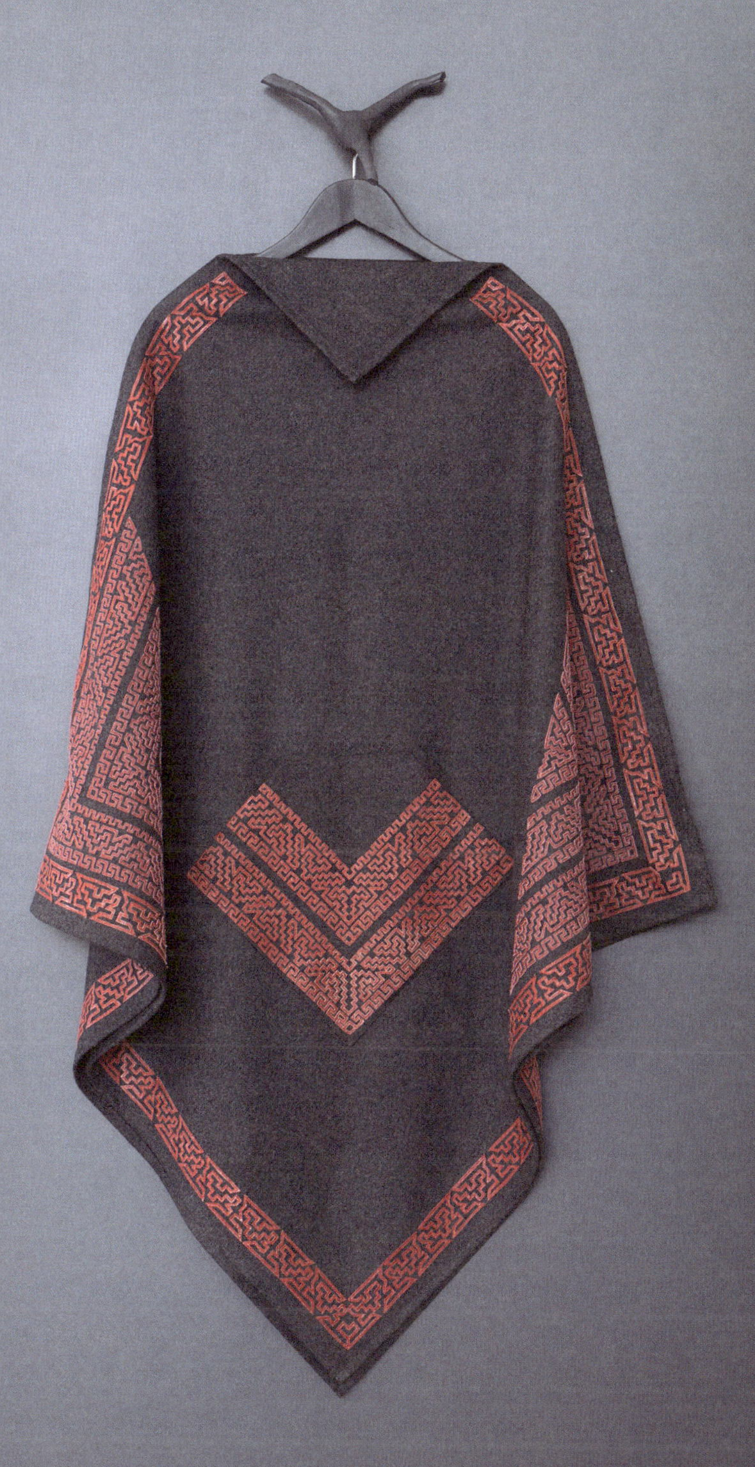

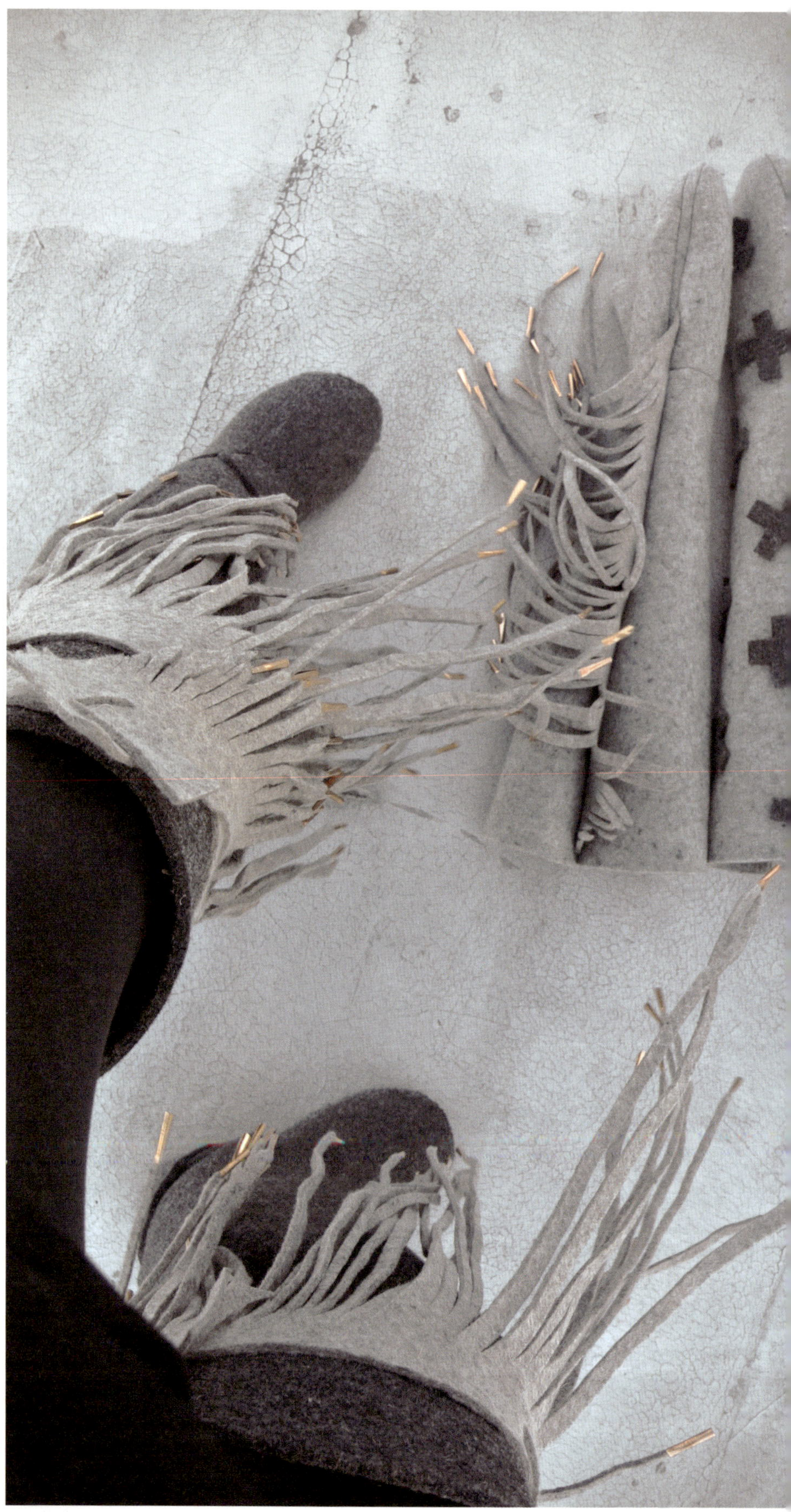

Contents

OPPOSITE:
Detail of performance, Maria Hupfield, *It Is Never Just about Sustenance or Pleasure*, 2016

PREVIOUS SPREAD:
Carla Fernández, *Charro Leather Fretwork Poncho*, 2016

The Ties That Bind Us

Irene Hofmann and Candice Hopkins

AN AMERICAS BIENNIAL AT SITE

At the forefront of the contemporary art scene for over twenty years, SITE Santa Fe opened in 1995 with what was then the only international contemporary art biennial in the United States. Over the intervening years, while the number of biennial exhibitions worldwide grew exponentially, the format of biennials, the lists of curators invited to organize them, and the rosters of exhibiting artists remained remarkably narrow. Recognizing these limitations, in the summer of 2011 we suspended our presentation for a cycle and announced that we were exploring a new identity for our signature show. In the process of revisiting our history, we challenged all previous assumptions and expectations, and what emerged was a groundbreaking new biennial model. Launched in 2014 and renamed SITElines: New Perspectives on Art of the Americas, the series has a new focus, curatorial approach, and set of principles to guide our work. Reimagining and transforming the international biennial template, SITE Santa Fe has again taken a leadership position and reaffirmed SITE's place at the vanguard of contemporary art.

In developing SITElines, our objectives were threefold: to establish a collaborative and multivocal approach to curating; to encourage continuity from one biennial exhibition to the next; and to create an infrastructure that would allow artists to spend more time on research and production than the sped-up time frame biennials normally entail. The expanded time frame also opened up the opportunity for artists to embed themselves within the context of New Mexico and create works beyond those destined for the biennial exhibition.

The most demonstrable and visible change in SITElines: New Perspectives on Art of the Americas is the shift in focus to the Western Hemisphere. The biennial now looks to geography as a structural framework for exploration, finding inspiration in the vast territory of the Americas, the region of New Mexico, and the city of Santa Fe and its surroundings. The region is a rich microcosm of the Americas: before statehood, New Mexico was first a Native-American land and then, successively, a Spanish kingdom, a Mexican province, and an American territory. With SITElines, we link this fertile ground to the rest of the Western Hemisphere, shifting from an east-west axis to one that runs south-north. Rejecting the notion of homogeneity in the Americas, we recuperate multiple histories and cosmologies, looking to artists to help us reveal and understand points of view that have often been sidelined in the international contemporary art world.

The 2014 *Unsettled Landscapes*, our first SITElines exhibition, took us boldly into uncharted terrain. The exhibition was curated by a team composed of two guest curators, Candice Hopkins and Lucía Sanromán, and two SITE Santa Fe curators, Janet Dees and Irene Hofmann. Adding to the dialogue was a council of five curatorial advisors whose fields of expertise covered Canada, the Caribbean, Central America, and South America. For the first time, SITE's biennial was organized collaboratively to invite multiple and varying voices into our curatorial discussions.

With the vast potential of the Americas before us as a source of inspiration and provocation, our team decided to begin with an investigation of the land—a subject that is elemental, universal, and intensely present to us in the American Southwest. The land established a context for concerns shared throughout the Americas and provided a literal grounding for future SITElines exhibitions. Through the themes of landscape, territory, and trade, *Unsettled Landscapes* probed the interconnections between representations *of* the land, movement *across* the land, and resources derived *from* the land. Using this lens, the exhibition revealed the social urgencies, political conditions, and historical narratives that informed the work of forty-five contemporary artists from fourteen countries across the Americas; our research took us from Nunavut to Tierra del Fuego. *Unsettled Landscapes* posited the land as a charged space, far from neutral or stable. The exhibition disputed the dominance of the visual conventions of European landscape traditions, made room for lesser-known narratives and readings of the land, and sought to destabilize Western notions of land ownership, use, and commodification through the introduction of Indigenous and decolonial understandings of land and territory.

In the process of organizing *Unsettled Landscapes*, we developed and tested a number of the structural elements of our new SITElines biennial. Supported by the diversity of voices at our curatorial table and in our exhibition spaces, we challenged ourselves and our audience to confront the biases and historical amnesia exacted by colonialism and interventionism. We developed new competencies and strategies for collaborative work and expanded our curatorial conversations to include input from artists and educators.

Strengthening our institutional infrastructure to support greater research and production time for artists and curators became an important priority in our work. Frustrated by the all-too-common phenomenon of the biennial artist who "parachutes" into a community with minimal involvement in context and place, we decided to create a new way of supporting artists who are interested in producing site-responsive works. This resulted in the formation of SITE Center, a research and programming hub of SITE Santa Fe's Education Department that works with our SITElines team in the production of community-based and site-responsive projects. Through long-term residencies, artists are provided with the necessary facilities and research support—along with the possibility of open-ended timelines for production—to create works that connect to place in ways that are informed, meaningful, and satisfying. During the development of *Unsettled Landscapes*, Pablo Helguera became our first SITE Center artist, and in that capacity has devoted the past four years to a series of research-based projects. In workshops and performances during the first phase of his residency, an interactive installation in *Unsettled Landscapes*, and a new work planned for the current SITElines exhibition, *much wider than a line*, Helguera has thoughtfully examined New Mexico's early history and intimately engaged with its contemporary community.

MUCH WIDER THAN A LINE

Not long after *Unsettled Landscapes* opened to the public, work on SITElines.2016 began. A new curatorial team was formed, each of its five members bringing an accomplished career, expertise in a particular region in the Americas, and a willingness to embrace the unpredictable nature of a collaborative process. Our team included Rocío Aranda-Alvarado, Kathleen Ash-Milby, Pip Day, Pablo León de la Barra, and Kiki Mazzucchelli.

The work of our SITElines.2016 team resulted in an exhibition that tacks away from images and histories of landscape to a more universal exploration of the interconnectedness of the Americas. The curators identified such essential shared experiences as the recognition of colonial legacies, the expression of the vernacular, the influence of Indigenous understandings, and the importance of our relationship to the land. *much wider than a line* takes its title from Leanne Simpson's *Dancing on Our Turtle's Back*, a book about the lifeways of the Nishnaabeg people.[1] In her accounts of non-colonial conceptions of nationhood and sovereignty, Simpson points to the joint caretaking required of different nations within their overlapping territorial boundaries. The relationships that emerge are indeed, like the borders themselves, much wider than a line.

Three potent threads run through *much wider than a line*: vernacular strategies, Indigenous understandings, and shared territories. Rather than firm categories into which we divide artists and artworks, these themes serve as points of connection. The vernacular implies the mobilization of local knowledge and the employment of expert manual technique, whether in design, architecture, or textiles. Stools with woven seats by Jorge González, for example, are distributed throughout the exhibition space, serving as welcome rest points while honoring the beauty of fine craft. These handmade objects short-circuit the craving of our increasingly consumptive society for mass-produced items that are cheap and disposable. They also highlight sustainable practices that have endured despite the transformation of goods that has taken place under capitalism. Carla Fernández uses the tradition of weaving to produce clothes—capes and robes—that incorporate Indigenous designs. The designs do not simply provide visual pleasure but demonstrate Indigenous cosmologies. They become a wearable display of Indigenous belief systems in a region known for this practice: in the nineteenth century, Navajo robes became the "Navajo rugs" that served, and still serve, trade and tourism markets. Local practices also inform the work of architect Lina Bo Bardi, whose interest in vernacular buildings and furnishings diverged from the concerns of her contemporaries in Brazil. Her solution for seating comprises four sticks bound together to form a simple and practical chair—a design solution for an everyday need. Responding to the vernacular more indirectly, William Cordova's installation is inspired by the so-called Pottery House in Santa Fe, built in 1984 from Frank Lloyd Wright's sketches and plans. Essentially a pottery vessel imagined at a grand scale, the adobe house reflects Wright's interest in both the ceramics and earth-building techniques of the Southwest.[2]

As its title implies, *much wider than a line* is informed by Indigenous understandings and decolonial practices, a theme that emerged with the first edition of SITElines. The 2001 feature-length film *Atanarjuat: The Fast Runner*, directed by Zacharias Kunuk, brings to life an ancient Inuit story of love and betrayal. The film, like many from Isuma Productions, emphasizes action over dialogue; for the Inuit, the demonstration of action is a way of teaching upcoming generations, whether it be how to properly hook up dogs to a *qamutik* (sled), hunt a seal, or build a snow house. (Inuit viewers' critique of television from "the south" is that "no one ever does anything; they only talk.") As a vehicle for transmitting traditions, the moving image acknowledges the malleability of customary practices and the significance of storytelling. Taking another approach, Abel Rodríguez disseminates knowledge of his home territory by annotating detailed drawings of the Amazon rainforest with the Indigenous names of the flora, their uses and medicinal properties, and their seasonal growth patterns. For Rodríguez, who was evicted from his homeland by an armed militia, drawing is a way to share this specialized information with similarly displaced compatriots. He does not consider himself an artist, concerned with aesthetics, but a recorder and communicator of knowledge.

In *Dancing on Our Turtle's Back*, Simpson introduces "communities of co-resistance," an idea whose implementation is essential to decolonialist efforts. It is not enough for Indigenous peoples to resist in isolation; they must shape change in solidarity with allies. The conjoined future of shared territories is the third thread that ties together *much wider than a line*. This aspect expands the dialogue to include all of us. By looking to other regions within the shared territory, artists can respond critically to questions of race and identity. Jonathas de Andrade adapts a 1952 UNESCO study titled *Race and Class in Rural Brazil* in a new version designed for Santa Fe and New York City. In conversations with the artist, subjects reveal the ways in which race is a social construct, one that is manifest throughout the Americas despite linguistic, regional, and social differences. Miguel Gandert too has pursued a cross-border study, photographing Native-American and Hispanic rituals and ceremonies in both the American Southwest and Mexico. His visual documentation reveals the generative sharing that has taken place in the border region's belief systems and aesthetics, resulting in hybrid ceremonies that become new traditions.

In shaping *much wider than a line*, our curatorial team pursued extensive research in Santa Fe and its surroundings, meeting with artists, archivists, and historians in order to gain a greater understanding of the rich regional context and cultural assets. Two discoveries that were particularly generative and inspirational for our team now serve as physical and metaphorical entry points to the exhibition: the Paolo Soleri Amphitheater in Santa Fe and the bilingual journal *El Corno Emplumado / The Plumed Horn*, both founded during the 1960s.

The Paolo Soleri Amphitheater was commissioned from the eponymous Italian architect by Lloyd Kiva New, then arts director of the newly founded Institute of American Indian Arts. The free-form concrete structure is located on the campus of the Santa Fe Indian School, which was established in 1890 to assimilate Native-American children from tribes throughout the southwestern United States. In conceiving the biomorphic amphitheater, Soleri drew on principles of Native-American design. Completed in 1970, it housed the Institute's groundbreaking curriculum in contemporary American Indian drama and was host to extraordinary performances of Indian theater. Today, the amphitheater is an empty, derelict, and contested site that is under threat of demolition despite its significance to the architecture of the Southwest: its maintenance puts a prohibitive burden on the Santa Fe Indian School on whose grounds it stands. This architectural achievement, then, serves as both a historically potent forum for an exploration of collaborative cross-cultural processes and a stand-in for the geopolitical tensions that presently exist in the region and throughout the Americas.

During the same decade that the Paolo Soleri Amphitheater was built in Santa Fe, a small poetry quarterly issued in Mexico City gave voice to progressive poets and writers from all over the Americas. *El Corno Emplumado / The Plumed Horn*, co-founded and edited by Margaret Randall and Sergio Mondragón, was on the cutting edge of independent publishing. Distributed throughout the Americas, *El Corno* established an international network of like-minded writers and artists who found a supportive venue for their language of rebellion. With striking and provocative cover art and topical writings, the thirty-one issues of *El Corno* powerfully reflect the energy of a tumultuous era. Today, Randall is a resident of New Mexico, where—as poet, writer, and activist as well as *El Corno* co-publisher—she was an early inspiration for our curatorial team. Meeting Randall in Albuquerque in the summer of 2015 set the tone for a show that seeks to capture her dynamism, fearlessness, and vision of connectivity in the Americas.

Where SITElines.2014 concentrated on instances of radical difference—the Americas as a nonhomogeneous space—the organizers of the second edition are motivated by moments of connectivity: the cross-cultural exchanges that have led to the development of visionary artworks, objects, and buildings; a community of poets, artists, and writers; and innovations in ceremonies and rituals that remain a vital part of the fabric of contemporary life. This intricate connectivity represents the web of ties that bind us, however diverse our origins and outlook. It is our willingness to learn from one another that will inevitably teach us more about ourselves.

Los lazos que nos unen

Irene Hofmann y Candice Hopkins

UNA BIENAL DE LAS AMÉRICAS EN SITE

A la vanguardia de la escena del arte contemporáneo desde hace más de veinte años, SITE Santa Fe abrió en 1995 con lo que era en ese entonces la única bienal internacional de arte contemporáneo en los Estados Unidos. A lo largo de años intermedios, mientras que el número de exposiciones bienales a nivel mundial creció de manera exponencial, el formato de bienales, las listas de curadores y curadoras invitadas a organizarlas y los listados de artistas expositores permanecieron remarcablemente limitados. Reconociendo estas limitaciones, en el verano de 2011 suspendimos nuestra presentación por una temporada y anunciamos que estábamos explorando una nueva identidad para nuestra exposición central. En el proceso de revisar nuestra historia, desafiamos a todas las presunciones y expectativas anteriores, y lo que surgió fue un nuevo e innovador modelo para bienales. Lanzada en 2014 y renombrada SITElines: New Perspectives on Art of the Americas, la serie tiene un nuevo enfoque, abordaje curatorial, y conjunto de principios para guiar nuestro trabajo. Re-imaginando y transformando el esquema internacional para bienales, SITE Santa Fe ha tomado otra vez una posición de liderazgo y ha reafirmado el lugar de SITE en la vanguardia del arte contemporáneo.

Al desarrollar SITElines, nuestros objetivos eran tres: establecer un abordaje colaborativo y multivocal para la curaduría; alentar la continuidad de una exposición bienal a la siguiente; y crear una infraestructura que permitiera a las y los artistas pasar más tiempo en investigación y producción en lugar del plazo de tiempo acelerado que las bienales generalmente permiten. El plazo extendido de tiempo también abrió la oportunidad para que las y los artistas se insertaran dentro del contexto de Nuevo México y crearan obras más allá que aquellas destinadas para la exposición bienal.

El cambio más demostrable y visible en SITElines: New Perspectives on Art of the Americas es el giro en el enfoque al hemisferio occidental. La bienal ahora mira hacia la geografía como un marco estructural para la exploración, encontrando inspiración en el vasto territorio de las Américas, la región de Nuevo México y la ciudad de Santa Fe y sus alrededores. La región es un rico microcosmos de las Américas: antes de convertirse en estado, Nuevo México fue primero una tierra nativo americana, y después, sucesivamente, un reino español, una provincia mexicana, y un territorio norteamericano. Con SITElines, vinculamos este terreno fértil al resto del hemisferio occidental, cambiando de un eje este-oeste a uno que corre de sur a norte. Al rechazar la noción de la homogeneidad en las Américas, recuperamos múltiples historias y cosmologías, buscando que las y los artistas nos ayuden a revelar y entender puntos de vista que a menudo han sido marginados en el mundo del arte contemporáneo internacional.

La exposición *Unsettled Landscapes* (*Paisajes inquietos*) en 2014, la primera de SITElines, nos llevó intrépidamente a un territorio inexplorado. La exposición fue curada por un equipo compuesto de dos curadoras invitadas, Lucía Sanromán y Candice Hopkins, y dos curadoras de SITE Santa Fe, Irene Hofmann y Janet Dees. Se añadió al diálogo un consejo de cinco asesores y asesoras curatoriales cuyas áreas de especialización cubrían Canadá, el Caribe, Centroamérica, y Sudamérica. Por primera vez, la bienal de SITE fue organizada colaborativamente para invitar a voces múltiples y variadas a las conversaciones curatoriales.

Con el vasto potencial de las Américas antes nosotras como fuente de inspiración y provocación, nuestro equipo decidió empezar con una investigación de la tierra—un tema que es elemental, universal y está intensamente presente para todas las personas en el suroeste norteamericano. La tierra (*land*) estableció un contexto para preocupaciones compartidas en todas las Américas y proporcionó una base literal para futuras exposiciones de SITElines. Mediante los temas de paisaje, territorio y comercio, *Unsettled Landscapes* exploró las interconexiones entre las representaciones *de* la tierra, el movimiento *a través de* la tierra, y recursos derivados *de* la tierra. Usando esta lente, la exposición reveló las urgencias sociales, condiciones políticas y narrativas históricas que informaron el trabajo de cuarenta y cinco artistas contemporáneos de catorce países a través de las Américas: nuestra investigación nos llevó de Nunavut a Tierra del Fuego. *Unsettled Landscapes* postuló a la tierra como un espacio cargado, lejos de ser neutral o estable. La exposición cuestionó la dominancia de las convenciones visuales de tradiciones europeas del paisaje, hizo espacio para narrativas y análisis de la tierra menos conocidas, y buscó desestabilizar las nociones occidentales de la propiedad, uso y mercantilización de la tierra mediante la introducción de concepciones indígenas y decoloniales de la tierra y el territorio.

En el proceso de la curaduría de *Unsettled Landscapes*, desarrollamos y probamos varios de los elementos estructurales de nuestra nueva bienal SITElines. Con el apoyo de una diversidad de voces en nuestra mesa curatorial y en nuestros espacios de exposición, nos desafiamos a nosotras mismas y a nuestro público para enfrentar los prejuicios y la amnesia histórica impuestos por el colonialismo y el intervencionismo. Desarrollamos nuevas capacidades y estrategias para el trabajo colaborativo y expandimos nuestras conversaciones curatoriales para incluir las aportaciones de artistas y educadores.

El fortalecer nuestra infraestructura institucional para apoyar más investigación y tiempo de producción para las y los artistas y curadores, se volvió una prioridad importante en nuestro trabajo. Frustradas por el muy común fenómeno del artista bienal que entra como "paracaidista" a una comunidad con un mínimo involucramiento en cuanto al contexto y lugar, decidimos crear una nueva manera de apoyar a artistas quienes tenían interés en producir obras que respondían directamente al entorno. Esto resultó en la creación del SITE Center, un núcleo de investigación y programación del Departamento de Educación de SITE Santa Fe que trabaja con nuestro equipo SITElines en la producción de proyectos comunitarios y que responden al entorno. Mediante residencias de largo plazo, se proporciona a las y los artistas con las facilidades necesarias y apoyo para la investigación—junto con la posibilidad de plazos abiertos para producción—para crear obras que conecten al lugar de manera informada, significativa y satisfactoria. Durante el desarrollo de *Unsettled Landscapes*, Pablo Helguera se convirtió en el primer artista del SITE Center, y en esa capacidad ha devotado los últimos cuatro años a una serie de proyectos basados en la investigación. En talleres y perfomances durante la primera fase de su residencia, una instalación interactiva en *Unsettled Landscapes*, y una nueva obra planeada para la exposición actual *much wider than a line* (*mucho más ancho que una línea*), Helguera ha examinado cuidadosamente la historia temprana de Nuevo México y se ha involucrado íntimamente con su comunidad contemporánea.

MUCH WIDER THAN A LINE

Poco después de que *Unsettled Landscapes* abriera al público, empezó el trabajo para SITElines.2016. Se formó un nuevo equipo curatorial, cada uno de sus cinco miembros contando con destacadas trayectorias, experiencia en una región particular de las Américas, y la voluntad para adherirse a la impredecible naturaleza de un proceso colaborativo. Nuestro equipo incluyó a Rocío Aranda-Alvarado, Kathleen Ash-Milby, Pip Day, Pablo León de la Barra, y Kiki Mazzucchelli.

El trabajo de nuestro equipo SITElines.2016 resultó en una exposición que se aleja de imágenes e historias del paisaje hacia una exploración más universal de la interconexión de las Américas. Las y los curadores identificaron aquellas esenciales experiencias compartidas como el reconocimiento de legados coloniales, la expresión vernácula, la influencia de concepciones indígenas, y la importancia de nuestra relación con la tierra. *much wider than a line* debe su título a *Dancing on Our Turtle's Back* (*Bailando sobre la espalda de nuestra tortuga*) de Leanne Simpson, libro que trata sobre el estilo de vida del pueblo Nishnaabeg.[3] En sus relatos de concepciones no coloniales de nación y soberanía, Simpson apunta hacia el cuidado colectivo requerido de diferentes naciones dentro de sus límites territoriales superpuestos. Las relaciones que surgen son, efectivamente, como las mismas fronteras, mucho más anchas que una línea.

Tres potentes hebras corren a través de *much wider than a line*: estrategias vernáculas, concepciones indígenas, y territorios compartidos. Más que categorías fijas en las cuales dividimos a las y los artistas y sus obras, estos temas sirven como puntos de conexión. Lo vernáculo implica la movilización del conocimiento local y el uso de técnica manual experta, ya sea en diseño, arquitectura o textiles. Por ejemplo, se distribuyen en todo el espacio de la exposición, bancos con asientos tejidos por Jorge González, los cuales sirven como bienvenidos lugares de descanso mientras se honra la belleza de la tradición artesanal. Estos objetos hechos a mano hacen un cortocircuito con la apetencia de nuestra sociedad cada vez más consumista por objetos producidos en masa que son baratos y desechables. También resaltan las prácticas sustentables que han perdurado a pesar de la transformación de bienes que se ha producido bajo el capitalismo. Carla Fernández usa la tradición del tejido para producir ropa—capas y túnicas—que incorporan diseños indígenas. Los diseños no proporcionan simplemente placer visual, sino que demuestran cosmologías indígenas. Se vuelven una exhibición portátil de los sistemas de creencias indígenas en una región conocida por esta práctica: en el siglo XIX, las túnicas Navajo se volvieron "alfombras Navajo" que servían, y aún sirven, a mercados de comercio y de turismo. Las prácticas locales también informan el trabajo de la arquitecta Lina Bo Bardi, cuyo interés en edificios y muebles vernáculos diverge de los intereses de sus contemporáneos en Brasil. Su solución para los asientos consiste en cuatro palos amarrados para formar una simple y practica silla—una solución de diseño para un uso diario. Respondiendo a lo vernáculo de modo más indirecto, la instalación de William Cordova está inspirada en la llamada "Pottery House" en Santa Fe, la cual fue construida en 1984 usando esbozos y planos de Frank Lloyd Wright. Básicamente una vasija de cerámica imaginada a gran escala, la casa de adobe refleja el interés de Wright tanto en la cerámica como en las técnicas de construcción en tierra del Suroeste.[4]

Como el título lo indica, *much wider than a line* está informada por concepciones indígenas y prácticas decoloniales, un tema que surgió con la primera versión de SITElines. El largometraje de 2001, *Atanarjuat: The Fast Runner* (*Atanarjuat. El corredor veloz*), dirigido por Zacharias Kunuk, da vida a una antigua historia inuit de amor y traición. La película, como muchas otras de Isuma Productions, enfatiza la acción por encima del diálogo; para las y los inuit, la demostración de acción es una manera de educar a nuevas generaciones, ya sea sobre cómo enganchar a perros a un *qamutik* (trineo), cazar una foca, o construir una casa de nieve. (La crítica de las y los espectadores inuit respecto a la televisión del "sur" es que "nadie hace nada, sólo hablan"). Como un vehículo para transmitir tradiciones, la imagen en movimiento reconoce la maleabilidad de las prácticas habituales y la importancia de la narración. Tomando otro enfoque, Abel Rodríguez divulga conocimiento de su territorio de origen al inscribir detallados dibujos de la selva del Amazonas con los nombres indígenas de la flora, sus usos y propiedades medicinales, y sus patrones de crecimiento de temporada.

Para Rodriguez, quien fue desalojado de su tierra natal por una milicia armada, dibujar es una forma de compartir esta información especializada con compatriotas desplazados de semejante manera. Él no se considera un artista, preocupado por la estética, sino un registrador y comunicador de conocimiento.

En *Dancing on Our Turtle's Back*, Simpson presenta "comunidades de co-resistencia", una idea cuya implementación es esencial para los esfuerzos decolonizadores. No es suficiente que los pueblos indígenas resistan en aislamiento; deben dar forma al cambio en solidaridad con aliados y aliadas. El futuro que va de la mano de territorios compartidos es la tercera hebra que enlaza a *much wider than a line*. Este aspecto expande el diálogo para incluirnos a todas y todos nosotros. Al ver hacia otras regiones dentro del territorio compartido, las y los artistas pueden responder de manera crítica a cuestiones de raza e identidad. Jonathas de Andrade adapta un estudio de la UNESCO de 1952 llamado *Race and Class in Rural Brazil (Raza y clase en el Brasil rural)* en su nueva versión diseñada para Santa Fe y la ciudad de Nueva York. En conversaciones con el artista, los sujetos revelan las maneras en que la raza es una construcción social, una que está presente a lo largo de las Américas a pesar de diferencias lingüísticas, regionales y sociales. Miguel Gandert también ha perseguido un estudio transfronterizo, fotografiando rituales nativo americanos e hispanos y ceremonias tanto en el suroeste norteamericano como en México. Su documentación visual revela el intercambio generativo que se ha llevado a cabo en el sistema de creencias y estética en la región de la frontera, resultando en ceremonias híbridas que se convierten en nuevas tradiciones.

Al darle forma a *much wider than a line*, nuestro equipo curatorial hizo investigación extensiva en Santa Fe y sus alrededores, reuniéndose con artistas, archivistas e historiadores con el fin de lograr una mayor comprensión del rico contexto regional y patrimonio cultural. Dos descubrimientos que fueron particularmente generativos e inspiradores para nuestro equipo sirven ahora como puntos de partida físico y metafísico para la exposición: el anfiteatro Paolo Soleri en Santa Fe y la revista literaria bilingüe *El Corno Emplumado / The Plumed Horn*, ambos fundados durante los años sesenta.

El Paolo Soleri Amphitheater fue comisionado del epónimo arquitecto italiano por Lloyd Kiva New, entonces director artístico del recién fundado Institute of American Indian Arts. La estructura, improvisada de concreto, está localizada en el campus de la Santa Fe Indian School (Escuela Indígena de Santa Fe), la cual fue establecida en 1890 para asimilar a niños y niñas nativo americanas de tribus en todo el suroeste de los Estados Unidos. Al concebir el anfiteatro biomorfico, Soleri se basó en principios de diseño nativo americano. Terminado en 1970, el anfiteatro alojó el innovador currículo en drama Indígena Americano contemporánea del Instituto y recibió perfomances extraordinarios de teatro indígena. El día de hoy, el anfiteatro es un sitio vacío, abandonado y controvertido que está bajo amenaza de demolición a pesar de su significado para la arquitectura del suroeste: su mantenimiento pone una carga prohibitiva a la Santa Fe Indian School en cuyos terrenos están ubicados. Este logro arquitectónico, entonces, sirve tanto como un potente foro histórico para una exploración de procesos colaborativos transculturales que como un suplente para las tensiones geopolíticas que existen actualmente en la región y a través de las Américas.

Durante la misma década en que se construyó el Paolo Soleri Amphitheater en Santa Fe, una pequeña publicación trimestral de poesía realizada en la Ciudad de México dio voz a poetas y escritores progresistas de todas las Américas. *El Corno Emplumado / The Plumed Horn*, co-fundada por Margaret Randall y Sergio Mondragón, estaba en la vanguardia de publicaciones independientes. Distribuida a lo largo de las Américas, *El Corno* estableció una red internacional de escritores y artistas afines, quienes encontraron un espacio de apoyo para su lenguaje de rebelión. Con sorprendente y provocativa arte de portada y escritos temáticos, los treinta y un números de *El Corno* reflejan de manera poderosa la energía de una época tumultuosa. El día de hoy, Randall es residente de Nuevo México, donde—como poeta, escritora y activista, así como coeditora de *El Corno*—fue una inspiración temprana para nuestro equipo curatorial. Conocer a Randall en Albuquerque en el verano de 2015 estableció el tono para una exposición que busca capturar su dinamismo, audacia, y visión de conectividad en las Américas.

Mientras que SITElines.2014 se concentró en instancias de diferencia radical—las Américas como un espacio no homogéneo—las y los organizadores de la segunda versión, están motivados y motivadas por momentos de conectividad: los intercambios transculturales que han llevado a un desarrollo de obras artísticas, objetos y edificios visionarios; una comunidad de poetas, artistas y escritores; e innovaciones en ceremonias y rituales que continúan siendo una parte vital del tejido de la vida contemporánea. Esta compleja conectividad representa la red de lazos que nos unen, sin importar lo diverso de nuestros orígenes y perspectivas. Es nuestra voluntad para aprender de las demás personas lo que de manera inevitable nos enseña más sobre nosotros mismos.

— traducido por Ana Paula Noguez Mercado

Les liens qui nous unissent

Irene Hofmann et Candice Hopkins

UNE BIENNALE DES AMÉRIQUES À SITE

Au premier plan de la scène artistique contemporaine depuis plus de vingt ans, SITE Santa Fe a ouvert en 1995 en lançant ce qui était à l'époque la seule biennale internationale d'art contemporain des États-Unis. Au cours des années suivantes, le nombre d'expositions biennales a eu beau s'accroître de façon exponentielle dans le monde entier, leur format, la liste des commissaires invités à les organiser, et l'éventail des artistes exposés sont demeurés étrangement étriqués. À l'été 2011, conscients de ces limitations, nous avons suspendu notre présentation le temps d'un cycle et annoncé notre volonté d'explorer une nouvelle identité pour notre exposition phare. Dans l'optique de revisiter notre histoire, nous nous sommes attachés à remettre en question tous les postulats et attentes préexistants, et il en a résulté un modèle de biennale complètement neuf et sans précédent. Lancée en 2014 et rebaptisée SITElines : New Perspectives on Art of the Americas, la série s'est dotée d'un nouvel axe, d'une nouvelle approche du commissariat, et d'un nouvel ensemble de principes directeurs. En réimaginant et en transformant le modèle international de la biennale, SITE Santa Fe a retrouvé une position de tête et réaffirmé sa place à l'avant-garde de l'art contemporain.

En développant SITElines, nous nous sommes donné un triple objectif : établir une approche collaborative et multivoque du commissariat ; encourager la continuité d'une biennale à l'autre ; et enfin créer une infrastructure autorisant les artistes à consacrer davantage de temps à la recherche et à la production que ce que permettent en général les calendriers frénétiques des biennales. Ce cadre temporel élargi a également offert aux artistes l'opportunité de s'immerger dans le contexte du Nouveau-Mexique et de créer des œuvres dont la destination dépasse le contexte strict de la biennale.

Le changement le plus évident de SITElines: New Perspectives on Art of the Americas est l'accent mis sur l'hémisphère ouest. La biennale prend désormais la géographie pour cadre structurel d'exploration et cherche son inspiration dans le vaste territoire des Amériques, la région du Nouveau-Mexique, et la ville de Santa Fe et ses environs. Cette région représente un formidable microcosme des Amériques : avant d'être un état, le Nouveau-Mexique a d'abord été une terre amérindienne, puis, successivement, un royaume espagnol, une province mexicaine, et un territoire américain. À travers SITElines, nous relions ce terreau fertile à l'ensemble de l'hémisphère ouest : nous sommes passés d'un axe est-ouest à un axe sud-nord. En rejetant l'idée d'une homogénéité des Amériques, il s'agit de nous ressaisir d'une multiplicité d'histoires et de cosmologies, en comptant sur les artistes pour nous aider à révéler et à comprendre des points de vue souvent négligés dans le monde de l'art contemporain au niveau international.

En 2014, *Unsettled Landscapes* (*Paysages incertains*), la première exposition de SITElines, nous a hardiment lancés sur un terrain inexploré. Le commissariat de l'exposition était assuré par une équipe constituée de deux commissaires invitées, Lucía Sanromán et Candice Hopkins, et de deux commissaires de SITE Santa Fe, Irene Hofmann et Janet Dees. Pour enrichir le dialogue, venait s'y ajouter un comité de cinq conseillers, avec pour domaines d'expertise respectifs le Canada, les Caraïbes, l'Amérique Centrale et l'Amérique du Sud. Pour la première fois, la biennale de SITE était organisée de manière collaborative afin d'inviter des voix multiples et variées dans nos discussions commissariales.

Avec pour source d'inspiration et élément catalyseur l'immense potentiel des Amériques, notre équipe a résolu de commencer par une analyse de la question de la terre (*land*) – un thème fondamental, universel et intensément présent pour nous, dans le sud-ouest des États-Unis. La terre posait un contexte où inscrire des préoccupations partagées dans toutes les Amériques et fournissait une base concrète pour les futures expositions de SITElines. À travers les thèmes du paysage, du territoire, et du commerce, *Unsettled Landscapes* interrogeait les interconnexions entre les représentations *de* la terre, le déplacement *sur* la terre, et les ressources puisées *dans* la terre. Par ce biais, l'exposition révélait les urgences sociales, les conditions politiques, et les récits historiques sous-tendant le travail de quarante-cinq artistes contemporains venus de quatorze pays des quatre coins des Amériques : notre recherche nous a amenés du Nunavut à la Terre de Feu. *Unsettled Landscapes* postulait que, loin d'être neutre ou stable, la terre que l'on occupe est un espace chargé. L'exposition s'élevait contre la domination des conventions visuelles venues des traditions européennes du paysage ; elle s'ouvrait à des récits et des lectures de la terre moins connus ; et elle visait à déstabiliser les concepts occidentaux de possession, d'utilisation et de marchandisation de la terre à travers l'introduction de visions autochtones et décoloniales de la terre et du territoire.

En travaillant au commissariat de *Unsettled Landscapes*, nous avons déployé et testé un bon nombre des éléments structurels de notre nouvelle série biennale, SITElines. Encouragés par la diversité des voix autour de notre table de discussion et dans nos espaces d'exposition, nous nous sommes donnés à nous-mêmes, ainsi qu'au public, le défi de regarder en face les préjugés et l'amnésie historique imposés par le colonialisme et l'interventionnisme. Nous avons développé de nouvelles compétences et stratégies afin de favoriser le travail collaboratif et élargi nos discussions commissariales pour y inclure le point de vue des artistes et des éducateurs.

Renforcer notre infrastructure institutionnelle afin de promouvoir des temps de recherche et de production plus importants pour les artistes et les commissaires est devenu une priorité dans notre travail. Frustrés par le phénomène bien trop commun de l'artiste de biennale « parachuté » dans une communauté, qui ne s'inscrit qu'a minima dans le contexte et le lieu, nous avons décidé d'inventer une nouvelle manière de venir en aide aux artistes désireux de produire des œuvres en dialogue avec le site. Cette démarche a abouti à la création du SITE Center, un pôle de recherche et de programmation du Département d'Éducation de SITE Santa Fe qui travaille, aux côtés de notre équipe de SITElines, à la production de projets ancrés dans la communauté et en dialogue avec le site. Dans le cadre de résidences de longue durée, les artistes se voient fournir les équipements et l'aide à la recherche indispensables – ainsi que la possibilité d'une temporalité dégagée du diktat des échéances pour la production – afin de créer des œuvres qui entrent en lien avec le lieu de façon éclairée, significative et satisfaisante. Au cours de l'élaboration de *Unsettled Landscapes*, Pablo Helguera est devenu le premier artiste du SITE Center et, à ce titre, il a consacré les quatre dernières années à une série de projets axés sur la recherche. À travers des ateliers et performances durant la première phase de sa résidence, une installation interactive dans *Unsettled Landscapes*, et une nouvelle œuvre prévue pour l'exposition actuelle *much wider than a line* (*bien plus larges qu'une ligne*), Helguera a consciencieusement ausculté l'histoire des origines du Nouveau-Mexique et s'est engagé intimement auprès de sa population actuelle.

MUCH WIDER THAN A LINE

Peu après l'ouverture au public de *Unsettled Landscapes*, nous avons commencé à travailler sur SITElines.2016. Une nouvelle équipe commissariale a été formée : chacun de ses cinq membres, fort d'une carrière déjà bien remplie, apporte son expertise dans une région particulière des Amériques et sa volonté de jouer le jeu du processus collaboratif, avec sa nature imprévisible. Notre équipe comprend Rocío Aranda-Alvarado, Kathleen Ash-Milby, Pip Day, Pablo León de la Barra, et Kiki Mazzuchelli.

Le travail de l'équipe de SITElines.2016 a débouché ne exposition qui se détourne un peu des images et histoires du paysage pour se lancer dans une exploration plus universelle de l'interconnexion des Amériques. Les commissaires ont identifié des expériences partagées, aussi essentielles que la reconnaissance des héritages coloniaux, l'expression du vernaculaire, l'influence des conceptions autochtones, et l'importance de notre relation à la terre. *much wider than a line* emprunte son titre à *Dancing on Our Turtle's Back* (*En dansent sur le dos de notre tortue*)[5], de Leanne Simpson, un livre sur le mode de vie du peuple Nishnaabeg. Dans sa description des conceptions non coloniales des idées de nation et de souveraineté, Simpson met l'accent sur la collaboration indispensable de différentes nations à l'intérieur de limites territoriales qui se chevauchent. Les relations qui en résultent sont effectivement, de même que les frontières elles-mêmes, bien plus larges qu'une ligne.

Trois axes puissants traversent *much wider than a line* : les stratégies vernaculaires, les conceptions autochtones, et les territoires partagés. Plutôt que des catégories rigides visant à diviser les artistes et les œuvres, ces thèmes servent de points de jonction. Le vernaculaire implique la mobilisation des savoirs locaux et l'usage de techniques manuelles sophistiquées, que ce soit dans le domaine du design, de l'architecture, ou des textiles. Répartis dans tout l'espace d'exposition, les tabourets aux sièges tissés de Jorge González, par exemple, servent de haltes bienvenues pour le visiteur tout en faisant honneur à la beauté de leur artisanat. Ces objets faits main court-circuitent l'appétit insatiable de notre société toujours plus avide de consommation pour des objets fabriqués en série, bon marché et jetables. Ils mettent également en valeur des pratiques durables qui ont survécu malgré le mode de transformation des biens qui fait loi dans le système capitaliste. Carla Fernández utilise la tradition du tissage pour produire des vêtements - capes et tuniques - qui incorporent des motifs autochtones. Ces motifs, outre le plaisir visuel qu'ils procurent, montrent les cosmologies autochtones. Ils deviennent une représentation « portable » sur soi des systèmes de croyances autochtones, dans une région connue pour cette pratique : au dix-neuvième siècle, les tuniques Navajo sont devenues les « tapis Navajo » qui ont nourri, et nourrissent encore, le commerce et les marchés du tourisme. Les pratiques locales influencent également le travail de l'architecte Lina Bo Bardi, que son intérêt pour les bâtiments et le mobilier vernaculaires distingue de ses contemporains au Brésil et de leurs préoccupations. Pour s'asseoir, elle propose quatre bâtons attachés l'un à l'autre, qui forment une chaise simple et pratique - une solution *design* pour un usage quotidien. L'installation de William Cordova, qui répond de manière plus indirecte à la culture vernaculaire, s'inspire de la « Pottery House » de Santa Fe, construite en 1984 à partir des esquisses et plans de Frank Lloyd Wright. Semblable à une poterie conçue à grande échelle, la maison d'adobe reflète l'intérêt de Wright pour les techniques de céramique et d'architecture en terre du sud-ouest des États-Unis[6].

Comme l'implique son titre, *much wider than a line* est pétri par les conceptions autochtones et les pratiques décoloniales, un thème apparu dès la première édition de SITElines. Le long-métrage de 2001 *Atanarjuat : The Fast Runner* (*Atanarjuat. Le coureur rapide*), réalisé par Zacharias Kunuk, ressuscite une ancienne légende inuite d'amour et de trahison. Ce film, comme souvent chez Isuma Productions, privilégie l'action sur le dialogue ; pour les Inuits, la démonstration par l'action est une manière d'enseigner aux nouvelles générations, qu'il s'agisse de la bonne façon d'attacher des chiens à un *qamutik* (traîneau), de chasser le phoque, ou de construire un igloo. (La critique de la télévision « du sud » par des spectateurs inuits consiste à dire que « personne ne fait jamais rien; ils se contentent de parler. ») En tant que véhicule de transmission des traditions, l'image mouvante rend compte de la malléabilité des pratiques coutumières et du poids de la narration. Optant pour une autre approche, Abel Rodríguez propage le savoir de son territoire d'origine en annotant des dessins détaillés de la forêt amazonienne, y ajoutant les noms indigènes de la flore, l'usage des plantes et leurs propriétés médicinales, ainsi que leur cycle de développement saisonnier. Pour Rodríguez, qui a été expulsé de son territoire par une milice armée, le dessin est une manière de partager ces informations spécialisées avec des compatriotes déracinés comme lui. Il ne se considère pas comme un artiste, qui se soucie d'esthétique, mais comme un archiviste et un passeur de savoirs.

Dans *Dancing on Our Turtle's Back*, Simpson introduit les « communautés de corésistance », un concept dont l'application est indispensable aux efforts décolonialistes. Pour les peuples autochtones, il ne suffit pas de résister dans l'isolement ; ils doivent donner forme au changement en se solidarisant avec des alliés. Le futur conjoint des territoires partagés est le troisième axe qui donne son unité à *much wider than a line.* Il s'agit grâce à lui d'élargir le dialogue afin de nous inclure tous. En se tournant vers d'autres régions à l'intérieur du territoire partagé, les artistes peuvent répondre de façon critique aux questions de race et d'identité. Jonathas de Andrade adapte une étude de l'UNESCO datant de 1952 intitulée *Race and Class in Rural Brazil (Race et classe dans les régions rurales du Brésil)* pour en faire une nouvelle version conçue pour Santa Fe et New York. Lors de conversations avec l'artiste, des sujets révèlent à quel point la race est une construction sociale, qui se manifeste dans toutes les Amériques en dépit des différences linguistiques, régionales, et sociales. Miguel Gandert a lui aussi entrepris une étude transfrontalière, photographiant des rituels et cérémonies amérindiens et hispaniques dans le sud-ouest des États-Unis et au Mexique. Sa documentation visuelle révèle le partage fructueux qui s'est instauré entre les systèmes de croyances et les esthétiques des régions frontalières, avec pour résultat des cérémonies hybrides qui deviennent de nouvelles traditions.

En préparant *much wider than a line*, notre équipe commissariale a entrepris des recherches approfondies à Santa Fe et dans les environs, et rencontré des artistes, des archivistes, et des historiens afin d'acquérir une meilleure compréhension de la richesse du contexte de la région et de ses atouts culturels. Deux découvertes se sont avérées particulièrement fécondes et inspirantes pour notre équipe ; elles servent à présent de points d'entrée, physique et métaphorique, à l'exposition : le Paolo Soleri Amphitheater à Santa Fe et la revue bilingue *El Corno Emplumado / The Plumed Horn*, tous deux fondés dans les années 1960.

Le Paolo Soleri Amphitheater a été commandé à l'architecte italien éponyme par Lloyd Kiva New, alors directeur artistique de l'Institute of American Indian Arts, qui venait juste d'être fondé. La structure de béton à la forme atypique est située sur le campus de la Santa Fe Indian School, fondée en 1890 dans le but d'assimiler les enfants amérindiens des tribus de tout le sud-ouest des États-Unis. En concevant l'amphithéâtre biomorphique, Soleri s'est inspiré des principes de l'architecture amérindienne. Achevé en 1970, le bâtiment a abrité le programme de théâtre amérindien contemporain, un programme d'études sans précédent, et il a été le cadre d'extraordinaires représentations de théâtre amérindien. Aujourd'hui, l'amphithéâtre est un site vide, délabré, et contesté qui fait face à une menace de démolition malgré son importance historique dans l'architecture du sud-ouest américain : son entretien représente un fardeau exorbitant pour la Santa Fe Indian School, sur le terrain de laquelle il est situé. Cette réussite architecturale, par conséquent, sert à la fois de forum chargé d'histoire à l'exploration des processus collaboratifs transfrontaliers et de symbole des tensions géopolitiques qui existent à l'heure actuelle dans la région et dans toutes les Amériques.

Au cours de la même décennie où fut construit le Paolo Soleri Amphitheater à Santa Fe, une petite revue trimestrielle de poésie publiée à Mexico s'est mise à donner la parole à des poètes et écrivains progressistes issus de toutes les Amériques. *El Corno Emplumado / The Plumed Horn*, cofondée et éditée par Margaret Randall et Sergio Mondragón, était à la pointe de l'édition indépendante. Distribuée dans toutes les Amériques, *El Corno* a créé un réseau international d'écrivains et d'artistes réunis par une même sensibilité, qui y trouvèrent un espace accueillant pour leur langage de rébellion. Avec leurs couvertures au design singulier et intrigant et leurs écrits thématiques, les trente et un numéros de *El Corno* reflètent l'énergie d'une époque tumultueuse. Aujourd'hui, Randall vit au Nouveau-Mexique, où – en tant que poète, écrivaine, activiste, et coéditrice d'*El Corno* – elle a inspiré dès le début notre équipe commissariale. Notre rencontre avec Randall à Albuquerque à l'été 2015 a donné le ton d'une exposition qui vise à faire siens son dynamisme, son audace, et sa vision de l'interconnectivité dans les Amériques.

Là où SITElines.2014 se concentrait sur les cas de différences radicales – les Amériques en tant qu'espace non homogène – les organisateurs de cette seconde édition se sont appliqués à chercher les moments de lien : les échanges transculturels qui ont conduit au développement d'œuvres, d'objets, et de bâtiments visionnaires ; une communauté de poètes, d'artistes, et d'écrivains ; et des innovations dans les cérémonies et les rituels qui demeurent une part vitale du tissu de la vie contemporaine. Cette connectivité complexe représente le réseau des liens qui nous unissent, aussi divers soient nos origines et points de vue. Inévitablement, c'est notre volonté à apprendre les uns des autres qui nous en apprendra plus long sur nous-mêmes.

— tranduit par Héloïse Esquié

Os elos que nos ligam

Irene Hofmann e Candice Hopkins

UMA BIENAL DAS AMÉRICAS NO SITE

Na vanguarda do circuito da arte contemporânea há mais de vinte anos, o SITE Santa Fe foi inaugurado em 1995 como a única bienal de arte contemporânea internacional nos EUA da época. Nos anos subsequentes, embora o número de bienais no mundo tenha crescido exponencialmente, o seu formato e as listas de curadores convidados e artistas participantes permaneceram notavelmente restritos. Reconhecendo essas limitações, no verão de 2011, suspendemos nossa apresentação por um ciclo e anunciamos que estávamos explorando uma nova identidade para a nossa emblemática exposição. Durante o processo de revisitar nossa história, questionamos todas as suposições e expectativas anteriores dando espaço para o desenvolvimento de um modelo inédito e inovador de bienal. Lançada em 2014, e rebatizada SITElines: New Perspectives on Art of the Americas, a série atualmente conta com inovações no seu enfoque, abordagem curatorial e conjunto de princípios orientadores. Repensando e transformando o modelo de bienais internacionais, o SITE Santa Fe mais uma vez assume uma posição de liderança e reafirma seu lugar na vanguarda da arte contemporânea.

Ao desenvolver a SITElines, nossos objetivos se basearam em três vertentes: estabelecer uma abordagem curatorial colaborativa e com múltiplas vozes; incentivar a continuidade entre uma bienal e a próxima; e criar uma infraestrutura que permita que os artistas passem mais tempo pesquisando e produzindo do que sob os cronogramas restritos normalmente impostos pelas bienais. O cronograma mais longo também proporciona aos artistas a oportunidade de imersão no contexto do Novo México, para criar trabalhos que vão além das obras destinadas para exibição na bienal.

A mudança mais evidente e visível na SITElines: New Perspectives on Art of the Americas é a mudança de foco para o Hemisfério Ocidental. A bienal agora olha para a geografia como um quadro estrutural a ser explorado, buscando inspiração no vasto território das Américas, na região do Novo México e na cidade de Santa Fé e seus arredores. Essa região é um rico microcosmo das Américas: antes de se tornar um estado americano, o Novo México foi habitado pelas populações nativas, passando posteriormente a ser um reino espanhol, uma província mexicana e finalmente um território americano. Com a SITElines, criamos um elo entre esse terreno fértil e o resto do Hemisfério Ocidental, deslocando o eixo Leste-Oeste para Sul-Norte. Ao rejeitar a noção de homogeneidade nas Américas, recuperamos várias histórias e cosmologias, buscando nos artistas formas de revelar e entender pontos de vista tipicamente marginalizados pela arte contemporânea internacional.

A edição de 2014, intitulada *Unsettled Landscapes* (*Paisagens inquietas*), a primeira exposição da SITElines, audaciosamente nos levou para territórios desconhecidos. A curadoria foi realizada por uma equipe composta por duas curadoras convidadas, Lucía Sanromán e Candice Hopkins, e duas curadoras do próprio SITE Santa Fe, Irene Hofmann e Janet Dees. Como parte do diálogo, contamos também com uma equipe de cinco consultores curatoriais cujas especialidades abrangiam o Canadá, o Caribe, a América Central e a América do Sul. Pela primeira vez, a bienal do SITE foi organizada de forma colaborativa, integrando vozes diversas e múltiplas às discussões curatoriais.

Com o vasto potencial das Américas como grande fonte de inspiração e provocação, nossa equipe decidiu começar com uma investigação sobre o conceito de terra (*land*), um tópico que é elementar, universal e intensamente presente para nós no sudoeste americano. Terra serviu de contexto para preocupações compartilhadas por todo o continente americano e forneceu uma base literal para as futuras exposições da SITElines. Tendo paisagem, território e comércio como temas, *Unsettled Landscapes* investigou as interconexões entres as representações *da* terra, os movimentos *pela* terra e os recursos *derivados da* terra. Sob essa lente, a exposição revelou as urgências sociais, as condições políticas e as narrativas históricas que informaram o trabalho de quarenta e cinco artistas contemporâneos de quatorze países do continente americano: nossa pesquisa nos levou de Nunavut à Tierra del Fuego. *Unsettled Landscapes* abordou a ideia de terra como um espaço carregado, longe de ser neutro ou estável. A exposição questionou o domínio das convenções visuais das paisagens europeias tradicionais, dando espaço para narrativas e leituras menos conhecidas de território, buscando desestabilizar as noções ocidentais de posse, uso e comoditização da terra por meio da introdução de entendimentos indígenas e decolonizados.

Durante a curadoria de *Unsettled Landscapes*, desenvolvemos e testamos uma série de elementos estruturais da nova edição da bienal SITElines. Com o apoio da diversidade de vozes que compunham nossa equipe curatorial e em nossos espaços expositivos, lançamos o desafio de repensar nossos próprios pontos de vista e os de nosso público, confrontando os preconceitos e a amnésia histórica impostos pelo colonialismo e o intervencionismo. Desenvolvemos novas competências e estratégias para um trabalho colaborativo e expandimos nosso diálogo curatorial para incluir a contribuição de artistas e educadores.

Fortalecer nossa infraestrutura institucional para proporcionar mais tempo de pesquisa e produção para artistas e curadores se tornou uma grande prioridade de nosso trabalho. Frustradas com o habitual fenômeno em que artistas de bienais "caem de paraquedas" em uma comunidade, sem o mínimo de envolvimento com o contexto ou o lugar, decidimos criar uma nova forma de apoiar artistas que estivessem interessados em produzir obras sensíveis ao local da exposição. Isso resultou na formação do SITE Center, um centro de pesquisa e programação do Departamento de Educação do SITE Santa Fe que trabalha com a equipe da SITElines na produção de projetos comunitários e sensíveis às especificidades locais. Por meio de residências a longo prazo, os artistas têm acesso às instalações e apoio à pesquisa necessários, bem como a possibilidade de usufruir de cronogramas sem prazos de produção definidos, para criar trabalhos que se relacionam com o lugar de maneira esclarecida, significativa e gratificante. Durante o desenvolvimento de *Unsettled Landscapes*, Pablo Helguera se tornou o primeiro artista do SITE Center e, como tal, dedicou os últimos quatro anos a uma série de projetos baseados em pesquisa. Em workshops e performances realizados durante a primeira fase de sua residência, uma instalação interativa na *Unsettled Landscapes* e um novo trabalho planejado para a atual exposição *much wider than a line* (*muito mais largo do que uma linha*), Heguera examinou ponderadamente a história da formação do Novo México e se envolveu intimamente com sua comunidade contemporânea.

MUCH WIDER THAN A LINE

Pouco tempo após a abertura de *Unsettled Landscapes* para o público, foi iniciado o trabalho para a SITElines.2016. Foi formada uma nova equipe curatorial, com cada um dos seus cinco membros contribuindo com sua experiência e especialização em uma região específica das Américas, bem como uma grande disposição para abraçar a natureza imprevisível de um processo colaborativo. Nossa equipe inclui Rocío Aranda-Alvarado, Kathleen Ash-Milby, Pip Day, Pablo León de la Barra, e Kiki Mazzucchelli.

O trabalho da equipe da SITElines.2016 resultou em uma exposição que se afasta de imagens e histórias de paisagens para abrir caminho para uma exploração mais universal da interconexão nas Américas. Os curadores identificaram experiências comuns, tais como o reconhecimento dos legados coloniais, a expressão do vernáculo, a influência de entendimentos indígenas e a importância de nossa relação com a terra. *much wider than a line* empresta seu título do livro *Dancing on Our Turtle's Back* (em tradução livre, *Dançando no casco da nossa tartaruga*) de Leanne Simpson, que trata dos modos de vida do povo Nishnaabeg.[7] Em suas descrições dos conceitos não coloniais de nação e soberania, a autora destaca o cuidado conjunto necessário por parte dos diferentes países nas suas fronteiras territoriais comuns e sobrepostas. As relações que emergem daí são certamente, assim como as próprias fronteiras, muito mais amplas do que uma linha.

Três potentes tópicos atravessam *much wider than a line*: estratégias vernaculares, entendimentos indígenas e territórios compartilhados. Ao invés de categorias fixas que funcionam para classificar artistas e obras, esses temas servem como pontos de conexão. O vernacular sugere a mobilização do conhecimento local e o emprego de técnicas manuais especializadas, sejam elas de design, arquitetônicas ou têxteis. Bancos com assentos de palha trançada criados por Jorge González, por exemplo, estão distribuídos pelo espaço expositivo, servindo como pontos de pausa para descanso ao mesmo tempo em que celebram a beleza do acabamento artesanal. Esses objetos feitos à mão contrastam com o desejo da nossa sociedade cada vez mais consumista por itens produzidos em massa que sejam baratos e descartáveis. Também destacam práticas sustentáveis que sobrevivem apesar das transformações dos bens trazidas pelo capitalismo. Carla Fernández usa a tradição da tecelagem para produzir roupas - capas e mantos - que incorporam designs indígenas. Além de proporcionar prazer visual, os desenhos apresentam cosmologias indígenas e transformam-se em demonstração usável de crenças indígenas numa região conhecida por essa prática: no século XIX, os mantos dos Navajos viraram os "tapetes Navajo" que serviram, e ainda servem, os mercados de comércio e turismo. As práticas locais também informam o trabalho da arquiteta Lina Bo Bardi, cujo interesse em construções e interiores vernaculares diverge das preocupações de seus contemporâneos no Brasil. Sua solução para assento é composta de quatro paus amarrados para formar uma cadeira simples e prática: uma solução de design para uma função rotineira. Respondendo ao vernacular de uma forma mais indireta, a instalação de William Cordova é inspirada na chamada "Pottery House" em Santa Fé, que foi construída em 1984 a partir de esboços e plantas de Frank Lloyd Wright. Tendo sido imaginada, essencialmente, como um vaso de cerâmica em grande escala, a casa de adobe reflete o interesse de Wright tanto na cerâmica quanto nas técnicas de construção em adobe do sudoeste americano.[8]

Como sugere o título, *much wider than a line* contempla entendimentos indígenas e práticas decoloniais, um tema que surgiu com a primeira edição da SITElines. O longa-metragem *Atanarjuat: The Fast Runner* (em tradução livre, *Atanarjuat: O corredor rápido*) de 2001, dirigido por Zacharias Kunuk, dá vida a uma antiga história de amor e traição entre os inuítes. O filme, como vários outros realizados pela Isuma Productions, enfatiza ações em detrimento de diálogos. Para os inuítes, a demonstração de uma ação é uma forma de ensinar às próximas gerações como amarrar corretamente os cachorros ao *qamutik* (trenó), pescar uma foca ou construir uma casa de gelo (a crítica dos inuítes contra a televisão do "Sul" é que "ninguém nunca faz nada, só falam"). Como um veículo para transmitir tradições, a imagem em movimento reconhece a maleabilidade das práticas tradicionais e a importância do contar histórias. Por meio de outra abordagem, Abel Rodríguez dissemina o conhecimento de seu território natal ao anotar em desenhos detalhados da floresta tropical amazônica os nomes indígenas da flora, seu uso, propriedades medicinais e padrões de crescimento sazonais. Para Rodríguez, que foi expulso de sua terra natal por uma milícia armada, desenhar é uma forma de compartilhar essas informações especializadas com outros compatriotas igualmente exilados. Ele não se considera um artista, preocupado com a estética, mas sim um gravador e comunicador de conhecimentos.

No livro *Dancing on Our Turtle's Back*, Simpson introduz o conceito de "comunidades de coresistência", cuja implementação é essencial para os esforços decolonialistas. Não é suficiente para os povos indígenas apenas resistirem isoladamente, eles devem forjar a mudança em solidariedade com aliados. O futuro conjunto de territórios compartilhados é a terceira vertente que atravessa *much wider than a line*. Esse aspecto expande o diálogo para incluir todos nós. Ao olhar para outras regiões dentro do território compartilhado, os artistas são capazes de responder criticamente a questões de raça e identidade. Jonathas de Andrade adaptou um estudo da UNESCO de 1952 intitulado *Race and Class in Rural Brazil (Raça e classe no Brasil rural)* em sua nova versão concebida para Santa Fé e Nova York. Em conversas com o artista, os sujeitos revelam como a raça é uma construção social que se manifesta em todo o continente americano independentemente das diferenças linguísticas, regionais e sociais. Miguel Gandert também se dedicou a um estudo transfronteiriço, fotografando rituais e cerimônias nativos americanos e hispânicos no sudoeste americano e no México. Sua documentação visual revela a partilha generativa das crenças e estéticas na região fronteiriça, cujo resultado são cerimônias híbridas que se transformam em novas tradições.

Ao desenvolver *much wider than a line*, nossa equipe curatorial investigou extensivamente Santa Fé e seus arredores, trabalhando com artistas, arquivistas e historiadores a fim de adquirir um maior entendimento do rico contexto regional e seus bens culturais. Duas descobertas particularmente frutíferas e inspiradoras para nossa equipe agora servem como pontos de entrada físicos e metafóricos para a exposição: o Anfiteatro Paolo Soleri em Santa Fé e o periódico bilíngue *El Corno Emplumado / The Plumed Horn*, ambos fundados na década de 1960.

O Anfiteatro Paolo Soleri foi concebido pelo arquiteto italiano de mesmo nome a pedido de Lloyd Kiva New, que era, na época, diretor de artes do recém-fundado Institute of American Indian Arts. A estrutura de concreto em forma livre fica no campus da Santa Fe Indian School, que foi fundada em 1890 com a finalidade de assimilar crianças das tribos espalhadas pelo sudoeste dos EUA. Ao idealizar o anfiteatro biomórfico, Soleri usou princípios do design nativo americano. Finalizado em 1970, recebeu o inovador currículo de dramaturgia contemporânea nativo americano e foi palco de extraordinárias performances de teatro indígena. Hoje, o anfiteatro é um espaço vazio, abandonado e disputado, que está sob ameaça de demolição apesar de sua importância para a arquitetura do sudoeste americano. Sua manutenção é inviável para a Santa Fe Indian School. Portanto, essa conquista arquitetônica serve tanto como um fórum historicamente potente para a exploração de processos colaborativos entre culturas quanto um exemplo das tensões geopolíticas que existem atualmente na região e em todo o continente americano.

Na mesma década em que o Anfiteatro Paolo Soleri foi construído em Santa Fé, uma pequena publicação trimestral de poesia da Cidade do México deu voz a poetas e escritores progressistas de todas as partes das Américas. *El Corno Emplumado / The Plumed Horn*, fundado e editado por Margaret Randall e Sergio Mondragón, assumiu uma posição de vanguarda em termos de edições independentes. Distribuído em todo o continente americano, *El Corno* estabeleceu uma rede internacional de escritores e artistas com ideias semelhantes, que encontraram na revista uma plataforma para sua linguagem de rebelião. Com capas e textos contundentes e provocativos, as trinta e uma edições de *El Corno* refletiram vigorosamente a energia de uma era tumultuada. Hoje, Randall vive no Novo México - como poeta, escritora e ativista, além de coeditora de *El Corno* - e foi uma das primeiras inspirações para nossa equipe curatorial. O encontro com Randall em Albuquerque no verão de 2015 deu o tom para uma exposição que busca captar o seu dinamismo, coragem e visão de conectividade para as Américas.

Enquanto a SITElines.2014 enfatizava exemplos de diferenças radicais - as Américas como um espaço não homogêneo - os organizadores da segunda edição são motivados por momentos de conectividade: as trocas interculturais que levaram ao desenvolvimento de obras de arte, objetos e construções visionários; de uma comunidade de poetas, artistas e escritores; e de inovações nas cerimônias e rituais que continuam a ser uma parte essencial do tecido da vida contemporânea. Essa complexa conectividade representa a rede de vínculos que nos liga, independentemente da diversidade de nossas origens e opiniões. É nossa disposição em aprendermos uns com os outros que inevitavelmente irá nos ensinar mais sobre nós mesmos.

— traduzido por Adriana Francisco

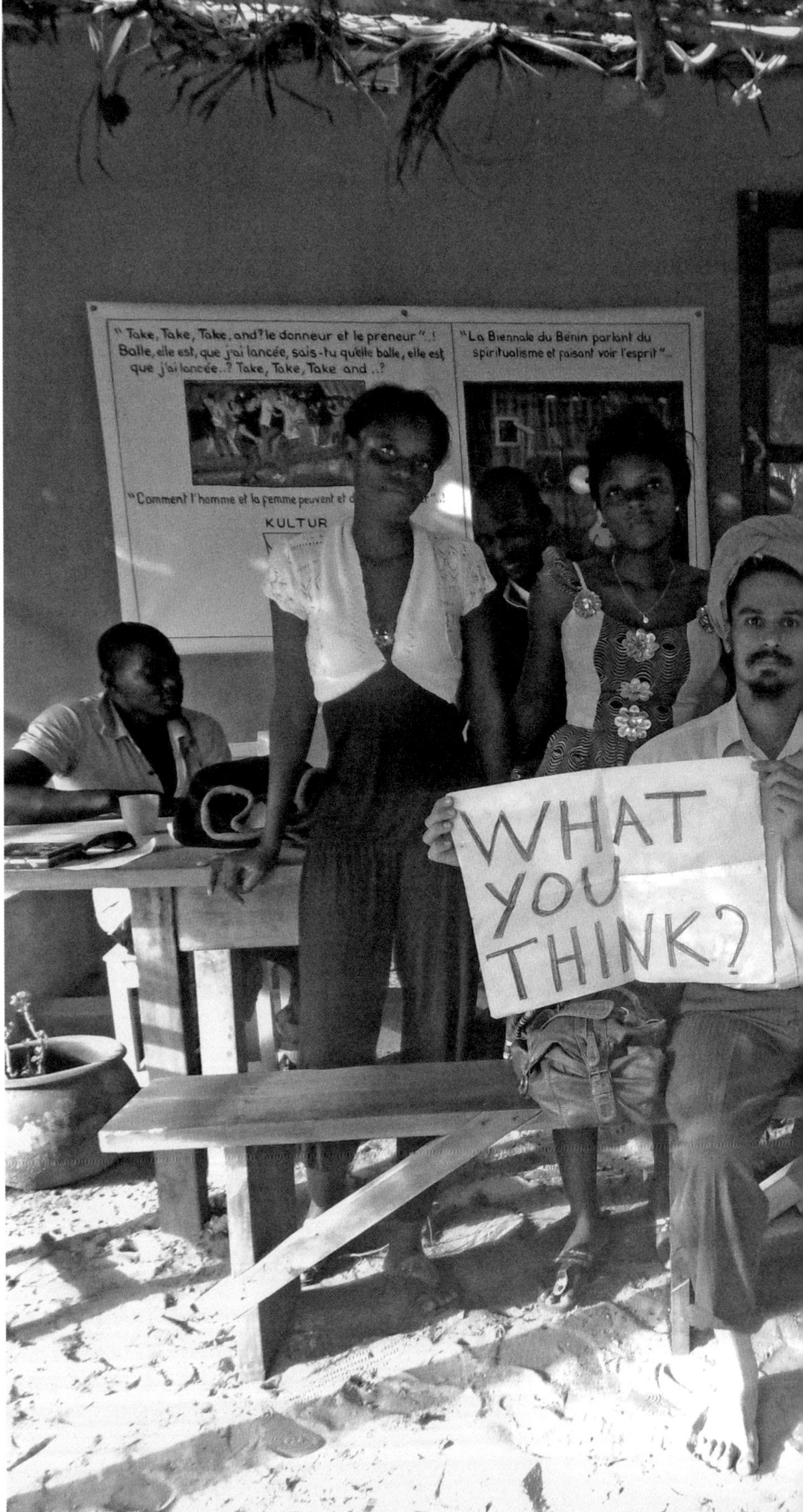
" Take, Take, Take, and? le donneur et le preneur "..!
Balle, elle est, que j'ai lancée, sais-tu quelle balle, elle est, que j'ai lancée..? Take, Take, Take and ..?
"La Biennale du Bénin parlant du spiritualisme et faisant voir l'esprit"...
"Comment l'homme et la femme peuvent et
KULTUR
WHAT
YOU
THINK?

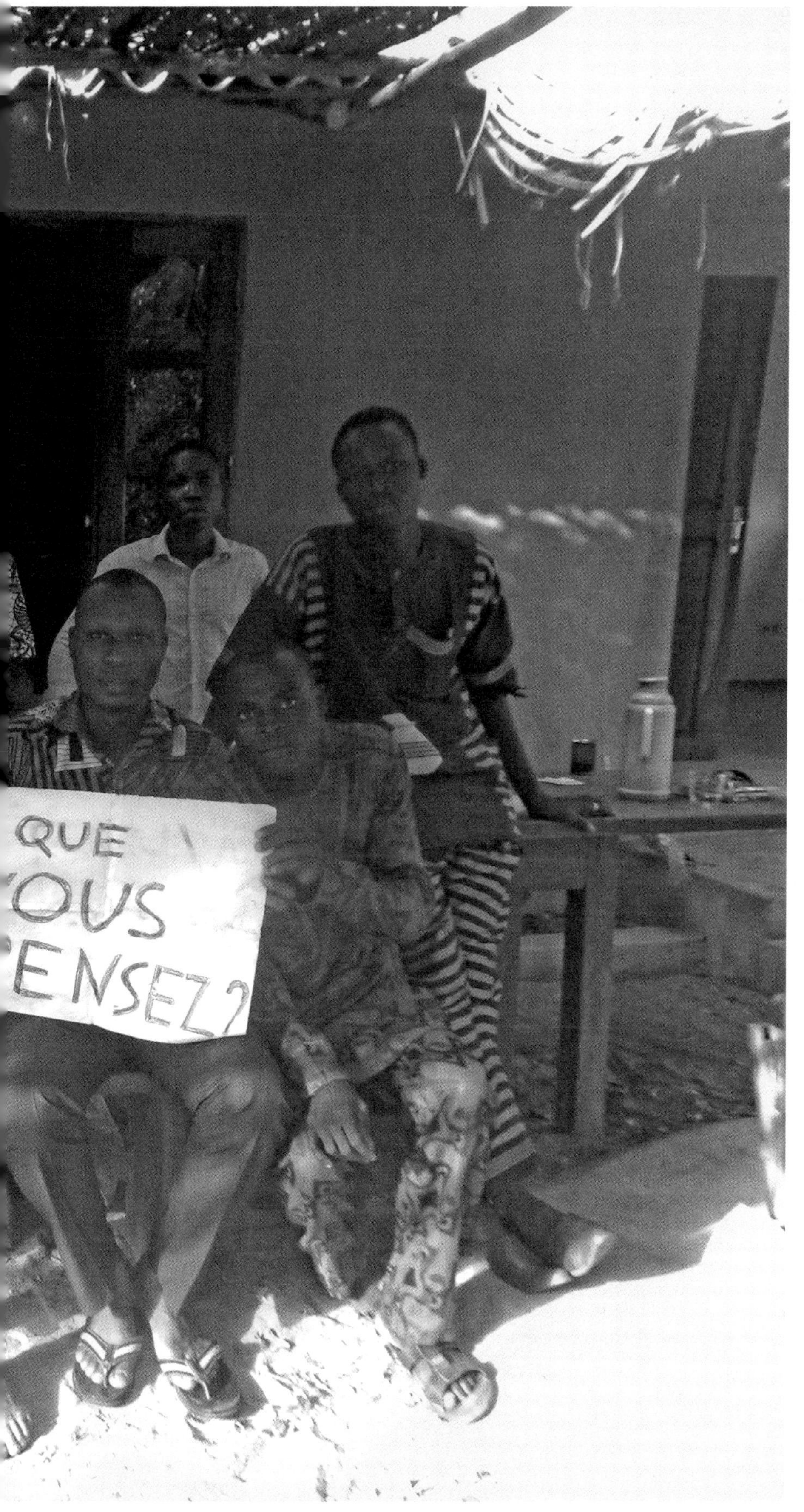
QUE
OUS
ENSEZ?

el corno emplumado

MISS FINCH'S HOME, OR RATHER STUDI
WAS WITH HER FAMILY IN EAST TWEN
SIXTH STREET, WHERE SHE OCCUPIED
NORTH ROOM ON THE THIRD FLOOR, BUT
HER PRESENCE IN THE BOSOM OF THA
FAMILY DID NOT PREVENT [illegible]
[illegible] AND AN EX-
CLUSIVENESS WHICH WAS MOST ILLUMINATI
TO EUGENE. HER ROOM WAS DONE IN
SILVER, [illegible] AND [illegible] WITH A GREA
WAX-FESTOONED CANDLESTICK FULLY F
FEET HIGH STANDING IN ONE CORNE
AND A MAGNIFICENT CARVED CHEST OF
EARLY FLEMISH WORKMANSHIP STANDI
IN ANOTHER. THERE WAS A BROWN CO
BINATION WRITING DESK AND BOOK-SHE
WHICH WAS ARRAYED WITH SOME OF TH
MOST CURIOUS VOLUMES — PATER'S "MARI
THE EPICUREAN," DAUDET'S "WIVES OF
MEN OF GENIUS," RICHARD JEFFERIES'
"STORY OF MY HEART," STEVENSON'S "AE
TRIPLEX," "THE KASIDAH" OF RICHARD
BURTON, "THE HOUSE OF LIFE" BY DANT
GABRIEL ROSSETTI, "ALSO SPRACH ZARA-
THUSTRA" BY FRIEDRICH NIETZSCHE. THE

Curatorial Perspectives

Through the discussions and deliberations that guided their work together, our curatorial team brought forward urgent ideas, bold proposals, and an extraordinary group of artists. While they each came to the table with significant knowledge and strong ideas about exhibition-making, they were incredibly open to the collaborative process and to learning from each other. Much to our delight, they were also very curious about Santa Fe and New Mexico, letting the treasures and histories of the region inspire them. Additionally, they invited voices from the past to inform the framework and direction of their show.

In the final months of exhibition planning, we asked the team to reflect on their curatorial process, the exhibition model, themes, and artists, and what it was about the region that so powerfully engaged them.

PREVIOUS SPREAD:
Paulo Nazareth, *C'que vous pensez*, from the project *Cadernos de África (Africa's Notebooks)*, 2012–13

OPPOSITE:
El Corno Emplumado / The Plumed Horn, no. 3 (July 1962)

Rocío Aranda-Alvarado

Interpreting place

Loco Local is a painting by Luis Cruz Azaceta (b. 1942 in Havana, Cuba) in the collection of the museum where I work—El Museo del Barrio—which powerfully presents the artist's impression of New York City when he first moved there in the late 1960s. Depicting a deranged person riding on a local subway train, the Spanglish-titled work is an excellent vehicle for studying the concept of the "local" in various parts of the Hispanic States of America. The idea of encountering, exploring, and making reference to local color is an interpretive approach that can be brought to any city-specific project that involves art. Portions of *much wider than a line* respond directly to the landscape, culture, and history of Santa Fe, including works by Margarita Cabrera, William Cordova, Jonathas de Andrade, Miguel Gandert, and Sonya Kelliher-Combs.

The character of this place in the southwestern United States has been (over) determined by its architecture, the proximity of the national border, the painted-earth landscape, and the complex history of the state of New Mexico. The region is a contested site in which layers of Indigenous America, Spain, Anglo-America, and Mexico have all competed for prominence.

Through his photography, Miguel Gandert exposes the falseness of the notion that Spanish bloodlines have passed directly to contemporary Hispanic New Mexicans, a belief that continues to permeate society in the state.[9] Gandert's photographs explore aspects of daily life as experienced by the diverse racially and ethnically coded bodies of New Mexicans. Both Gandert and his counterpart in Mexico, Graciela Iturbide, have worked on government-sponsored projects that catalogue local populations. In the process, Iturbide occupies a somewhat more distant relationship to her subjects than Gandert, who was born and raised in the region he studies.

Taken only a couple of years apart, Iturbide's *Los que viven en la arena* (*Those Who Live in the Sand*), 1981, and the images that Gandert took in Albuquerque in 1983 for the project *The Essential Landscape: The New Mexico Photographic Survey* depict local populations who typically have been underserved and marginalized—rarely the subject of art. Iturbide photographed the Seri of the Sonora Desert for a documentary project organized by the Instituto Nacional Indigenista of Mexico. The *Essential Landscape* project was funded by the National Endowment for the Arts as a mini-inventory of New Mexico's culture. Evident in both bodies of work is the dignity with which the photographers portray their subjects, the participation of the subjects in their own representation, and the role of location in expanding the artists' vision. In one of Gandert's photographs, the unyielding brutalist architecture of Albuquerque's Civic Plaza harbors various kinds of bodies of Nuevo Mexicanos. Iturbide's proud subjects reflect a time when capitalism has forever changed their nomadic way of life. Both photographers' subjects are formidable presences that are meant to be seen, understood as bodies of evidence and subjects for introspection.

Saying America, and meaning all of it

Creating a coherent picture of the Americas is virtually impossible. But there are some interesting moments in the modern art history of the hemisphere that point to concerns that remain relevant. The period of the 1920s to the 1940s saw the development of important publications throughout the hemisphere that addressed concerns about art and culture and how national identity, race, and ethnicity played into conceptions of new or modern national cultures. Among these publications are *The Crisis* and *Opportunity*, from Harlem; *Revista de Avance*, from Havana; *Irradiador* and *Horizonte*, from Mexico City (issued by the Estridentista group); *Amauta*, from Lima; *Martin Fierro*, from Buenos Aires; and the *Revista de Antropofagia*, from Brazil. These publications, issued mostly between 1910 and 1930, show a shared interest in modernity—defining its characteristics and locating it within the artistic production of each of these American capitals. Almost all are concerned with the concept of an "American" identity, and two of them, *The Crisis* and *Revista de Avance*, asked readers to contribute to its definition. The period signaled a moment when questions about national identity were paramount, not only in visual art but also in literature and music.

Such early efforts showed the urgency of persistent questions. Modernists throughout the American hemisphere, such as Tarsila do Amaral, Wifredo Lam, Emilio Pettoruti, Fermín Revueltas Sánchez, and José Sabogal, carefully considered how they would represent the contemporary culture of their countries and, often, how the body would participate in this important endeavor. The presence or absence of the (racialized) body has been one of the most relevant subjects in art of the twentieth and twenty-first centuries throughout the Americas. Indeed, we still seem to be trapped at the outer edges of a genuine exploration of subjects like Blackness and Indigeneity and what they mean to contemporary geopolitical culture. The possibilities and deeper meanings of the brown body continue to be explored today through the work of artists like William Cordova (Peru/U.S.A); Nicolás Dumit Estévez, Charo Oquet, and Raquel Paiewonsky (Dominican Republic/U.S.A.); Claudia Joskowicz (Bolivia/U.S.A.); Milagros de la Torre (Peru); Paulo Nazareth (Brazil); and countless others.

In her search for the Americas, Marta Minujín (Argentina) organized a transposition of earth from the sacred Inca site of Machu Picchu to twenty-four other locations across Latin America and back again. This tangible but essentially invisible gesture embraces movement, transnationalism, similarity and difference, history and permanence, and—most importantly for the artist—a kind of "oneness." She gave form to this holistic view by burying at the Inca site the names of the artists who returned to her their local soil mixed with the Machu Picchu earth she had sent them. For Minujín, the mixture symbolizes the earth of all Latin America, belonging to everyone for all eternity.

The artist being an artist or a purveyor of ideas

Research, experimentation, and fearlessness are essential to the working process of all the artists in *much wider than a line*. Research is the crucial tool for telling stories with a deep understanding of the human context. This is true for artists of different generations in this exhibition.

In creating his works for the series *Congelados* (*Frozen*), Benvenuto Chavajay closely examined the construction of pistols. Using clay rather than molten metal to produce a replica, he found it difficult to remove the material from the crevices of the weapon; in the end, there was much additive work involved in the fabrication of his pistols. Working in a similar medium, Juana Valdes experimented with many options in creating her porcelain "rags," which hang from hooks on the wall. Using an actual rag, the artist left the fabric in the porcelain during firing, which burned it away, leaving only the porcelain shell. Broadening the meanings implicit in her conventional material, she also "racialized" the cloths by adding pigment to the porcelain.

As always, artists continue to ask questions and explore alternative ways of seeing old problems. Margarita Cabrera and Carla Fernández both work with textiles, communities, and focus groups. Cabrera studies the politics of the U.S.-Mexico border, the paths across it, and the flora and fauna of the American desert. She has hosted workshops in which women visually narrate their own stories of crossing the border or living away from their families by embroidering them on soft "cactuses." Fernández researches the handmade textile traditions and pattern-making of groups from all parts of Mexico. Exploring the ways historical geometric patterns have developed through generations of Indigenous groups across the country, her work relates to that of many other artists throughout the hemisphere who uphold the significance of geometry, the handmade, and Indigenous or African traditions. In many cases, the embrace of these traditions also signals a desire to rescue the planet from almost-certain death. The deeply troubling state of the earth's environment and atmosphere is of concern to artists across the continents.

Research has always been at the heart of William Cordova's working process. For this project, he has paired his history of activism with an exploration of architectural history, the history of a place, and the emotional bearing of sound. Frank Lloyd Wright, the Black Panther Party, a colony of ants, and the ubiquitous Southwestern adobe all contribute to the meaning of his work, which examines interrelated ideas within the context of Santa Fe for audiences both local and international.

Thinking of it as a nightclub, we'd call it The Vernacular

The use of a vernacular visual language connects the work of Xenobia Bailey, Mariana Castillo Deball, Jeffrey Gibson, Jorge González, and celebrated figures such as Lina Bo Bardi and Marta Minujín. Bailey's crocheted works offer the visual equivalent of funk heralded by the rhythmic groove of the electric bass. Like her fellow sculptors, Castillo Deball and Gibson, Bailey asks important questions about process and history, and how to make these visible in work that explores not just this century, but deep histories of the past when bodies were enslaved, brutalized, and cast aside. The artist left her original calling in industrial design to pursue greatness through the ordinary process of crocheting yarn. Referencing rhythm and blues, a musical form developed in the United States during the 1960s, Bailey adapts funk as the ultimate signifier for race and the body. Her conception of funk, the voice, musical instruments, and implied movement creates conversations among sound, color, and form. The unassuming tool of the crochet hook becomes a conceptual weapon.

In their work, both Castillo Deball and Gibson allow us to see the unseen. In response to her own ambitious challenge—to tell the story of the universe in one day—Castillo Deball adapts the language of modernist and Indigenous forms. Stacking clay objects to form large totem poles, she makes physical versions of multilayered narrative histories. Gibson adapts the language of modern painting and geometric abstraction in materials used by Indigenous people in different parts of the hemisphere. The animal hide is a conveyer of pared-down patterns that pass on knowledge generationally and geographically.

The concept of harboring the body, using modest materials to provide a moment of respite, is at the core of contemporary art that evokes Indigenous knowledge. Taken together, works by artists like Bailey, Bo Bardi, Castillo Deball, Chavajay, Cordova, Gibson, and Minujín reflect the hemispheric interest in the past of our contiguous continents and the shared realities that affect us through the circulation of bodies, objects, ideas, and ways of making that flow into, across, and out of these regions.

Kathleen Ash-Milby

Sustaining relationships much wider than a line

Early in our conversations about exhibition themes, we talked about art that reflects a heightened awareness of how humankind's meddling with nature has caused an undeniable imbalance in the world. From the Western perspective, humans are supposed to be masters over nature, and we've done a pretty good job denying the gravity of our damage to this planet. A paradigm shift is beginning to occur, an end to the world as many people know it. So one of the expressions of the idea of blurred borders in the exhibition is a dissolution of the artificial boundary that Western culture had drawn between humankind and the environment, an idea dramatically expressed by Aaron Dysart in his sculptural works, especially *Second Growth*, a piñon tree bursting through the gallery wall.

Interestingly, Native cultural knowledge stresses that maintaining balance between all living beings and the environment is crucial to our survival, and consequently Indigenous teachings of ancient knowledge are now being recognized for their sagaciousness. Sonya Kelliher-Combs's installation *Remnant*, though beautiful, isn't a very comforting reflection on our insistent destruction of the environment. Her sculptural works are poignant when viewed in the context of her early memories of being taught to "respect and honor the natural world that provides for you, your family, and community." Maria Hupfield also draws on Anishinaabe teachings about the caretaking of our world in *It Is Never Just about Sustenance or Pleasure*, a performance and installation that uses the jarring contrast of the environment of the desert Southwest with materials designed for the wetlands of the Great Lakes.

Biennials repeating, reflecting, and generating

The space between biennials, by their very definition, is narrow—only two years. It is simply unimaginable that organizers wouldn't take previous biennial projects into careful consideration. What is both refreshing and forward-thinking is the idea of consciously linking the biennial cycle, as SITE has done. Instead of being constricting, setting the boundary of the Americas relieves the organizers of the task of surveying the world. It also creates an opportunity for a focus and depth that can be lacking in biennials that cast too wide a net and often pull together many of the same artists.

SITE Santa Fe has also escaped some of these pitfalls because the biennial is organized by an established museum with its own institutional memory, whose staff is conscious of building on, not repeating, its record of exhibiting important, challenging, and experimental art. Two years may seem like a long time in the fast-moving gallery and commercial art world, but for a museum it's a heartbeat. I think our audiences are more than capable of understanding the connection between the SITE biennials. They can each stand alone, but also, with the catalogues, they form a sequence that can reach new audiences who may be entering the conversation in the second or third iteration.

Grounding practice in research

Many of the most interesting works in the exhibition are rooted in both research and experience. In the series *Empire*, for example, Lewis deSoto's very intimate lived experience of the Inland Empire of Southern California imbues the work with a sensitivity that would be absent if the same landscapes and urban environments were looked at from a purely historical perspective. Jeffrey Gibson's in-depth research into the use of traditional Native-American hide painting and beadwork techniques deeply informs his practice, as does his awareness of the capitalist issues tied to the contemporary materials he utilizes. His work is powerful not because of his book knowledge, but because of his personal experience learning from other artists and from his own life as a Native person. For many Native people, it is the weight of our history that shapes and defines our identity, and it can't be overlooked as an influence in the work of Native artists.

As curators, we bring our lived experiences as art- and knowledge-seekers to each new project, one building on the other, but new paths also open to us through research. For *much wider than a line* we were able to share our research with one another, despite our geographical separation: an uncommon but welcome opportunity that deeply informed the course of the project.

Grounding curatorial work in artists

My curatorial practice is artist-based. By that, I mean that my experiences visiting artists, as well as seeing their work in exhibitions and publications, direct my scholarly work. I might have a general area of interest, but what really spurs my imagination is what I see artists creating in the studio. To that end, even after just a few early conversations, I schedule studio visits whenever and wherever the opportunity presents itself, always expanding my network with new artists. For this project, Rocío (Aranda-Alvarado) and I had many points of mutual interest in the artist communities that we work with, and, as we both live in the same city, we were able to visit some of these artists together. In Santa Fe, in different combinations of curators, we were also given the opportunity to visit artists together at various times.

The collaborative process of organizing this exhibition was challenging, in part because we were all seeing different things from disparate reaches of the art world, separated conceptually and philosophically, and often even geographically. Many of us were so close to and immersed in our own worlds that it took numerous conversations to get to a place where we could step back far enough to see where the connections existed. Once we did, many of the ideas coalesced and seemed obvious in retrospect.

Interrogating identity and race

By choosing to focus on art of the Americas, we could not ignore the fact that the subjectivity of race and racial boundaries would emerge as a subject in the work of many artists. We could have created an entire exhibition on the subject but instead chose to let it emerge in a variety of ways as another expression of the idea of artificial boundaries. Jonathas de Andrade's *A Study of Race and Class*, for example, explicitly demonstrates the futility of defining racial categories. Although the specifics may vary, the fixation on defining and classifying racial identification has been an obsession of sorts throughout the Americas—an important, though unfortunate, shared preoccupation.

What might be surprising to some is that the artists of Native heritage in the exhibition are not interrogating their own racial identity but are instead drawing on Indigenous knowledge about our relationships to one another and the environment, another shared concern for all people throughout the hemisphere and the planet.

Putting Santa Fe on the map

It's not just Santa Fe that is considered off the map for many in the mainstream art world—it's the entire state of New Mexico. How funny, when it is virtually the center of the world for so many Native people who live in New Mexico, by choice or because their families and their people have always lived here. Although I no longer live in New Mexico myself, it is my birthplace, and my family—both my Navajo and my Anglo ancestors—have been here for generations. For this reason, I have never been seduced by the beauty of the landscape or swept away by romantic or imaginative notions. New Mexico, and by extension Santa Fe, has always been a place of complexity and contrast for me.

Of course, the landscape is incredible, but it is also a harsh environment in which you need to protect yourself from the sun, the threat of dehydration, and sometimes poisonous critters. The intersection of cultures here creates a vibrant community, but there is also conflict, crime, and discrimination. It's a special place like no other, but complicated.

Santa Fe is known as a center for contemporary Native art. Growing that reputation to include a wider range of artists—and the scholars, curators, and critics who follow—should help demonstrate that many of the boundaries in the arts are artificial. SITE Santa Fe is playing an important role in decentering the art world by creating a space in New Mexico for contemporary art from all reaches of the art world. The biennial is a critical part of this process.

Pip Day

with Irmgard Emmelhainz and Pablo Lafuente

and Karen Barad, Ursula Biemann, Anna Boghiguian, Norman Cohn, Hu Fang, Lucy Flint, Hanay Geiogamah, Donna Haraway, Eduardo Kohn, Zacharias Kunuk, Achille Mbembe, Rolland Meinholz, Lloyd Kiva New, Abel Rodríguez, Leanne Simpson, Rebecca Solnit, Paulo Tavares, Zoe Todd, and Eve Tuck and K. Wayne Yang

In lieu of preparing essays, the much wider than a line *curatorial team responded to a set of questions proposed by SITE. In an attempt to answer, I collected thoughts from activists, thinkers, colleagues, and friends who have helped give shape to my contribution to the biennial. The diaristic text that follows includes abridged SITE questions.*

Note, March 3, 2016

much wider than a line

Moving away from one's center into unknown territory must be done with great care, and it involves acts of faith that need reciprocation in order to be fruitful. One's most pressing concerns and urgencies are, of course, not always shared by others. When concerns aren't cared for, the wide line as described by Leanne Simpson, and borrowed for the title of this biennial, narrows and ossifies—in relationships, institutionally, and politically.

SITE: How did Santa Fe and the region inform your curatorial work?

The Independent (London), January 15, 2015

On 16 July 1945 the first atomic-bomb test took place at the US Army testing range at Alamogordo in New Mexico, and with that first historic nuclear explosion a new geological epoch began on Earth, scientists have decided . . .

Note, January 15, 2015

The Anthropocene.

"Scientists have decided"!

Elders and Hunters in the North, whom Inuk filmmaker Zacharias Kunuk and Norman Cohn have been interviewing, describe a planet that has wobbled to such an extent that the sun no longer rises in the right place on the day that the long winter darkness breaks in the spring. Southern science calls this the effect of global warming and puts it down to the impact on perspective that even slightly higher temperatures would have. To them, the sun only *looks* like it is rising in the wrong place. To the Elders, the sun *is* rising in the wrong place, and this wobble is to be taken as a grave warning signal that the world urgently needs rebalancing.

Noted, May 6, 2015

Ursula Biemann and Paulo Tavares, *Forest Law*

"A territory that refuses to be represented by a single, hegemonic perspective. The first lines of this plurinational and multispecies contract are being currently drawn in Ecuador. [*Forest Law*] reflects upon this new constitutional space wherein both humans and nonhumans gather in a political assembly, the living forests of Amazonia."[11]

Note, May 6, 2015

The Inuit elders' "tilt" could equally be lodged in the forest, the rain forest, and the desert (and in physical, political, and historical landscapes of New Mexico). And in the colonial histories and presents of the Americas and the ways they are being upheld/told/untold/reconfigured.

E-mail, November 13, 2015

Dear team, a proposed title for the show: *Returning the Jaguar's Gaze.*

In *How Forests Think: Toward an Anthropology Beyond the Human*, Eduardo Kohn recounts the advice of the Ávila Runa of the Amazonian Ecuador, that when spending the night in the forest, you must always sleep face-up. That way, if a jaguar were to come across you in the night, you would be perceived as a thing that can look back, as a "you" and not an "it" that could be construed as prey. Kohn describes this awareness of being "seen" by the jaguar—really seen—as a moment that entirely defines one's relation to the world, to other creatures, and to the "things" of this earth (the living and thinking forest). We could argue that it is precisely Indigenous worldviews such as this that push through current theories of the Anthropocene, and are essential in dealing with—in even a small way—the ills that we're living and the damage that we're doing to the planet.

Noted, June 12, 2015

Hu Fang, "Why We Look at Plants in a Corrupted World"

"Anyone who slowly dissolves into the forest at night would believe that the legends of destiny are already inscribed into the body of the plant, which uses growth rings, scent, its own form, and the dirt in which it dwells to write history—a history that distantly echoes that of the earth's boiling core. . . . Anyone who sows seeds would deeply experience the hope promised by time: the future that starts from a single seed. . . .

Just as one's pulse registers the changing of the seasons, if we say that looking, like meditation, is an ancient technique based on bodily senses and the creation of the knowledge of the world, then looking, while surviving the night, does not only mean that humanity must wait patiently. It also means we get to see the arrival of daybreak. . . . In this way, looking is a kind of calm before the storm, like the quietude of ancient warriors preparing for battle.

It is only when we consider looking to be a technique for survival that we can grasp how looking at plants means becoming immersed in the world of the other, and without intruding. Looking is the reconciliation of divided existence, an exercise in survival manifesting as the searching of the world by the sensory apparatus. How might we write, through innumerable creases in the foliage, the remnants of the forest, the wastelands of the city, our current methods for coexisting with the world?"[12]

SITE: How did you approach your curatorial work on this project?

Response, March 20, 2016

Throughout the working process, much light has been shed on institutional ways and on the complex tangos that transpire in the attempt to find common ground, to seek the consensus (and dissensus), agonism (and antagonism), pleasure (and frustration), and compromise (and resistance) that emerge when negotiating an institution's needs. Parts of the curatorial team, for instance, were interested in bringing Aby Warburg's work on the Hopi Serpent ritual to the table; others believed that colonial material of this nature should remain firmly on the shelf, which it did. In another instance, the collaborative, cross-cultural processes that originally went into the design of the Soleri Amphitheater on the former grounds of the Institute of American Indian Arts and the present-day contentions around the amphitheater—not least of which is the question of whether it should be demolished or restored—echoed importantly, both locally and as a reflection of larger questions about colonial legacies across the Americas. The past and present histories of the amphitheater have provided productive models for the conceptual, political, and formal building of the exhibition.

Noted, March 18, 2016 (regarding the perceived wounds of Santa Fe)

Rebecca Solnit, *Hope in the Dark*

"This is an extraordinary time full of vital, transformative movements that could not be foreseen. It's also a nightmarish time. Full engagement requires the ability to perceive both."[13]

Achille Mbembe, *Decolonizing Knowledge and the Question of the Archive*

"A negative moment is a moment when new antagonisms emerge while old ones remain unresolved. It is a moment when contradictory forces—inchoate, fractured, fragmented—are at work but what might come out of their interaction is anything but certain. It is also a moment when multiple old and recent unresolved crises seem to be on the path towards a collision. Such a collision might happen—or maybe not. It might take the form of outbursts that end up petering out. Whether the collision actually happens or not, the age of innocence and complacency is over."[14]

SITE: What areas of overlap emerged? Were there any irreconcilable differences?

Response, March 12, 2016

Relationships to borders, which are foundational to questions of race and identity, as well as decolonial practices and discourses in the Americas, are as fundamentally varied as the cultures and groups of peoples engaging with the political processes involved. [Does this mean that the conception of borders and the way of inhabiting them, as well as the politics around them, vary because of the variety of people involved here? That is to say, there is no homogeneous notion of the border in the biennale or the artists' and the curators' work?][15] While the Americas share underlying settler colonial legacies, the regional specificities and discourses are as different as can be. This is reflected structurally in the SITElines.2016 biennial, in which artists' concerns are both extremely specific and general and in which five curators work together in an attempt to curate one exhibition and decide to curate four.

SITE: SITElines is a cumulative project, in that each edition expands and builds upon the one prior. How important is it to create a dialogue between the exhibitions? Do you think that a generative relationship is possible between an event that takes place every two years?

Response, March 20, 2016

Given the radical changes that occur over any given two-year period in the sociocultural and economic landscape of the Americas (that is, between one SITElines biennial and the next), the generative relationships that the institution seeks to establish must be supported on structural levels by that institution. For instance, the implications of the completion of the Truth and Reconciliation Commission report declaring a cultural genocide in Canada; a new panorama in which Black Lives Matter has gained traction as a major political movement against police racism and brutality; the emergence of the slogans "¡Vivos se los llevaron, vivos los queremos!" (They took them alive, and we want them back alive) and "Fue el estado" (It was the State) to channel social movements and popular discontent in response to the forty-three students disappeared in Ayotzinapa. These are instances that have created a structurally different world than the one in which SITElines.2014 was produced. In such a world, working methodologies conducive to generative practices must be integral to the host institution, or there will be little relation between one biennial and another.

SITE: Because of its geographic scope and divergent histories, it is hard to grasp a full picture of the Americas. Can an exhibition clarify this picture? Should it?

Noted, February 22, 2015

Donna Haraway, *When Species Meet*

"I think we learn to be worldly from grappling with, rather than generalizing from, the ordinary. I am a creature of the mud, not the sky."[16]

Noted, March 15, 2016

Eve Tuck and K. Wayne Yang, "Decolonization is not a metaphor"

"Decolonization, which we assert is a distinct project from other civil and human rights-based social justice projects, is far too often subsumed into the directives of these projects, with no regard for how decolonization wants something different than those forms of justice. . . . There is a long and bumbled history of non-Indigenous peoples making moves to alleviate the impacts of colonization. The too-easy adoption of decolonizing discourse (making decolonization a metaphor) is just one part of that history and it taps into pre-existing tropes that get in the way of more meaningful potential alliances. We think of the enactment of these tropes as a series of moves to innocence (Malwhinney, 1998), which problematically attempt to reconcile settler guilt and complicity, and rescue settler futurity."[17]

Noted, March 18, 2016

Achille Mbembe, *Decolonizing Knowledge and the Question of the Archive* (a bid to recall and decommission colonial myths of whiteness in South Africa's project of reconceiving democracy)

"For memory to fulfill this function long after the Truth and Reconciliation paradigm has run out of steam, the demythologizing of certain versions of history must go hand in hand with the demythologizing of whiteness.

This is not because whiteness is the same as history. Human history, by definition, is history beyond whiteness. Human history is about the future. Whiteness is about entrapment. Whiteness is at its best when it turns into a myth. It is the most corrosive and the most lethal when it makes us believe that it is everywhere; that everything originates from it and it has no outside."[18]

E-mail, November 13, 2015

Dear team: a possible title—*Some tunes will be hummed.*

Hanay Geiogamah, who was involved with IAIA in Santa Fe and established the Native American Theater Ensemble in New York in the early 1970s, presented his first play, *Body Indian*, at La Mama Experimental Theater Club in New York. "Some tunes will be hummed" forms part of the instructions to *Body Indian*.

A tune hummed contains much information, passed on without the need for language as such. This reference could capture our interest in making evident or pointing toward the vast range of modes of transmitting bodies of knowledge, across the Americas.

SITE: Is it possible to rethink the biennial?

SITE self-reflects.

Kiki Mazzucchelli

Giving context for a place-based contemporary biennial

In the case of SITElines.2016, one of the initial concerns shared by the curatorial team was to propose an exhibition project that could take place only in Santa Fe. Most of us were only vaguely familiar with the local context, and during our field trips we tried to identify certain dynamics, histories, or practices that could have some kind of resonance in other parts of the Americas. At the very beginning, Paolo Soleri's amphitheater emerged as an important reference in our research process. Conceived in 1965 as a venue for contemporary Native drama—a discipline that was just emerging, with the support of IAIA's visionary director, Lloyd Kiva New—the building was designed in close dialogue with Rolland Meinholz, who had conducted extensive research on ceremonial settings across different Native groups. Soleri's design allows for a certain use of the space—both in terms of opening up new possibilities for performance and in how the audience experiences the play—that does not derive from a conventional European conception of theater, while at the same time incorporating many Native-American forms. Although drawing on completely different sources, Lina Bo Bardi, the Italian-Brazilian architect who is also represented in the show, was also developing, at roughly the same time, a similarly decolonial approach to architecture and design that was based on the material culture of the populations of the Brazilian Northeast. To put it in very broad terms, both architects have actively researched and incorporated non-Western systems of knowledge in their practices, envisioning the possibility of an avant-garde grounded on cultural values that have been systematically despised and erased by the colonial establishment. Returning to Soleri's amphitheater and its relevance to this biennial, another important aspect is the current debate around its future, which encapsulates many of the sociopolitical tensions still present in the Santa Fe region today. On the other hand, Margaret Randall's fascinating trajectory, and particularly her work as co-editor (with Sergio Mondragón) of *El Corno Emplumado / The Plumed Horn*, shows a pioneering way of establishing informal networks and cultural exchange based on intellectual affinity across different countries in the Americas. *El Corno* was a truly DIY publication that relied on very limited resources, but nonetheless it managed to circumvent the official channels of circulation of culture and provided a much-needed platform to connect artists, poets, and writers in a pre-Internet era, when many American countries were still largely isolated.

Santa Fe inspiring site-responsive new works

All the artists we commissioned to create works have specific research interests that we felt could be further developed and expanded within the context of Santa Fe, although their methodologies might be quite different. Jonathas de Andrade, for instance, had shown a first iteration of the project he developed for *much wider than a line* in 2015 at Performa in New York. Using as his starting point a 1950s UNESCO-sponsored study on race relations in rural Brazil, de Andrade—himself a mixed-race Brazilian—inverted the equation and came to New York City more than a half-century after the original study to investigate U.S. race relations. New York, a cosmopolitan environment where the idea of race is subdued by the massive presence and heterogeneity of resident foreigners, offered different results than Santa Fe, which has a more distinctive racial makeup, and where groups assert their identity more emphatically. The 1950s study was conducted in a rural setting, and although there are enormous ethnic, geographical, and historical differences between the two places, New Mexico's peripheral position in relation to more urbanized, wealthier areas in the U.S. might be analogous to Bahia's standing in Brazil.

De Andrade arrived in the region of New Mexico with a prescribed methodology to carry out a specific project that, although involving a certain degree of unforeseeability, was pretty much resolved in terms of format and presentation. Paulo Nazareth, on the other hand, has a much looser approach, with his works mostly taking shape during epic wanderings he usually makes on foot. On the way, he encounters different communities with whom he shares the experience of a colonial past that still defines relations in contemporary societies. For *much wider than a line*, Nazareth has chosen to spend time in the Los Alamos region investigating the social and environmental impact of nuclear testing in Indigenous lands, a subject he first discussed a few years ago with a Navajo man in the Southwest. Nazareth has traveled extensively around the Americas, making connections with populations whose culture and histories are often marginalized. The end result of his experience in New Mexico remains unknown at the time of writing, entailing a great degree of experimentation and unpredictability.

Clarifying a picture of one vertical axis of the world

Rather than clarifying, I would say the most interesting thing the exhibition can achieve is to complicate or expand the very concept of "the Americas" by presenting unsuspected connections, relationships, or overlaps between practices across the territory. Any picture of the Americas will always be partial, and any attempt at a comprehensive view runs the risk of erasing fundamental differences between regions. Besides the profound socioeconomic disparity between North and South, there are a number of variable contexts that coexist within certain countries or regions. We took a realistic approach to our mission to produce an exhibition with a focus on the Americas that starts with the context of Santa Fe.

Though there is no categorical concept in this exhibition, it is sewn together with interconnected threads we picked up during our research trips to Santa Fe that we could follow to other parts of the hemisphere. One of our concerns has been to give visibility to artists and discourses from regions that have not been sufficiently explored in previous editions of the biennial, such as South and Central America. If we can think of a possible common denominator throughout the hemisphere, it is the shared colonial history of violence against Native populations. With this in mind, our interest is in the histories, practices, and knowledge that have been wiped out over the centuries, which do not necessarily correspond to a Western concept of nationality or geopolitical blocs.

Rooting ideas and practices in the vernacular

The idea that vernacular practices could articulate a kind of counternarrative to a Western discourse and to a developmentalist model of progress was widely discussed by prominent critics in Latin America between the 1960s and '80s, among them Aracy Amaral, Frederico Morais, and Mário Pedrosa. As many countries were still experiencing the effects of a new wave of industrialization in the postwar period, there was a lot of debate about how to conceive of a modernity that reflected the socioeconomic and cultural realities of the region. Lina Bo Bardi is part of this generation, and her practice was deeply influenced by her experience in Bahia, in northeast Brazil, a region characterized by conditions of acute material poverty but also great inventiveness. She lived in Bahia from the late 1950s until the beginning of the military regime in 1964. During this period, she came into close contact with local forms of production, folk expressions, and vernacular practices that would have a profound impact on her own avant-garde practice.

Bo Bardi was a prolific writer, and in several of her texts she openly criticizes the dominant processes of what she termed deculturation. Found in the great centers of São Paulo and Rio de Janeiro, deculturation was based on the emulation of European modernity—therefore structurally imported. In a text titled "Why the Northeast," Bo Bardi writes: "To search attentively for the real cultural bases of a country (whatever they are: poor, miserable, vernacular) does not mean to preserve the forms and materials; it means evaluating their original creative possibilities. Modern materials and modern production systems will later replace primitive means, preserving not the forms but the underlying structure of these possibilities."[19] She wanted to see existing vernacular practices inextricably rather than nominally incorporated into Brazil's ongoing process of industrialization. During her tenure at the Museu de Arte Moderna da Bahia (1959–64), Bo Bardi conceived a multidisciplinary program that encompassed a center for documenting popular art and another for technical studies focusing on the transition from what she called "pre-handicraft" to industrial manufacturing. However, these projects were abruptly suspended when the military took power in 1964 and she was forced to resign. Importantly, many of her ideas, such as the use of locally sourced materials and labor, today are central to the international debate around the failed promises of capitalism and the search for a fairer, more ecological and sustainable industrial model for the twenty-first century. Therefore, it's not surprising that her legacy has a great resonance with the works of some of the contemporary practitioners featured in *much wider than a line*, such as Carla Fernández and Jorge González, who incorporate vernacular techniques in fashion and furniture design.

Beyond the field of material culture, composer and artist Raven Chacon works with groups of Native-American teenagers from various reservations in the U.S. who create short musical pieces for a string quartet under his guidance within the framework of his Native-American Composers Apprentice Project. Most of his students have had no previous musical training, and they are not expected to write classical compositions. Rather than a hindrance, the lack of formal education opens up a space for real experimentation and the expansion of aural possibilities within one of the most traditional formats in Western music. The resulting pieces incorporate a wide range of sounds that are part of a young Native-American person's life today, from traditional music from their tribes to heavy metal tunes and video game soundtracks. As Chacon observes: "These students do not have the burden of needing to undo the influence of the tradition of Western classical knowledge. They were never given the opportunity to learn it, so any unlearning and bending of the ear is going to happen much easier." What I find particularly interesting about Chacon's project is that the Indigenous element in the students' compositions is not featured as a mere citation or appropriation of traditional musical forms and techniques, but as the source of a different kind of experimentalism that requires that new forms and techniques be constantly reinvented.

Pablo León de la Barra

Framing the biennial with landmarks from the past

There is a clear need for curatorial practices to create dialogues with other disciplines and temporalities. In relation to *El Corno Emplumado / The Plumed Horn* and Paolo Soleri's amphitheater for the Institute of American Indian Arts (on the current Santa Fe Indian School campus), as a team we all had an interest in researching recent historical cases that would resonate at SITE, in Santa Fe, and in New Mexico. I was also interested in bringing forward particular forms of knowledge in the region that could serve as a reference for artists in the exhibition and that could also shed new light on forms of contemporary culture beyond the so-called "visual arts," expanding our understanding of what contemporary art practices can be today.

During my lengthy and ongoing research on artist magazines and publications, I have always admired *El Corno Emplumado*. I first heard of it from an artist I respect, Felipe Ehrenberg, who, like Margaret Randell and Sergio Mondragón, had to leave Mexico at the time of the student revolts of 1968 for fear of persecution. While in exile in England, he created Beau Geste Press, an artist-run imprint greatly influenced by *El Corno*. What makes *El Corno* different from other publications of the period is that the editors published poetry and literature from the entire American continent (and beyond) and invited artists to publish their work, creating a network of artists and thinkers that went beyond the traditional Euro- and North America–centric model. This strategy resonates with what SITE Santa Fe has been trying to do, starting with the last edition, which is to refocus exploration onto the American continent and to create connections between the artists, curators, and publics within it. While researching *El Corno*, I learned that Randall, who was born in New Mexico, now lives in Albuquerque. This made the inclusion of *El Corno* even more pertinent and provided an opportunity to recognize Randall's decades of work as a writer and activist.

In the case of Soleri, I have again been a long-time enthusiast, with a particular interest in his Arcosanti project, a functioning and sustainable utopian community in Arizona that he dedicated his life to building. (Another of my lines of research has been utopian communities in the Americas.) On my first visit to Santa Fe in January 2015, I met Conrad Skinner, who shared with me his passion for the amphitheater at the Santa Fe Indian School. The history of the theater on Indian land and its risk of demolition by those currently in charge of it are symbolic of a larger problem in New Mexico and the Americas: the physical occupation of Indigenous lands by those who came later. The amphitheater is also a metaphor for our view of SITElines as a conceptual space where opposition can be performed and negotiated. In the design of the Santa Fe amphitheater, Soleri replaced the traditional one-point Western perspective with multiple perspectives; it is our sense that similarly multiple perspectives can coexist at SITE Santa Fe.

Examining overlapping boundaries as in Leanne Simpson's Dancing on Our Turtle's Back

The area of intersection where artists stop being themselves in order to allow the cultural influence of the other—seeing not from a dominant perspective but from horizontal and multiple perspectives—acquires a special relevance in our exhibition. Differing from Hal Foster's idea of the artist as an ethnographer who, in a neocolonial, Eurocentric fashion, "speaks for the other," Simpson's idea is closer to Mary Louis Pratt's concept of "the contact zone" and Homi Bhabha's notion of the "in-between space or third space." This space can be seen in the pioneering photographs Graciela Iturbide made in 1979 of the Seri (Comcáac) Indigenous group on the coast of Sonora, Mexico, and in David Lamelas's 1974 film *The Desert People*, about the Papago (Tohono O'odham) in southeastern Arizona, which questions the voices that purport to speak for the disappearing other. In the exhibition, this intersection and collaboration with the others also appears in the work of contemporary artists, designers, and cultural practitioners, many of whom operate outside the traditional boundaries of art's domain: Mariana Castillo Deball's totemic ceramic sculptures, Carla Fernández's wearable textiles, Jorge González's stools, and Javier Téllez's recent film.

Santa Fe inspiring site-responsive new works

We responded to the context by incorporating works that connect aspects of Santa Fe and New Mexico with corresponding elements elsewhere in the Americas, intending to show new ways of seeing and doing that would resonate in Santa Fe. The artistic duo Rometti Costales, for example, who were guest resident artists at SITE Santa Fe, developed a new work that emerges from the New Mexico landscape as well as from readings such as Lucy Lippard's *Marks in Place: Contemporary Responses to Rock Art* (1989), which concerns the historical transmission of knowledge through hieroglyphics in the area, and Eduardo Viveiro de Castro's understanding of Amerindian cosmology via the notion of "perspectivism."

Reconciling differences in shared territories

From my early research for SITElines, I was interested in the case of Aby Warburg, a German art historian and cultural theorist who visited New Mexico in 1896. In 1923, Warburg described this experience in a lecture titled "Reminiscences from a Journey to the Pueblo Indians," which he delivered to a nonprofessional audience while he was interned in the Kreuzlingen Sanatorium in Kreuzlingen, Switzerland.[20] In the lecture, Warburg described the snake ritual of the Hopi, which he hadn't experienced, but knew of through photographs and the accounts of others. He connected the ritual to the iconography of the snake as cosmological and iconographical symbol in European antiquity—particularly in the figure of the Laocoön, but also in additional examples up to the Middle Ages—and used it to probe the disappearance of myth and ritual in modernity. The lecture ended with Warburg's plea for the recovery of ritual, myth, symbolism, poetry, and contemplation:

> The American of to-day no longer worships the rattle-snake. Extermination (and whisky) is his answer to it. Electricity enslaved, the lightning held captive in the wire, has produced a civilization which has no use for heathen poetry. But what does it put in its place? The forces of nature are no longer seen in anthropomorphic shapes; they are conceived as an endless succession of waves, obedient to the touch of a man's hand. With these waves the civilization of the mechanical age is destroying what natural science, itself emerging out of myth, had won with such vast effort—the sanctuary of devotion, the remoteness needed for contemplation.[21]

Warburg's visit to New Mexico was also to have a profound effect on his seminal, unfinished *Mnemosyne*, a visual atlas whose contents—a thousand images and photographs mounted on forty panels—trace aesthetic and historical connections from antiquity to modernity. Our curatorial research took us to the Warburg Institute in London, where we had access to the photographs Warburg took in New Mexico as well as to others he bought that portray Indigenous groups, ceremonies, handcrafts, landscapes, and buildings. Warburg's experience, and its outcome, has also inspired a number of contemporary artists to either follow his route or question his discourse, including Aurélien Froment, Goshka Macuga, Stefan Pente and Ines Schaber, and Stephen G. Rhodes.

The attempt to include Warburg's text or to incorporate him in some way in the SITE Santa Fe biennial was heavily contested by one of the co-curators. Today, we are aware of the historical and ethical flaws of Warburg's thought, which emerged from a context that still needs to be decolonized. Still, Warburg's demand for reintroducing ritual into modern life resonates with many works in the exhibition.

Hybridizing the vernacular

The production of handcrafts continues to be a means of economic survival for many Indigenous communities in the Americas. Often, the nature of the products has shifted from functional and symbolic objects to souvenirs turned out for the tourist market. On the one hand, contemporary handcrafts can be seen as the hybridization of Indigenous ways with modern materials or techniques—the creative result of an interchange between cultures—but on the other, they inevitably reflect the power imbalance of *mestizaje* and cultural colonization. Currently, artists and designers who are interested in gaining Indigenous and vernacular knowledge recognize that many forms of production that were lost during colonization and modernization are in fact more sustainable than industrial forms of production that are both destructive to the planet and reliant on economic and social exploitation. This relearning leads to the production, at a local level, of material forms that are requisite for living and thriving. Such handcrafts go beyond the decorative and mnemonic to regain their functional and symbolic meanings, and as such, they bring "folklore" to life again.

Challenging the model of the biennial

While the biennial exhibition provides a timely model for helping artistic communities at the semi-peripheries and peripheries gain visibility—allowing them to articulate local and regional concerns and practices in dialogue with a wider international network—today the format is in crisis. Since curators normally start work on exhibitions some eighteen months before they open, the biennial schedule allows very limited creative space and time for curators to conduct new research and for artists to develop new work. While it is urgently important to stretch the research and production time needed for organizing recurring exhibitions, it is more crucial still to question the conventional identity of the biennial as a survey of artistic practices. SITElines's concern is, instead, to provide a platform for raising questions and demonstrating how they resonate locally and internationally.

Cotton a plan
was dry to join W
Of Cotton is rich,
The fine Egypt

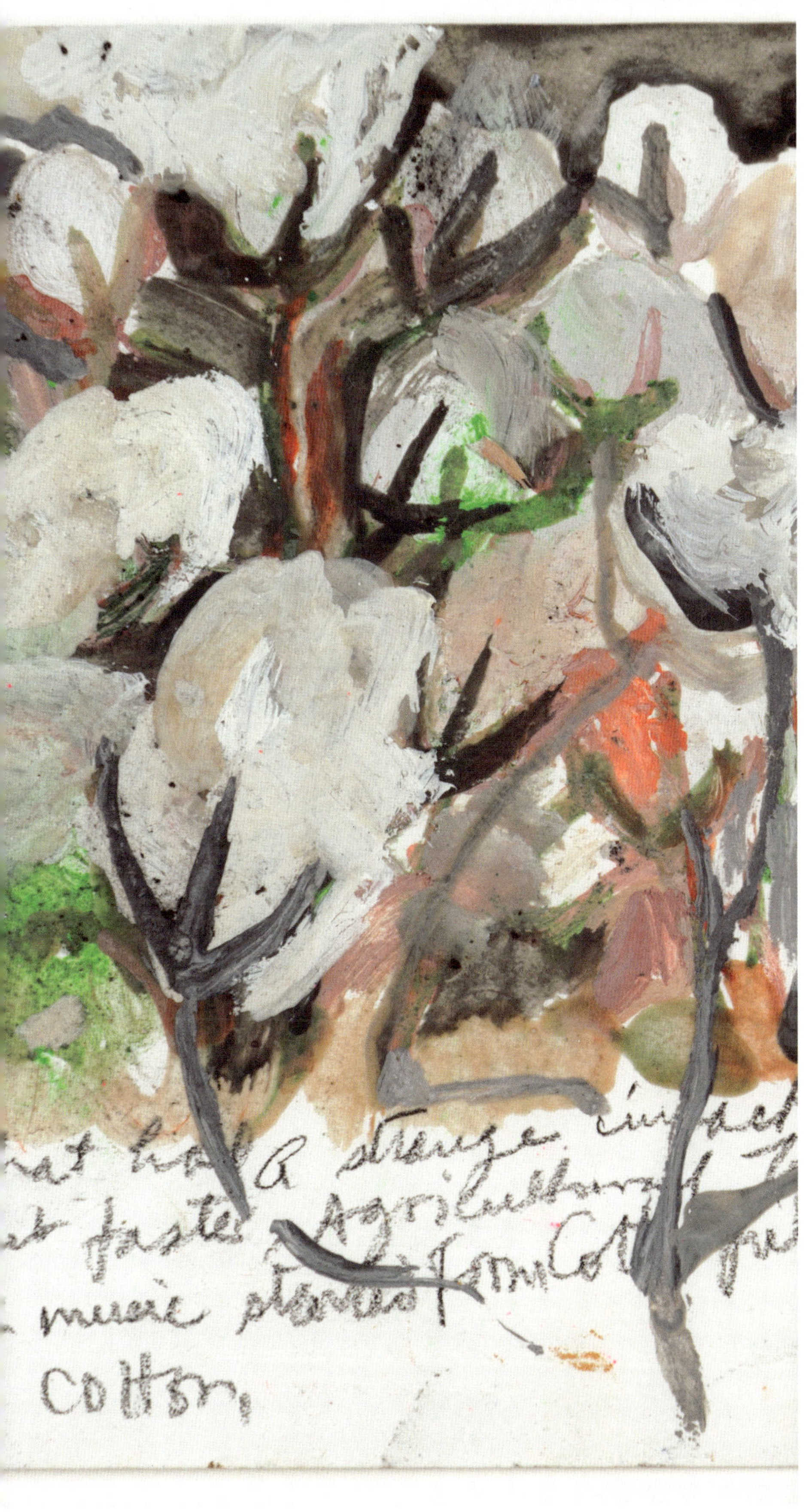
had a strange
faster
music stories from
Cotton.

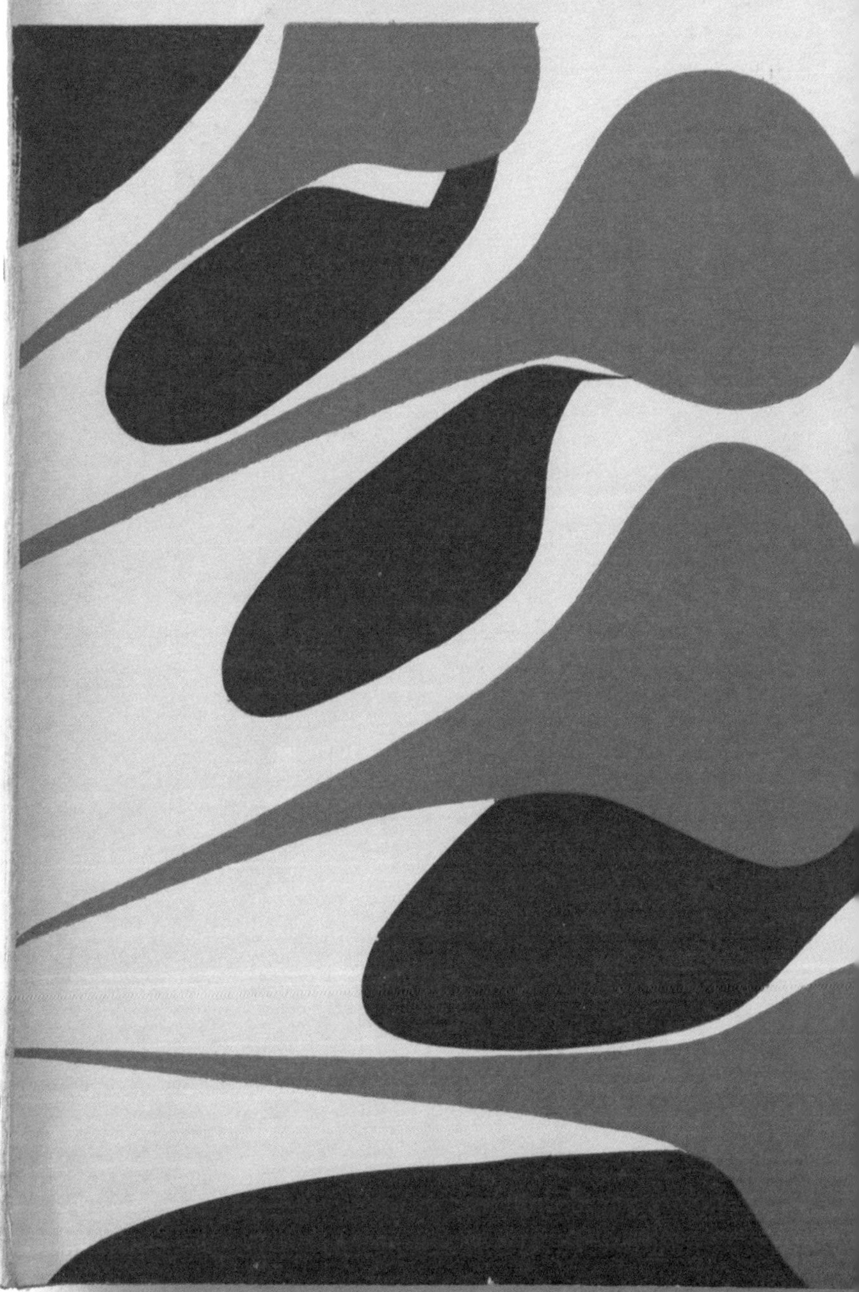
el corno emplumad

El Corno Emplumado / The Plumed Horn

Irene Hofmann

El Corno Emplumado / The Plumed Horn was a bilingual quarterly journal that in the 1960s provided a lively forum for vanguard poets, writers, and artists, primarily from the Americas. The periodical was named for the American jazz instrument embellished with the feathers of Quetzalcóatl, the iconic plumed serpent god of Mesoamerica's pre-Hispanic cultures. *El Corno*, as it became known, was launched in January 1962 by the American poet Margaret Randall and the Mexican writer and journalist Sergio Mondragón from their home in Mexico City. For close to a decade, the quarterly captured the political and artistic energy of the times through the voices of an international cohort of contributors.

A publication with thirty-one issues, *El Corno* was sustained by funds collected from poetry readings, the sale of donated art, subscriptions, and ads. Always seeking the best new work, *El Corno* championed both emerging and established talents: new Mexican poets, the Beats, Indigenous writers, and the surrealists. André Breton, Ernesto Cardenal, Leonora Carrington, Elaine de Kooning, Allen Ginsberg, Mathias Goeritz, Raquel Jodorowsky, Octavio Paz, and the architect Buckminster Fuller all found a platform in *El Corno*.

Writers and readers were drawn to *El Corno* because of its bold editorial stance, experimental typography, and provocative cover art reflecting issues of the period. Over the years, the journal found its way into bookstores in cities throughout the Americas, including Bogotá, Buenos Aires, Caracas, Havana, Lima, Managua, Montevideo, Santiago, São Paulo, and Quito. *El Corno* eventually reached Australia, Finland, and India. When the editors took a stand in defense of antigovernment student protests in Mexico in 1968, reprisals forced the journal to cease operation by the summer of 1969.

PREVIOUS SPREAD:
Anna Boghiguian, *Woven Wind*, 2016

OPPOSITE:
El Corno Emplumado / The Plumed Horn, no. 29 (January 1969)

Once an American Indian Theater

Conrad Skinner

I gave them an Elizabethan theater.

— Paolo Soleri

Embedded in the alluvial cobble of the Santa Fe watershed plain, the Paolo Soleri Amphitheater—located on the Santa Fe Indian School (SFIS) campus west of Cerrillos Road—lies in a geography of historical flux: Santa Fe has been variously inhabited, colonized, and governed by the Tewa, the Spanish, Mexico, and the United States. From 1890 until the early 1960s, the Bureau of Indian Affairs of the Department of the Interior ran the school, which served mostly Pueblo boarding students. In 1962, however, the Bureau relocated the students and converted the facility into the Institute of American Indian Arts (IAIA), a multitribal high school of the arts augmented by two years of postgraduate offerings. In 1964, IAIA Arts Director Lloyd Kiva New (Cherokee) commissioned an Italian emigré, architect Paolo Soleri, to design a cultural center as home for the performing arts program. New had two years earlier visited Soleri's Cosanti Foundation, where he and the architect discussed building a theater using Soleri's earth-formed building techniques, which New felt were appropriate for the Indian theater. The 2,000-seat Paolo Soleri Amphitheater was completed in 1970.

Until 1980, when IAIA closed, Paolo Soleri's singularly imaginative building provided a venue for the first curriculum in the country to professionally train young American Indians in playwriting, acting, modern dance, and stagecraft. As Daystar/Rosalie Jones, choreographer and former IAIA faculty member, has noted, Native-American performing arts at IAIA were a conscious, deliberate invention.[22] Following an IAIA architectural program, Soleri designed the theater so that it would invite players and audience to physically engage and interact over, around, and through its biomorphic and geometric forms. Standing at the lip of the steep bowl seating, one sights across the theater bowl north to the twelve-thousand-foot Sangre de Cristo peaks. Looking downward, the rusticated concrete shell backing the circular stage reflects the bowl's curve. Beyond the stage, the bowl's excavation spoils pile up to form an artificial hill, rising in gentle arabesque. On the slope, actors may perform, animals may play roles, and, imparting a two-faced aspect to the theater, audiences may sit. A concrete bridge, broken by a scooping balcony whose upturned horns frame the sky, limns the shell's arc. Construe this scooping balcony as the equivalent of an Elizabethan theater's upper stage.

In an architectural sketch, Soleri annotated the main stage "physical" and the upper zone "ghostly." He traced across the top-level stage a diurnal cycle from morning star to dawn to day to a moon bridge. This intersected, at a geometric sun sculpture, with a representation of a succession of weather conditions: cloud, sun, lightning, thunder. Subterranean tunnels effected a vertical transition, embodying stages of being. As players emerged through openings at the foot of the stage, they could ascend hollow columns or broad staircases penetrating the shell to reach the upper level. In this stage without a proscenium, the vitality of creation and nature coexisted with the artifice of a new American drama.

New articulated IAIA's pedagogical philosophy that guided the architectural design, explaining that "cultural traditions . . . can be used creatively as a springboard to a meaningful and productive contemporary life."[23] Drama instructor Rolland Meinholtz, metalwork instructor Charles Loloma, and Daystar/Rosalie Jones joined New in developing a theory of contemporary Native dramaturgy based in research into ancient and traditional forms that contemporaneously spawned the Indian amphitheater, a new building type. As part of their research, the three attended ceremonies at the Hopi and Rio Grande Pueblos. They admired the pin-drop acoustics of the great kiva at the Aztec Ruins. Meinholtz contributed information on Northwest coastal tribe rituals set in large timber houses, and New brought knowledge of Plains Indian ceremonial settings.[24]

Meinholtz's "Notes on Indian Theatre and Theatre Practice" delineates the program he, New, and Loloma conceived for the architecture of Native-American performing arts: "The audience should feel that they have been somewhat crowded into a large lodge or partially underground chamber . . . The theater should be designed in such a way that theatrical action is not necessarily localized to the stage area. . . . The arrangement of spectator and performer should make it plain that the theater is a three-dimensional art."

Paolo Soleri (1919–2013), graduate of Torino Politecnico in Turin, Italy, had apprenticed to Frank Lloyd Wright in 1946 and in 1956 settled in Scottsdale, Arizona. There, he and his wife, Colly (1925–1982), established the nonprofit Cosanti Foundation. At this compound of earth-formed concrete studios and living quarters, Soleri ran workshops in which participants studied his casting techniques and learned his philosophy of modular, compact, self-sufficient cities termed *arcologies.*

IAIA's "outdoor theater classroom" would be the third of only six commissions Soleri undertook during his lifetime. His early sketches of the amphitheater depict a cluster of quarter-sphere apses resembling Cosanti. But as he absorbed the program of the IAIA "Notes" through intensive communication with New and Meinholtz and observation of IAIA students, he interpreted the prescription for a three-dimensional Native drama setting as a kinesthetic

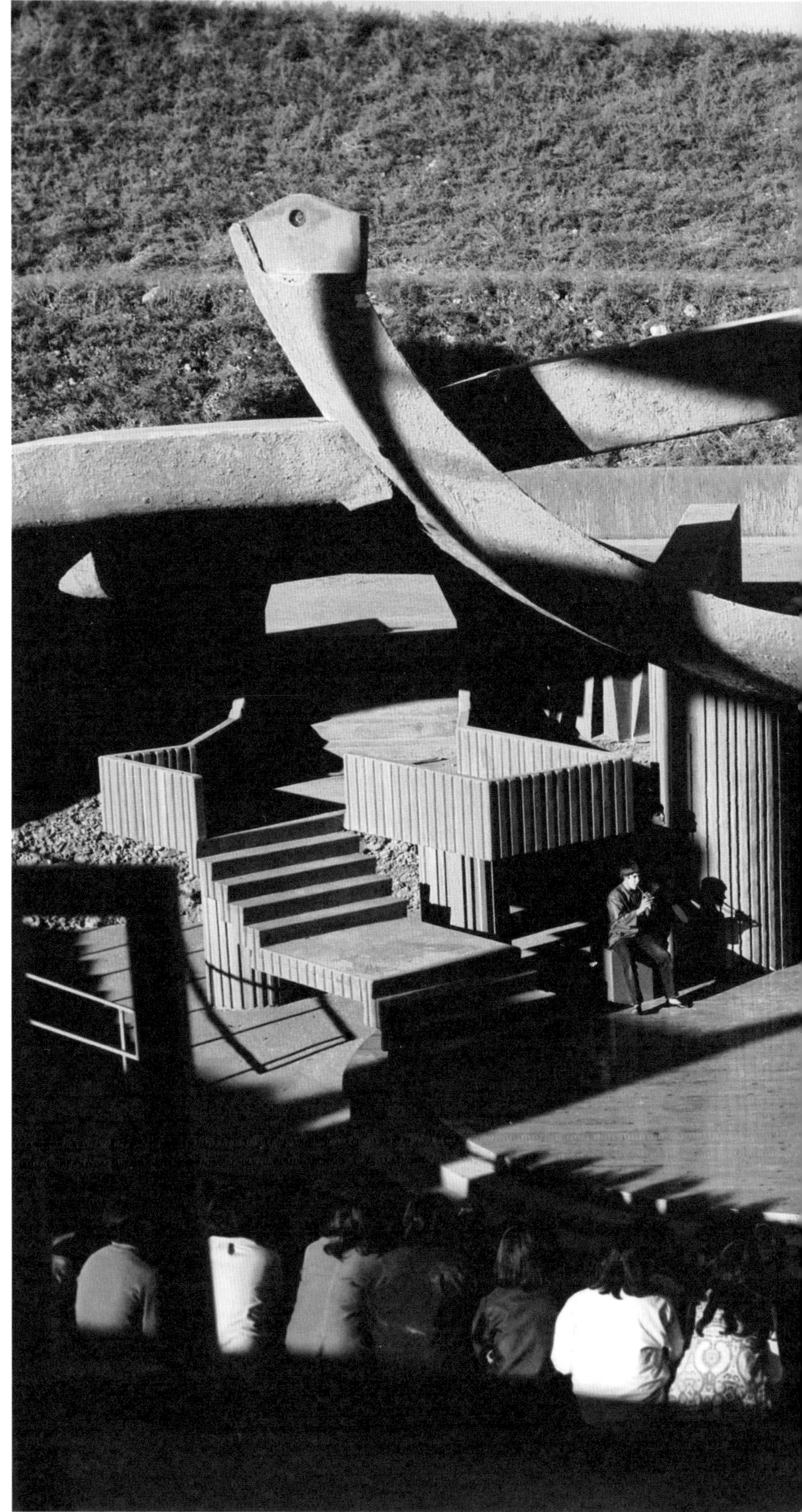

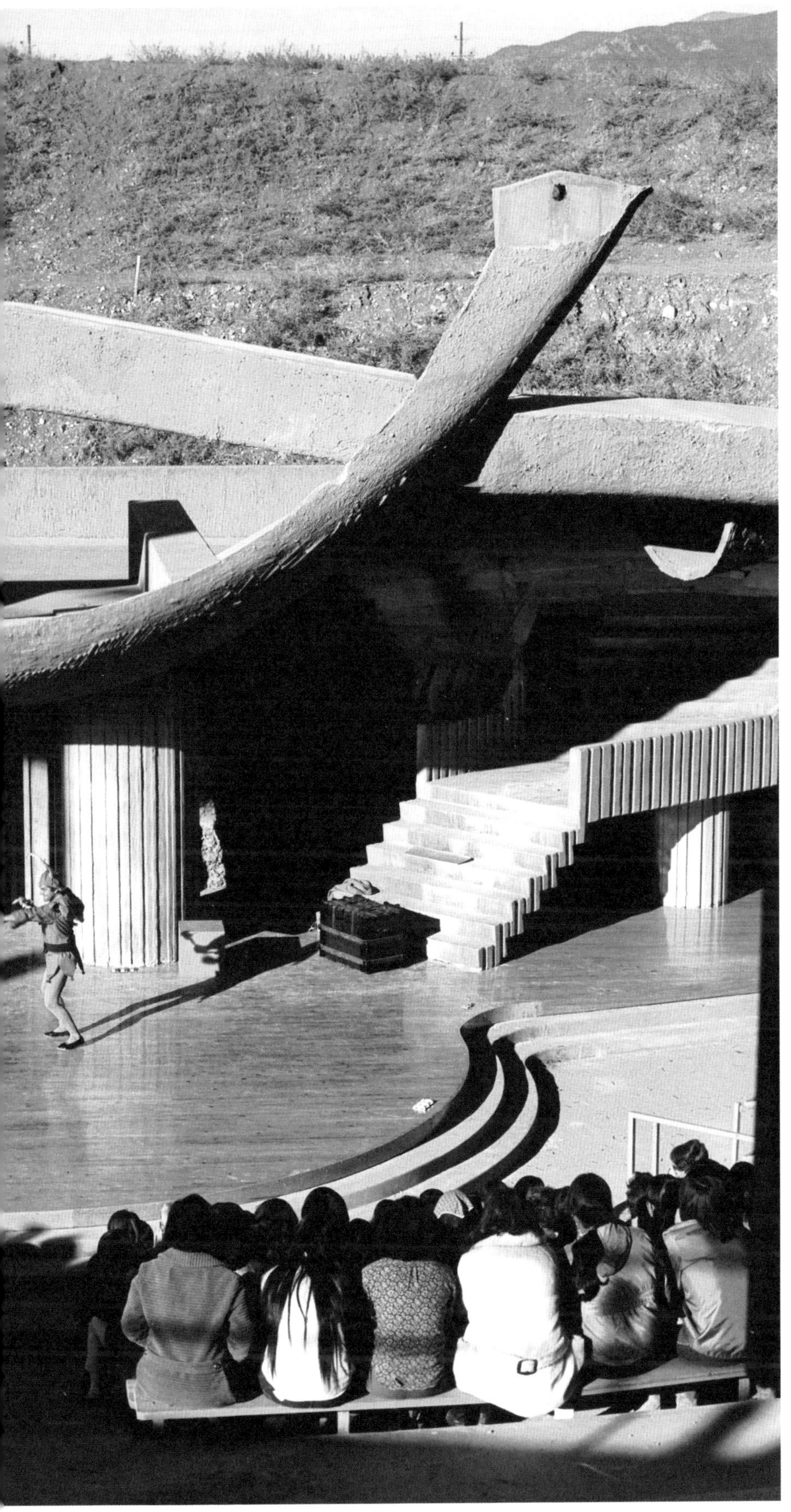

theater. Soleri planned construction as a series of workshops for IAIA over three summers. During the 1966 session, he and four of his Cosanti Foundation interns led IAIA staff and students in the massive work of carving into an open field in Santa Fe. Over a form of packed earth, they cast a concrete shell backing the stage. And they trenched an artificial canyon, smoothing its reticulated walls with clay before applying coats of concrete and a clay-glue slip.

For Soleri, working with the Native Americans of IAIA drew him closer to his adopted Southwest. The construction's Federal overseers, however, failed to understand either the collaboration or the earth-formed architecture. According to Soleri's project manager, Doug Lee, "They thought we were playing in the mud."[25] After the first summer, the Bureau of Indian Affairs took the project out of Soleri's hands and put it into those of executive architect Channell Graham of Albuquerque.

Construction of the theater marked a significant concentration of organization and energy within IAIA. Classes and events followed the 1970 opening performance by Swiss mime Jan Kessler. The "Indian Summer" workshops of 1971 featured choreographer Juan Valenzuela. In 1972, the American Indian Theater Ensemble (AITE), which was newly forming at LaMaMa Experimental Theater Club in New York, selected seven IAIA students to join the sixteen-member company.[26] Performances of Native dramaturgy, such as AITE founder Hanay Geiogamah's *Body Indian*, made the theater a vital part of campus life for the following decade. In July 1980, in commemoration of the fiftieth anniversary of D. H. Lawrence's death, Elizabeth Taylor and Trevor Howard joined other actors performing the British author's *Eagle in New Mexico* in the amphitheater. The event included the premier of Thea Musgrave's choral work *The Last Twilight* with a Lawrence text.

Despite these activities, New fell short in the funding of the institute's performing arts program.[27] Furthermore, the New Mexico Pueblos' nearly twenty-year opposition to IAIA culminated in House of Representatives hearings in 1979 that led to IAIA's expulsion from the campus and the restoration of SFIS occupancy the following year. When IAIA left, its theater, of course, had to stay behind. While the SFIS held poetry recitals as well as graduation and promotion ceremonies in the amphitheater's bowl, apparently the school's curriculum did not include professional drama instruction. For three decades, the SFIS rented "the Paolo" to impresarios such as Jamie Lenfestey for summer concerts; the qualities that were designed into it as an Indian theater—intimacy of the relationship between performer and audience, sensitive acoustics—pleased musicians and listeners alike. Promoter Seth Roffman held fourteen Native Roots and Rhythms Festivals at the venue. The amphitheater, hosting performances by Santana, Burning Spear, Bob Dylan, B. B. King, and Leonard Cohen, among many others, became a fixture in the cultural life of Santa Fe.

In 2010, however, the SFIS—now owned by the Pueblo Governors of New Mexico[28]—cited high maintenance costs, rowdy audiences, and the "expressionist" (a misinterpretation) architecture's incongruity with the Pueblo-style campus as grounds for closing the amphitheater and announcing its imminent demolition. Led by SFIS alumni, thousands of music lovers and Soleri admirers protested in the regional press and on social media. But it took an article in the *Santa Fe New Mexican* by actor/playwright Bruce King (Oneida), an IAIA alumnus and AITE founding member, to remind the public of the Paolo Soleri Amphitheater's founding purpose as the first contemporary Native-American theater. The *New Mexican* reported that in mid-July New Mexico Senators Tom Udall and Jeff Bingaman had negotiated with the Pueblos a reprieve for the amphitheater. Their intervention may have forestalled demolition but was inadequate to further its productive life. It now stands unused, forgotten, mothballed in chain-link, its concrete slowly spalling away in New Mexico's mercurial climate.

Navajo playwright Robert Shorty, an original AITE member, has expressed his hopes for an American-Indian drama that will be "as varied as pictures on canvas. We have to try and explain to Indians and non-Indians the turning points in their coexistent lives, where things happen and why, to try and make the communication between the two cultures more bearable."[29] These are not the words of a man who wishes his work to be confined within a cultural enclave, but one who hopes to generate an improved cultural understanding of a painful shared legacy.

The Paolo Soleri Amphitheater communicates the architecture of drama as a field or landscape of action, in contrast to the Western proscenium stage, which is a frame of action. One may even see its elements—stage, shell, bridge, canyon, hill—as performative themselves. As Santa Fean Dan Gibson wrote in 1993, "One finds a performance space at the Paolo Soleri that is as much a work of art as anything to be seen on the stage."[30]

Despite its obvious architectural power, the amphitheater seems to be unrecognized as a precedent for other Native theaters in which its qualities could recur. The question inevitably arises, will history see it as anomalous, or will it be one day exemplary?

PREVIOUS SPREAD:
Paolo Soleri Amphitheater, 1970

FOLLOWING SPREAD:
Paolo Soleri making design presentation to Rolland Meinholz, Lloyd Kiva New, and IAIA students, ca. 1965

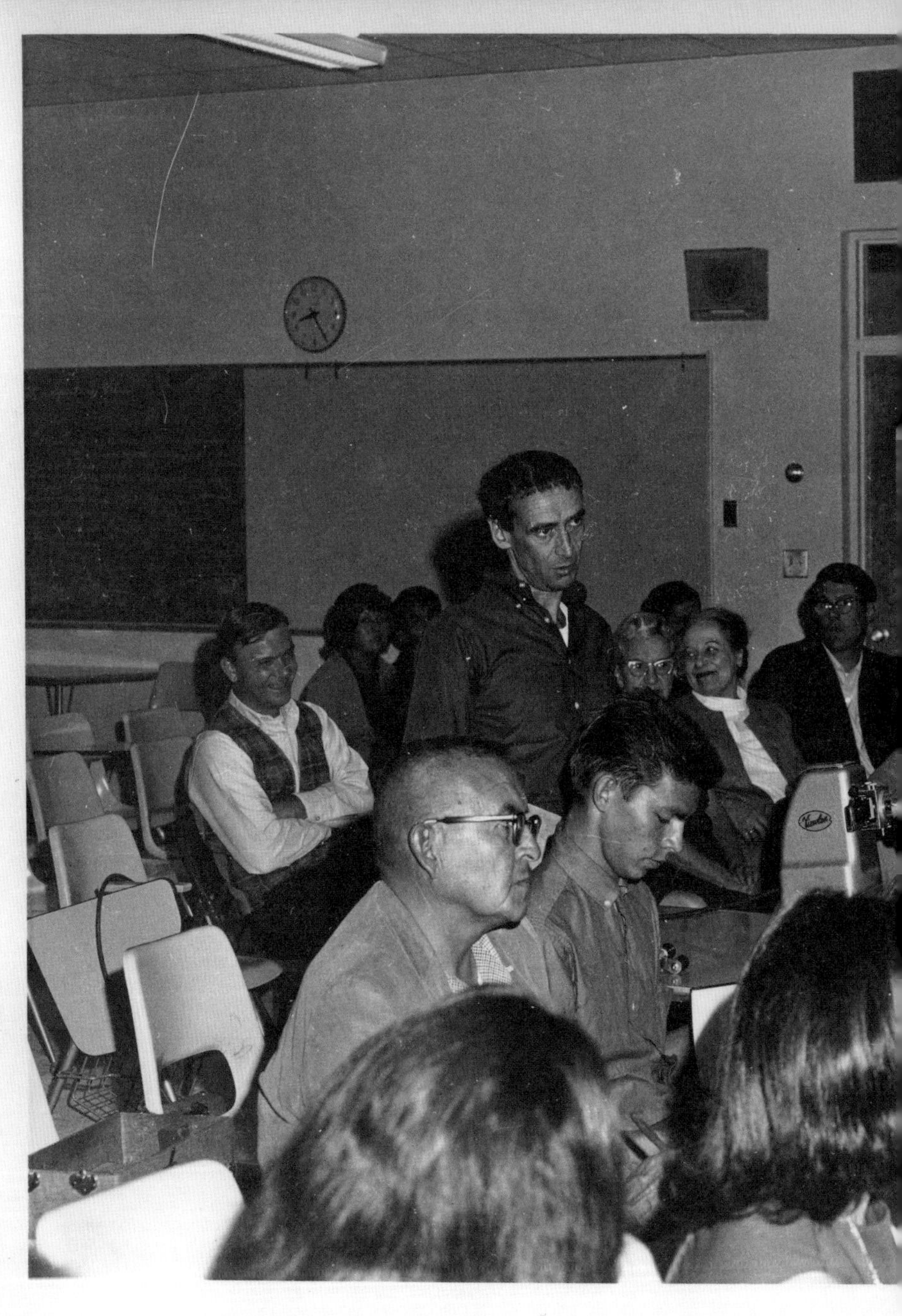

Mr. Soleri, architect from Phoenix discus

Kienholtz, Houser Smith Perry Harcourt Lin

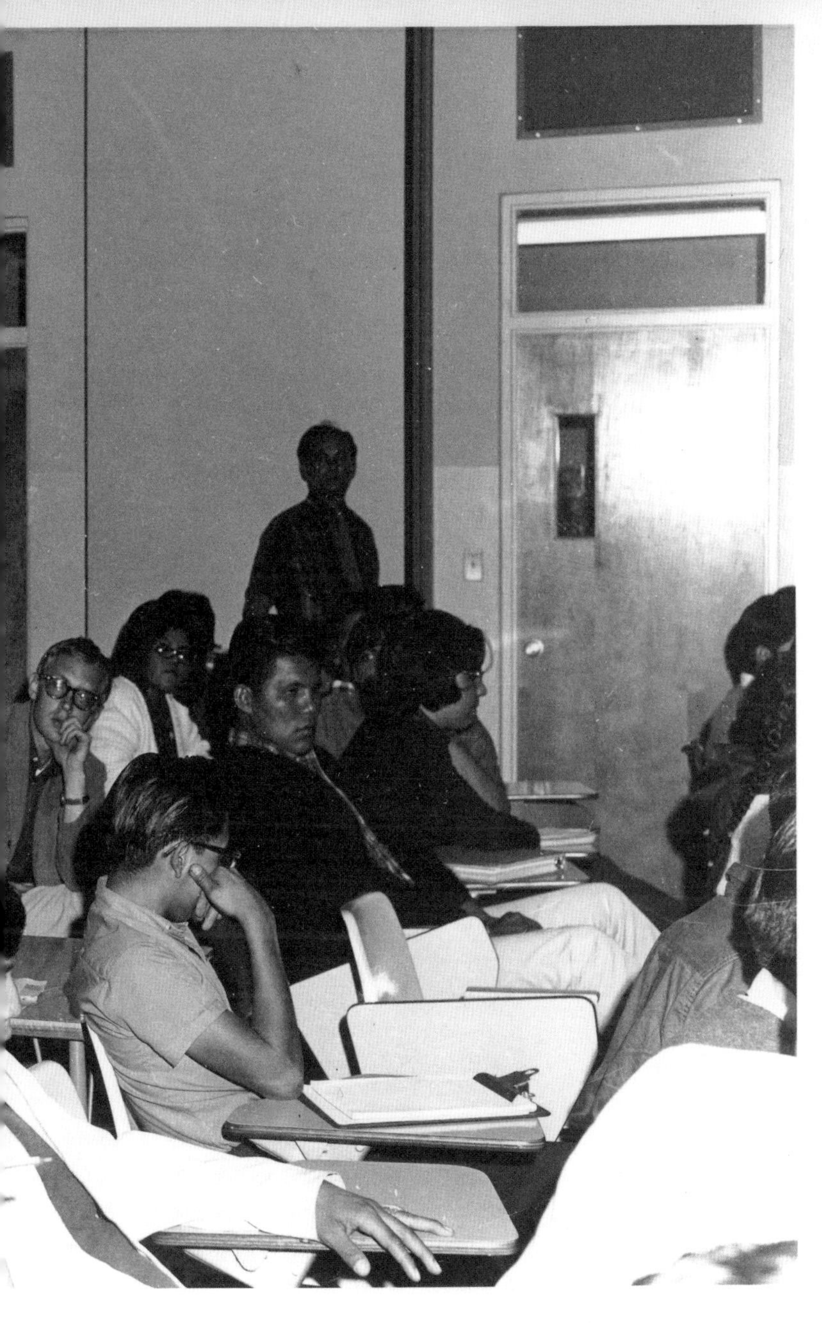

designs etc. of outdoor theatres

…lee McC.
…rmick

Pfoyd

and students

1964-65
'66

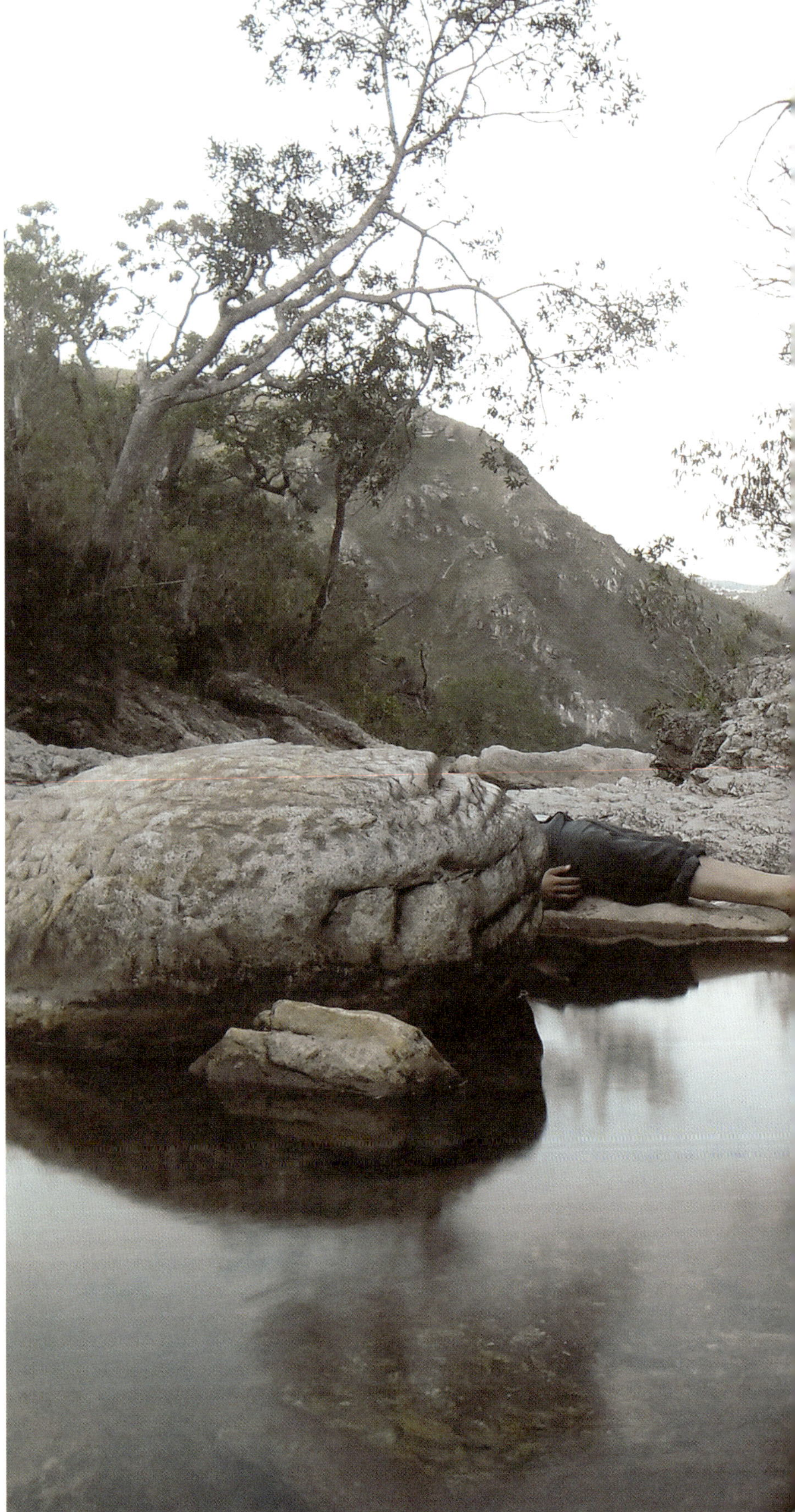

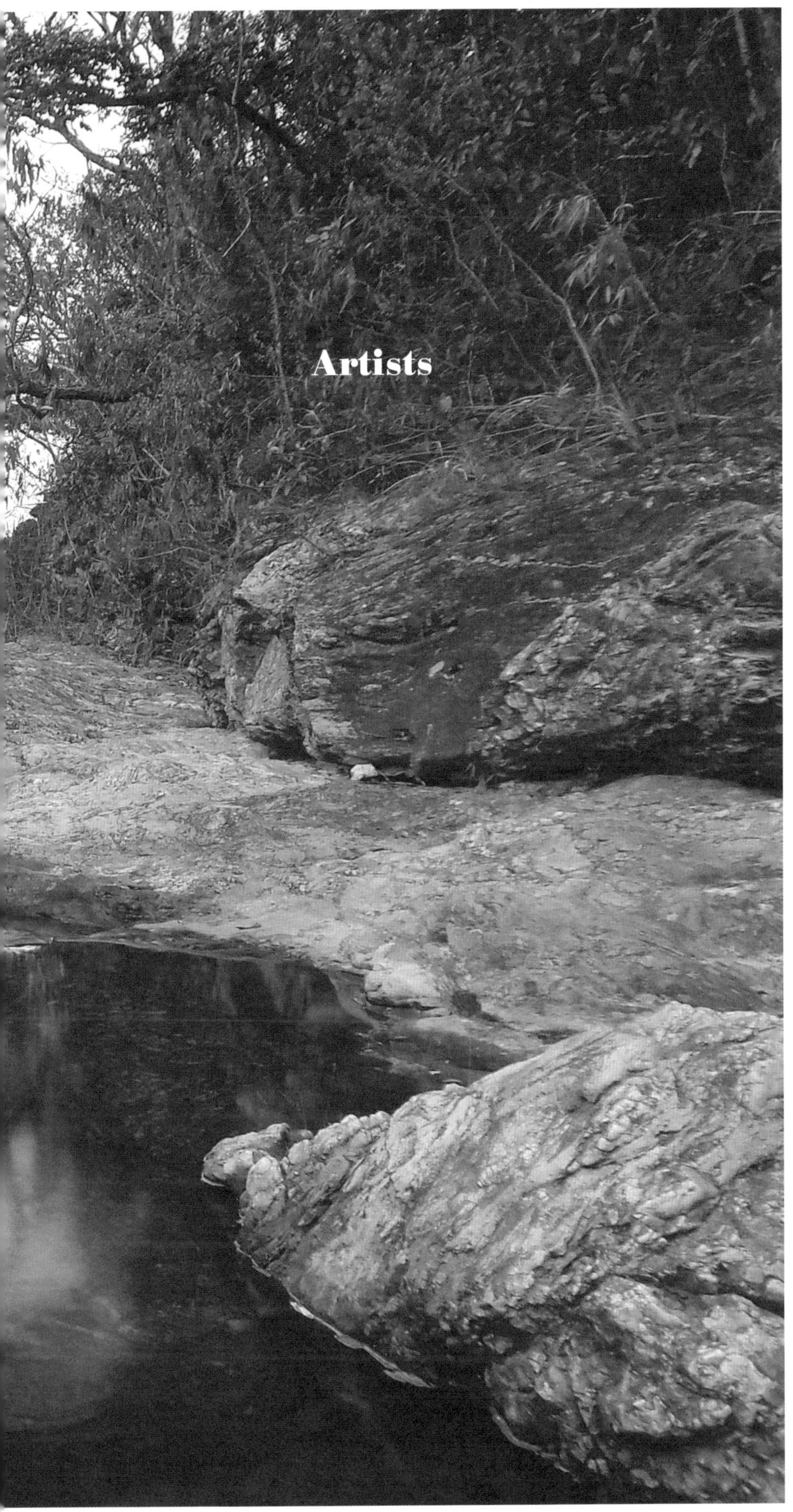

Artists

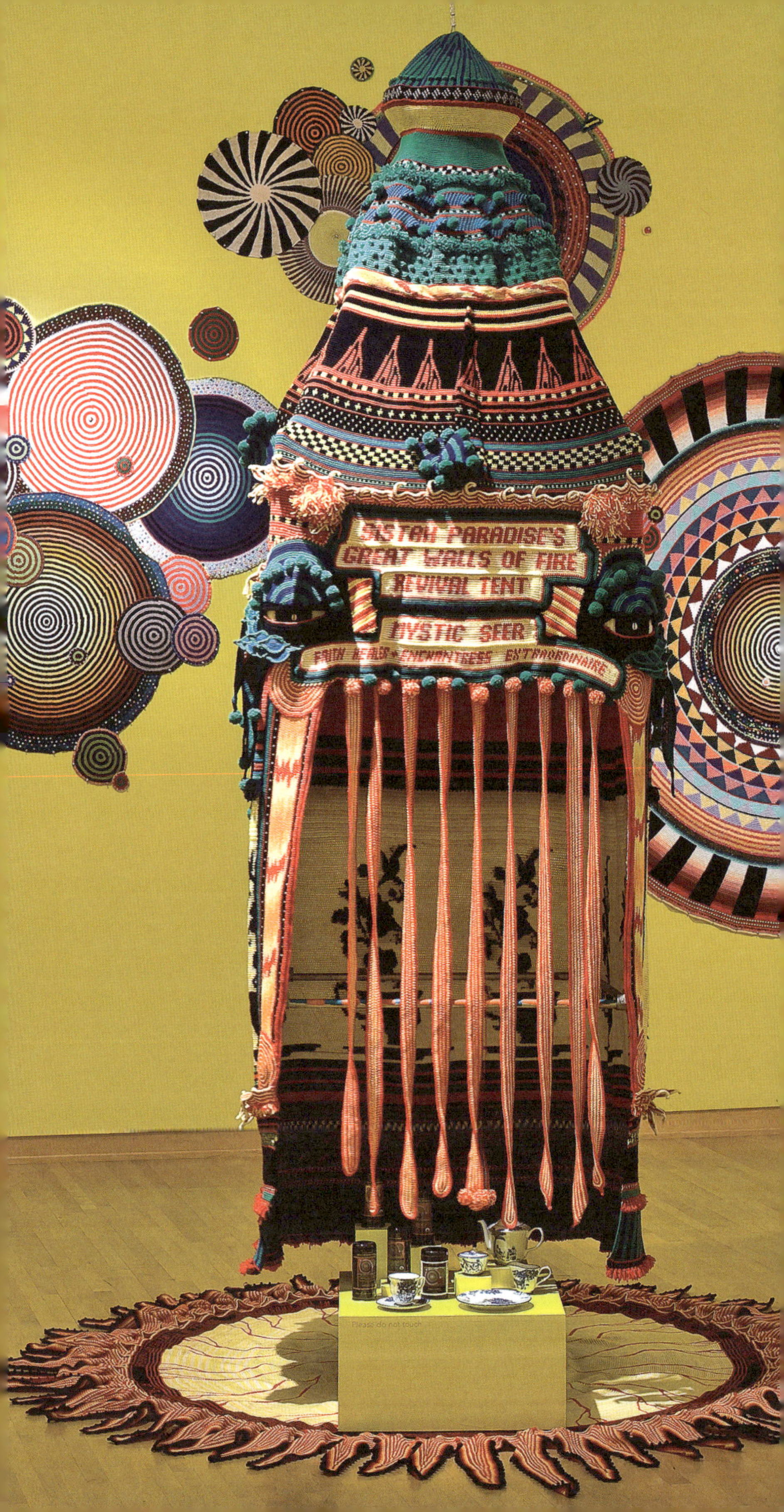
SISTAH PARADISE'S
GREAT WALLS OF FIRE
REVIVAL TENT
MYSTIC SEER

Xenobia Bailey

b. 1955 in Seattle, U.S.A.; lives in Philadelphia

Sistah Paradise's Revival Tent is a long-term project in which Xenobia Bailey addresses aspects of vernacular African-American history and culture. The revival, or missionary, tent originated in rural parts of the United States, particularly the South, where people once had limited access to social gatherings. Traveling evangelical ministries historically used these tents to engage ever-larger audiences. Bailey's work pays homage to these informal public gathering spaces and to the positive energy that has resonated from them throughout history. Creating her own version of myth and origins, the artist conjures the figure of Sistah Paradise as the ultimate healer—as well as a wizard in the aesthetic of funk—giving a feminist-inflected sense of being and place to African Americans within their own history.

Though Bailey began by studying sculpture, she switched from wood to yarn after learning to crochet, largely because of her interest in using ordinary, available, and affordable materials that reflect African-American popular culture. When in the 1980s she began crocheting objects as sculptures, they were large mandala-shaped works made from colorful, concentric circles; the form persists here as a backdrop for the revival tent.

Bailey's aesthetic comes from the "making something from nothing" sensibility that has been associated with the legacy of slavery. From the depths of humble materials, and through the work of the hands, a powerful form can be fabricated. Bailey's interest in funk was a product of growing up in the 1960s, and its influence is evident in her works' vibrations of color and rhythm and their reference to the shape of vinyl records. In addition to being inspired by African-American history and funk, the artist acknowledges the importance of Native-American and Asian influences, which inform both the colors and forms of her work.

— Rocío Aranda-Alvarado

PREVIOUS SPREAD:
Paulo Nazareth, *Untitled*, 2011–12

OPPOSITE:
Sistah Paradise's *Great Walls of Fire Revival Tent*, 1993, installed at John Michael Kohler Arts Center

Lina Bo Bardi

b. 1914 in Rome, Italy; d. 1992 in São Paulo, Brazil

Lina Bo Bardi was an architect, designer, editor, and writer, whose contribution to the field of modern architecture in Brazil has been internationally acknowledged for only a decade. After earning a degree in architecture in Rome, in 1940 Bo Bardi left the city to escape the rise of fascism, and moved to Milan. There, she worked at Gio Ponti's architecture practice and collaborated on several magazines before returning to Rome in 1946, where she married journalist and art dealer Pietro Maria Bardi (1900-1999). That same year, the couple emigrated to Brazil, where they were invited by communications tycoon Assis Chateaubriand to create the first modern museum in the country—the Museu de Arte de São Paulo (MASP), founded in 1947, with temporary offices in a commercial building in the city center. Lina's projects from the late 1940s and early '50s, such as the furniture and display systems created for MASP and her first built work, the 1951 Glass House—a home for her and her husband—show the modernist principles she absorbed during her formative years in Italy. In 1958, she was invited to become the director of the Museu de Arte Moderna da Bahia (MAM-BA) in Salvador, where she designed the renovation of the museum's headquarters at the old colonial complex of the Solar do Unhão, and conceived a radical education and exhibitions program for the institution. During her time in Bahia, Bo Bardi came into contact with the impoverished rural populations of the northeastern backcountry and their stripped-down yet highly inventive material culture. The Bahia experience intensified the architect's interest in reconciling the principles of European modernism with local practices and discouraging the country's increasing cultural dependency on the West, a concern that would permeate all her subsequent projects. In many of these—notably the new MASP building, 1968, the Centro de Lazer Fábrica da Pompéia (now simply called the SESC Pompeia), 1982, and the Teatro Oficina, 1991—Bo Bardi's involvement went far beyond the architectural to include programming and the design of display units, furniture, sets, and signage.

— Kiki Mazzucchelli

OPPOSITE:
Cadeira de Beira de Estrada (Roadside Chair), 1967

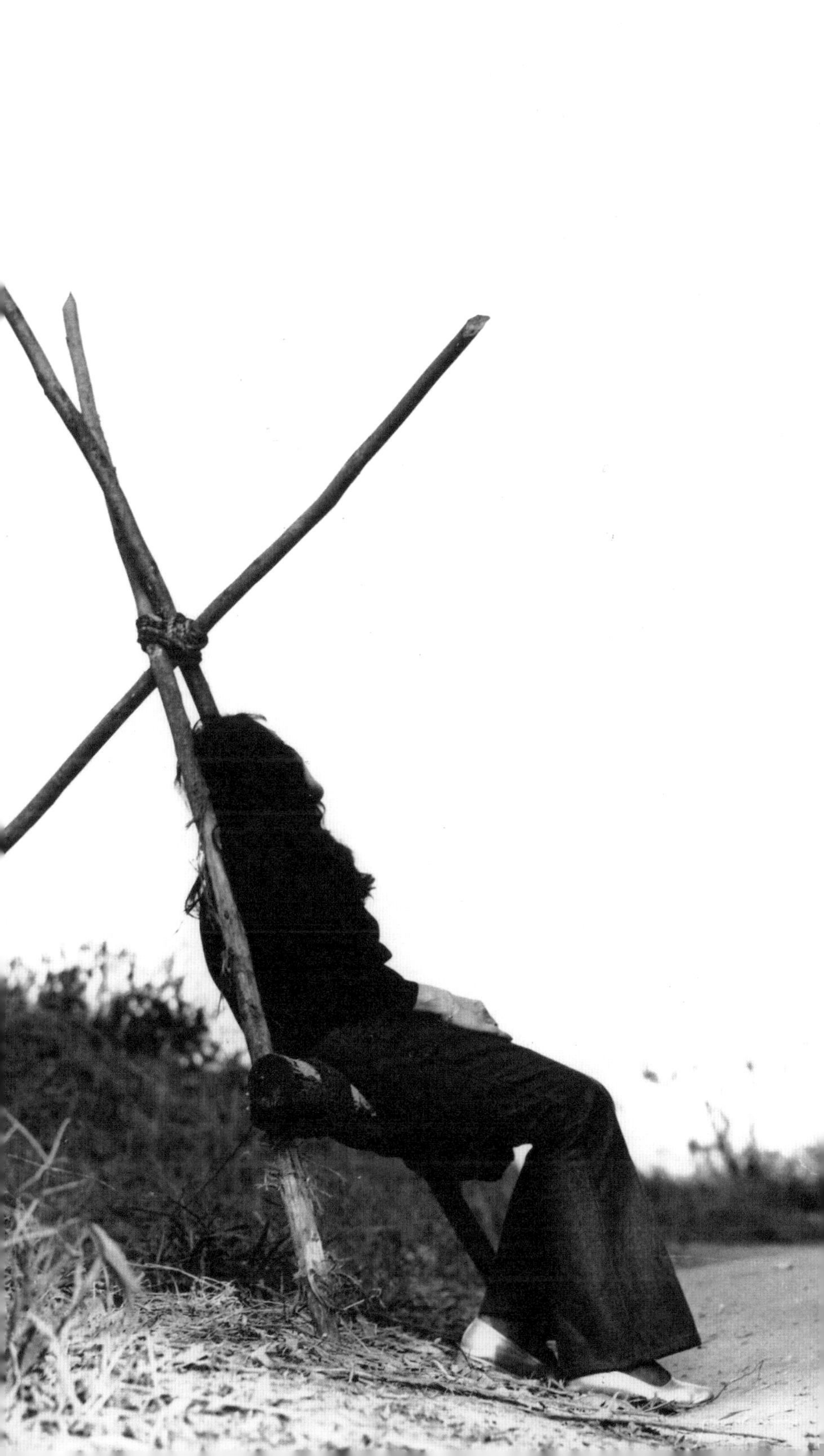

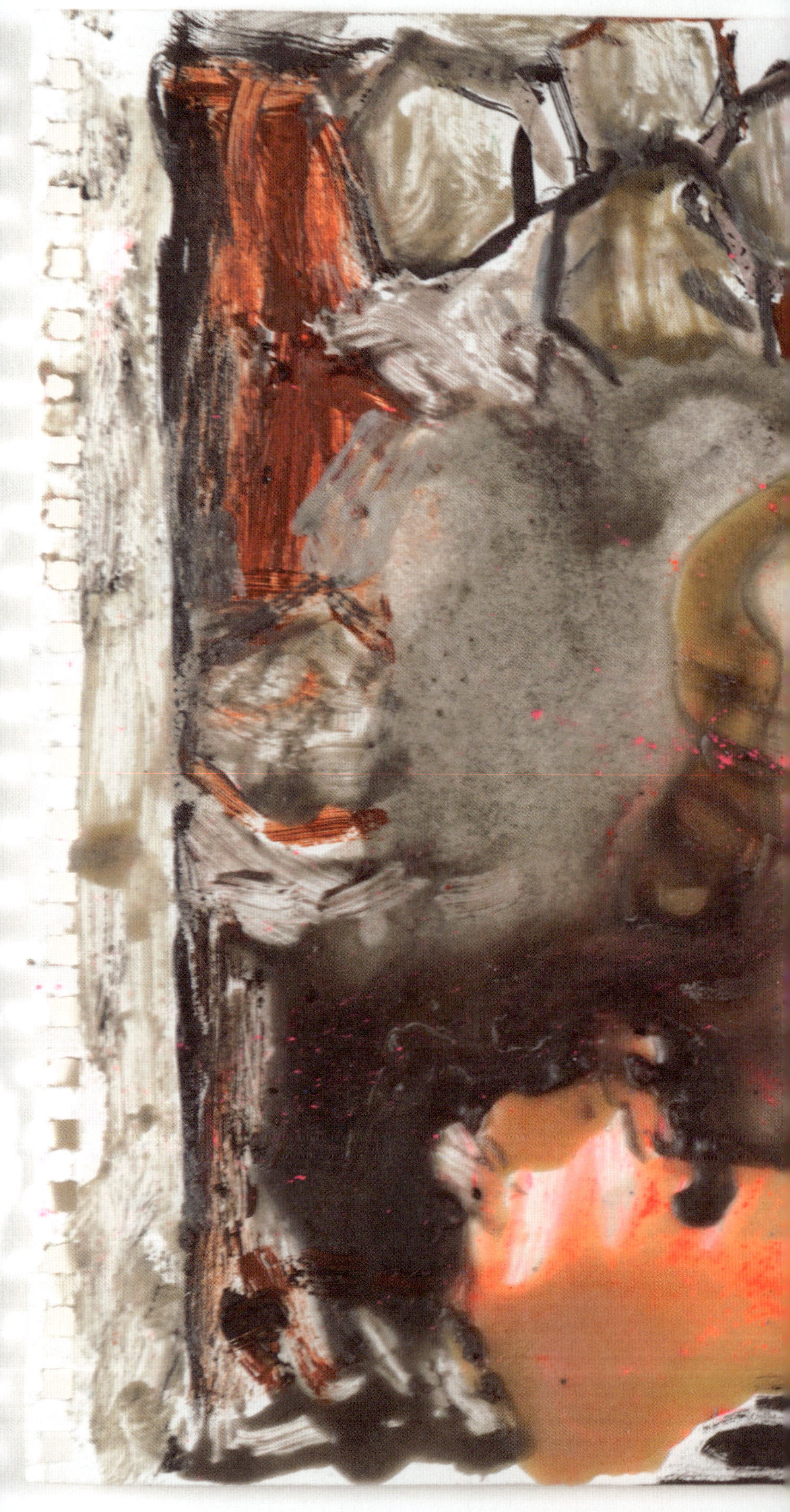

Anna Boghiguian

b. 1946 in Cairo, Egypt; based in Cairo

The simple cotton plant, grown across the globe—from India to Egypt, the Middle East, Peru, and the American South—came to dominate the textile industry, transforming itself into one of the earliest mass-consumer commodities and becoming the foundation for global economies as we know them today. The spice and salt markets had opened earlier international trade routes, as had luxury goods such as sugar and tobacco, but the economic revolution in whose service cotton was employed made it not only one of the first global industries, but also one whose profitability firmly established the large-scale workshop as a model for production, relying from its earliest days on exploitative and forced labor practices.

America's nineteenth-century economic growth depended largely on the commodification of the working bodies of slaves, brought to the South for cotton harvesting. America's slave-harvested crops in turn propped up Britain's textile-based economy, which depended on raw cotton imported from America. Cities like Cairo and Bombay were built on the profits of the cotton textile industry; cotton was central to industrialization in the United Kingdom. In the United States and Canada, textile mills sprang up, supplied with raw cotton from plantations in the fertile land of the American South. They were worked by Aboriginal laborers, Europeans, and other settlers displaced by World Wars I and II, and by children, who provided cheap labor for the garment and textile factories that were built in New England, Quebec, and elsewhere.

Anna Boghiguian's wall drawings and writings at SITE Santa Fe chart the history of this plant. After its harvest, raw cotton was shipped across land and sea, from port to port, destined for weaving workshops and factories. It was then transported in the form of woven textile products for local consumption or export. Boghiguian's drawings and cutout figures trace not only the trade routes that emerged with the international cotton trade, but also the displacement of people as laborers that accompanied the burgeoning industry. In doing so, Boghiguian maps the beginnings of the global markets that are now a defining structure of capitalism.

— Pip Day

OPPOSITE:
Woven Wind, 2016

Margarita Cabrera

b. 1973 in Monterrey, Mexico; lives in El Paso, Texas, U.S.A.

Margarita Cabrera makes these cactus works with groups of immigrants from various locations, but particularly from the southern United States and along the Mexico-U.S. border. In a series of workshops, participants embroider scenes from daily life, as well as symbolic imagery from the Mexican landscape, maps, the colors of the national flag, or more personal objects, such as driver's licenses, onto the surface of fabric cut in the shape of cactus areoles. The fabric is taken from decommissioned Border Patrol uniforms. The series shown in the 2016 version of SITElines includes cacti made by community workshop members in collaboration with the Santa Fe Art Institute. New cacti are added as participants in the workshops complete them.

The cactus species referenced in these sculptural forms are those found along the border, including the nopal, saguaro, and agave. Pockets, buttonholes, identification patches, and uniform labels remain visible, bringing to mind their previous function. Through the workshops, Cabrera encourages women from different community groups to share their narratives about life on the border, the in-between state that is neither Mexico nor the United States: the *nepantla* (in the Aztec language, "the space in between"). On the sculptures, Cabrera lists participants' names along with her own, recognizing them as fellow artists.

In her work, Cabrera brings the aesthetic of American pop art to a study of geopolitical boundaries and the informal networks of craft. She is particularly concerned with issues of immigration, industry, and the consumption of commodities at the border. This contested subject has been the long-standing focus of her soft sculpture: she is perhaps best known for her *Vocho (yellow)*, 2004, a full-scale soft sculpture of a Volkswagen Beetle, a car that was produced in Mexico from 1954 until 2003 for use as city taxis. One of the artist's central interests is the role that international politics have played in the global economy, particularly the reliance of the Mexican economy on its neighbor to the north.

— Rocío Aranda-Alvarado

OPPOSITE:
Space in Between—Saguaro, 2010-12, in collaboration with Maria Lopez

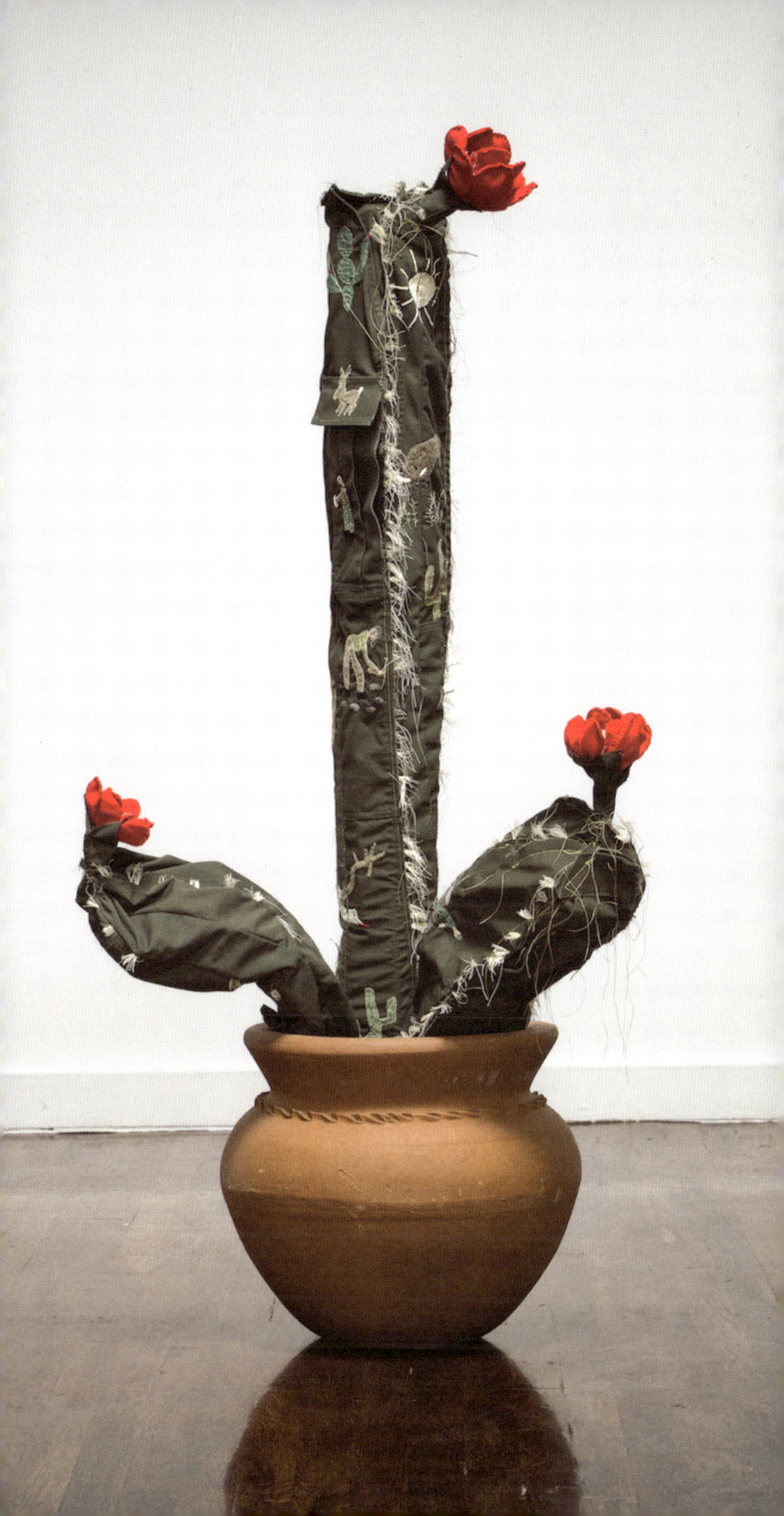

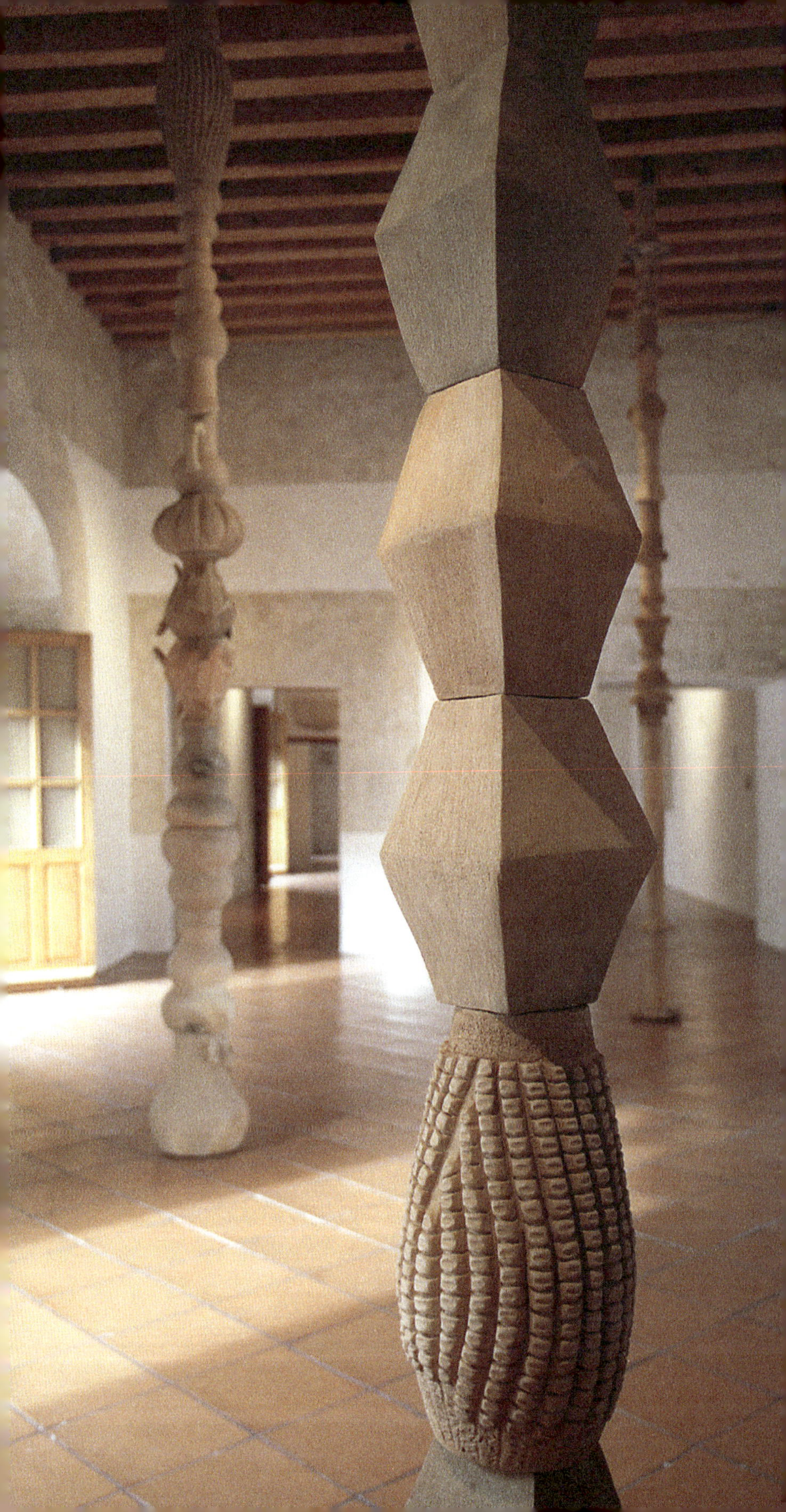

Mariana Castillo Deball

b. 1975 in Mexico City, Mexico; lives in Berlin, Germany

Mariana Castillo Deball developed *Who will measure the space, who will tell me the time?* in collaboration with the Coatlicue Ceramics Workshop (led by the Martínez Alarzón family) of the village of Atzompa, Oaxaca, and the ceramics cooperative Inovando la Tradición, a creative platform in which artisans, designers, and artists honor and adapt the ceramic traditions of the state of Oaxaca. The project was originally commissioned for Castillo Deball's exhibition of the same title at the Museo de Arte Contemporáneo de Oaxaca (MACO).

In preparation for making the work, the group visited the Museo Rufino Tamayo de Arte Prehispánico in Oaxaca City, which opened in 1974 as Tamayo's gift to his home city. In the exhibition spaces, which he developed with museographer Fernando Gamboa, the pre-Hispanic ceramics are not displayed in the conventional way—as relics organized in chronological order—but according to aesthetic considerations. After selecting their favorite pieces as inspiration, the workshop group discussed Atzompa potters' relationship with their own heritage, which led to a consideration of originality, copy, forgery, and the evolution of style as seen in Mexican archaeological findings. The workshop ended with the expression of answers, in ceramic form, to the questions of how to tell the story of the universe in a hundred years and in a single day. For this stage, the group split into two, each developing and rendering their own account in the form of clay objects assembled in totemic columns in the manner of a *corps exquis*. The column acts as a narrative device that resignifies the objects that form it and, in so doing, dismantles old narratives and allows for the construction of new histories.

SITElines presents three of the seven columns: one that resembles a *pochote* (Ceiba Aesculifolia), a thorned tree sacred in Oaxaca; another made of ceramic gear wheels, articulating a fusion of tradition and modernity; and a third that mixes various ceramics figures, including a bat, a dog, a warrior, a man, a gear, a pochote trunk, and Mother Earth, which when assembled tell the story of the universe.

— Pablo León de la Barra

OPPOSITE:
¿Quién medirá el espacio, quién me dirá el momento? (Who will measure the space, who will tell me the time?), 2015, installed at kurimanzutto, Mexico City

Benvenuto Chavajay

b. 1978 in San Pedro La Laguna, Guatemala; lives in Guatemala City

Guatemalan athlete Doroteo Guamuch Flores (1922-2011) was born in Cotió, Mixco, near Guatemala City. He trained himself to become a competitive long-distance runner with daily runs before and after his factory shift. When he participated in the Central American and Caribbean Games, held in Barranquilla, Colombia, in 1946, his name was "simplified" to Mateo Flores—at the time, it apparently was impossible for him to register with his father's Indigenous surname of Guamuch. After winning multiple international races, Guamuch gained international recognition and acknowledgment in his own country when he won the Boston Marathon in 1952. When interviewed in the press, he was consistently referred to as Mateo Flores, and on his return, the national stadium in Guatemala City was renamed Estadio Nacional Mateo Flores.

In the context of the many activist efforts to pressure the government to change the name of the stadium to the hero's original, Indigenous surname, Chavajay has tattooed Doroteo Guamuch Flores's original identification card on his own back. As the artist notes: "It is a demand for recognition and part of healing a wound for Indigenous communities."

In another of Chavajay's powerful works, *En Guatemala hay pueblos tan pequeños que caben en la mira de un fusil* (*In Guatemala There Are Villages So Small That They Fit within the Crosshairs of a Gun*), 2014, Chavajay annuls the weapons that trigger the collective memory of trauma and loss in Guatemala and other regions of Central America by rendering pistols in clay and suspending them from the ceiling. The title is taken from a quotation by poet Luis Alfredo Arango that Chavajay installs on the wall beside the array of whole and broken pistols, and refers to the disappearance of entire communities in Guatemala in the violence of the last half-century. In addition to being understood as an Indigenous material, clay serves as a metaphor for the vulnerability of humanity and the fleetingness of life. Over the last few years, Chavajay has made it his mission to honor Indigenous traditions and ways of thinking, being attentive to ancestral spirituality and to the structures and thoughts of his Mayan forebears.[31]

— Rocío Aranda-Alvarado

OPPOSITE:
Doroteo Guamuch, 2013

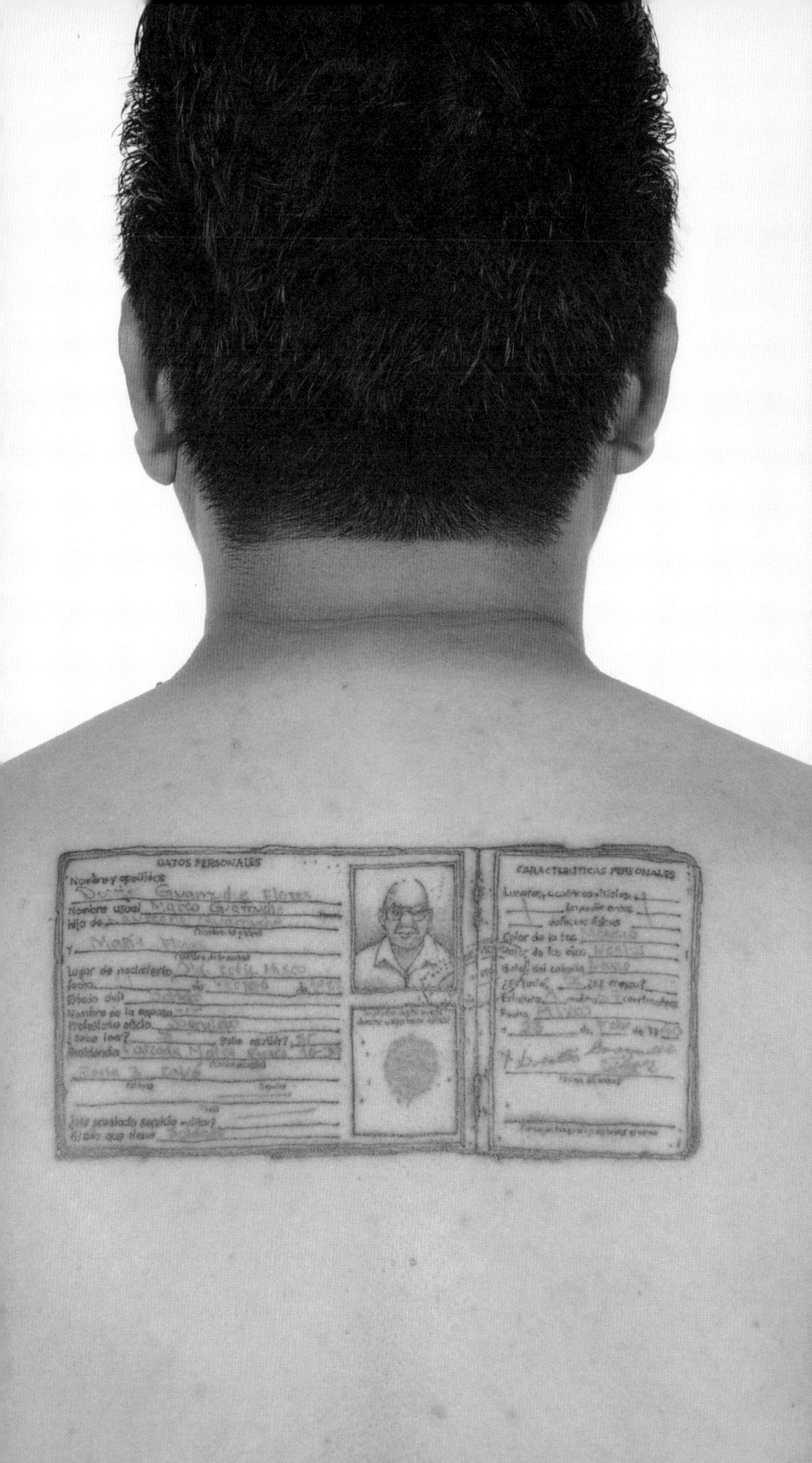
DATOS PERSONALES
CARACTERISTICAS PERSONALES

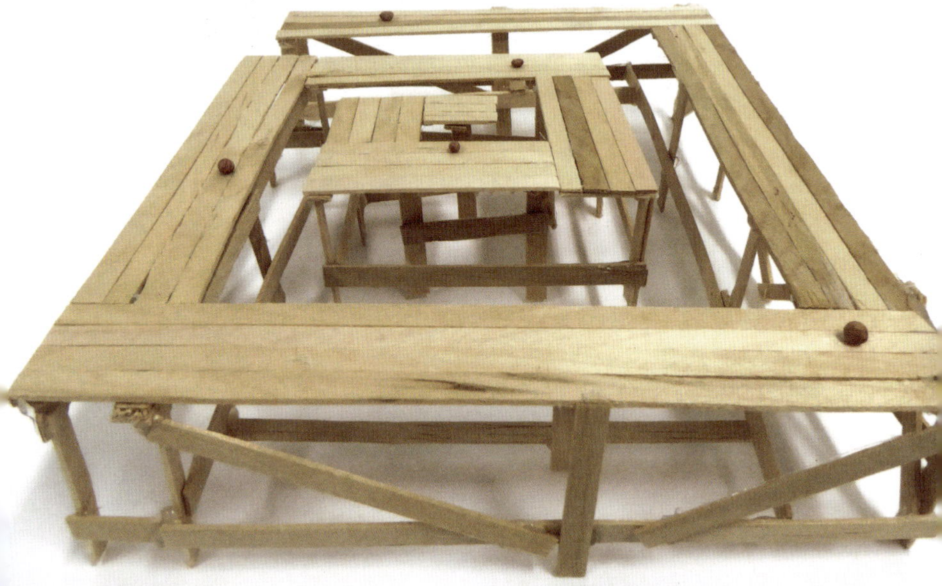

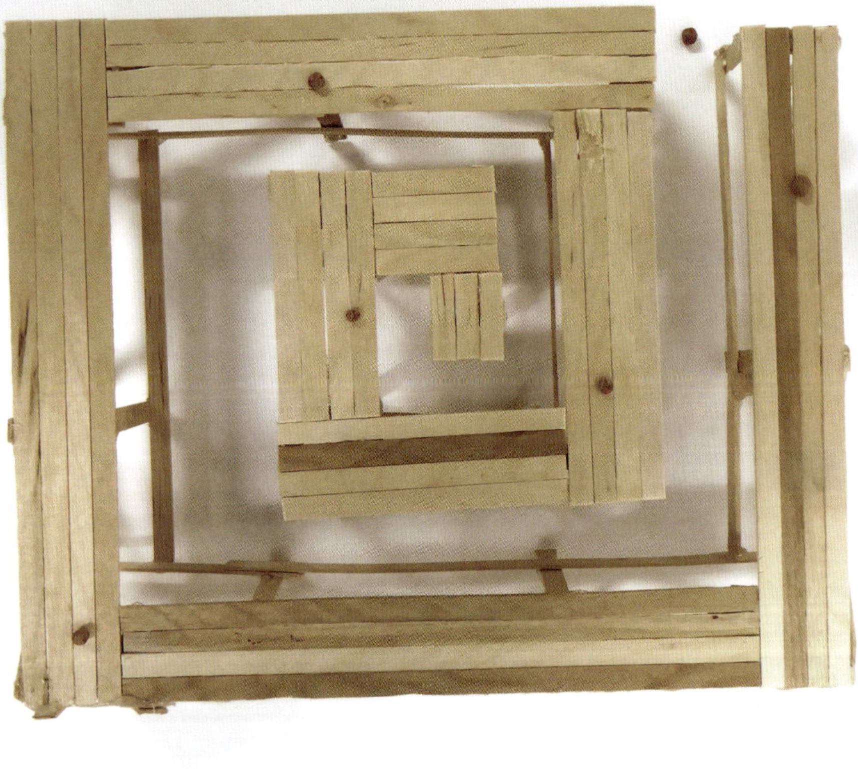

William Cordova

b. 1969 in Lima, Peru; lives in Lima/Miami/New York, U.S.A.

Interdisciplinary cultural practitioner William Cordova works at the intersection of architecture, politics, and social concerns, particularly those that seek to broaden participation in the definition and creation of culture. For Cordova, history is an archive of references with which to investigate ideological and artistic expressions. He is interested in serving the public through the fusion of artistic practice, archival documentation, and the production of knowledge.

With *yawar mallku: sculpting in time*, Cordova creates multiple connections that unite time and space through physical structures related to philosophy, geography, and spirituality. The work explores the influence of transcendental philosophers such as Ralph Waldo Emerson and Henry David Thoreau on two very different fronts. One is the architectural experimentation of Frank Lloyd Wright; the other is the socialist, communal, and non-Western thinking of young, radical political activists associated with the Black Panther Party, the Young Lords Organization, and the American Indian Movement of the late 1960s and early '70s.

The installation consists of interrelated parts, including a wooden scaffolding that alludes to Wright's so-called Pottery House in Santa Fe, the architect's only design in adobe. Wright created the plans for the house, but was unable to complete it prior to his death. The original scaffolding serves as the inspiration for Cordova's structure and for the drawings and embossed prints that surround it. Wright's practice is evident in the overall design and the organic forms. The top portion of the installation, however, features a wooden platform for clay spheres that suggest a celestial constellation and are made from materials found in historic locations in Santa Fe, Chicago, and Mexico. Cordova's investment in Andean, Pueblo, Aztec, and Japanese traditions is manifested in his choice of materials and in his references to labyrinths and portals.

Cordova incorporates Wright's architecture as a symbolic form to reevaluate assumptions about Western modernism and about standards of ownership and authenticity. Connections between structure, the land, political activism, and philosophical ideas are underscored by the harmony the installation creates between the man-made and natural worlds.

— Rocío Aranda-Alvarado

OPPOSITE:
yawar mallku: sculpting in time (maquette), 2016

Jonathas de Andrade

b. 1982 in Maceió, Brazil; lives in Recife, Brazil

Often drawing on historical and documental sources, Jonathas de Andrade combines textual and photographic material in works that operate in the gap between established narratives or codes of behaviors and our lived experience in contemporary society. Many of his projects are informed by his local context, directly referencing the rich cultural and intellectual history of Brazil's northeast region. In a country where colonial relationships and moralizing attitudes still prevail, de Andrade questions his own place and identity. Another distinctive feature in de Andrade's work is his fieldwork methodology. In projects such as *Educação para Adultos* (*Education for Adults*), 2010, and *Cartazes para o Museu do Homem do Nordeste* (*Posters for the Museum of the Man of the Northeast*), 2013, the artist recruited individuals from various northeastern communities to participate in activities designed to test ideas, in the first case related to educator Paulo Freire's *Pedagogy of the Oppressed* and in the latter to the representation of the northeastern population of Brazil.

A Study of Race and Class: Bahia><Santa Fe, 2015–16, commissioned by SITE Santa Fe, is titled after a homonymous study commissioned by UNESCO and conducted by Columbia University in 1952 in inland settlements in the state of Bahia and the Amazon Basin. In the original research, study participants were shown photographs of individuals from different racial backgrounds, and were asked to rate their physical and moral attributes. Drawing on the historical fieldwork, de Andrade has worked with communities across Santa Fe, photographing them as they dialogue with him about contemporary race relations. Though he loosely borrows scientific methodology, de Andrade declines the supposedly objective position of a social scientist to create multilayered work that reflects the complexity of deep-seated social relations.

— Kiki Mazzucchelli

OPPOSITE:
A Study of Race and Class: Bahia><Santa Fe (detail), 2015–16

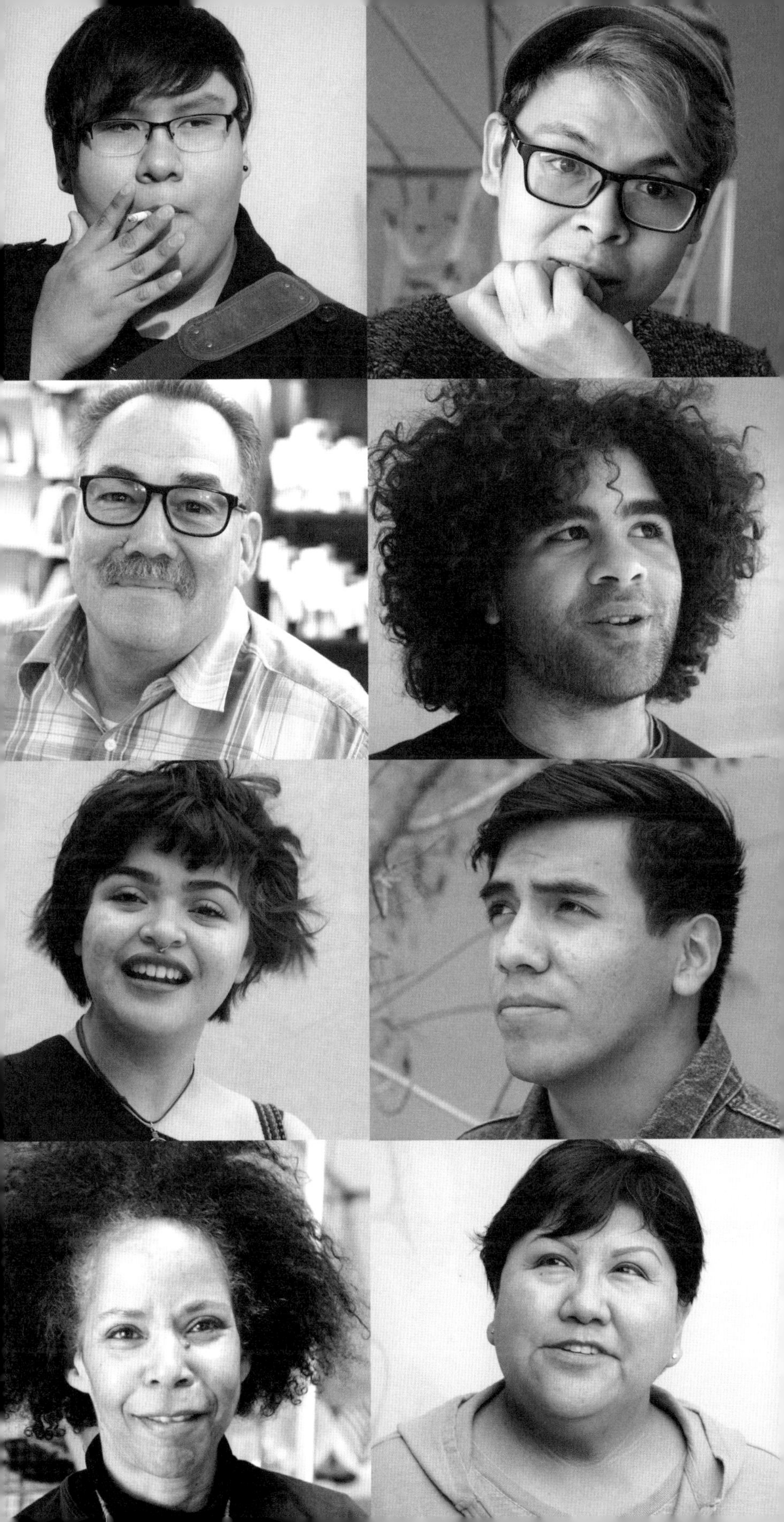

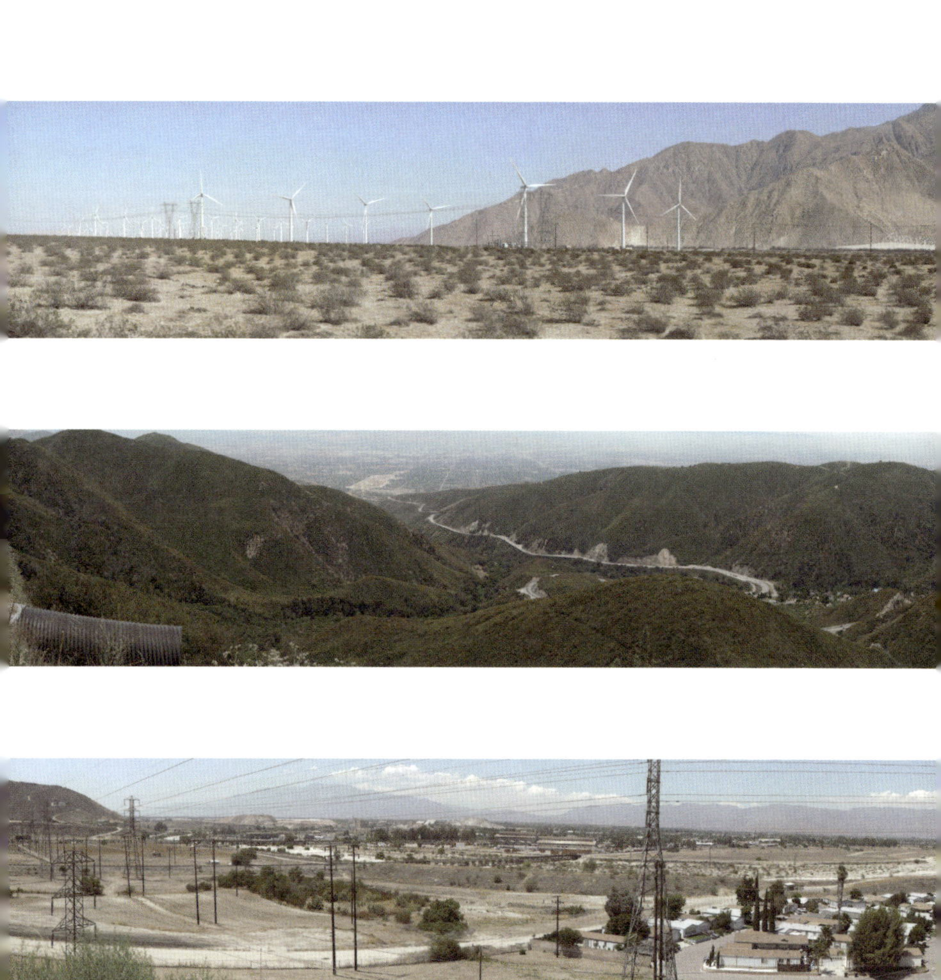

Lewis deSoto

b. 1954 in San Bernardino, California, U.S.A.; lives in Napa, California

No place I have experienced offers the full range of elements that compel and inspire—the vast public works, the neighborhoods both grand and beat down, the air fragrant with citrus and acrid from smog and industry. Cool pine breezes waft off the snow, and hot blasts of wind are scented with creosote. It is the Empire. It is everything.[32]

— Lewis deSoto

Though best known for his conceptually complex multimedia work, Lewis deSoto returned to his early practice of photography in the 2012–15 series *Empire*. These meditative landscapes capture both the profound beauty and the tragedy of the land known as the Inland Empire of Southern California. Far from coolly objective records, these vistas are infused with formal elegance and record multifaceted histories of loss. DeSoto first surveyed this landscape as a student of Joe Deal, one of the photographers who participated in the iconic documentation project *New Topographics* in the 1970s. DeSoto's first *Empire* series, 1979, centers on a drab environs of eerie, plastic interiors and mid-century architecture. Void of people, the images show old cars and worn buildings that recall a glamorous past. In his mature *Empire* series, consisting of sweeping panoramas and single-frame vignettes, deSoto returns to some of the same locales, but this time probing more deeply. Towns such as San Bernardino, Ontario, Rialto, and Palm Springs look tired and forlorn. Landscapes that are embued with personal memories and dramas for the artist are also suffused with the forgotten histories of failed industries, conflicts between settlers and Indigenous communities, and environmental desecration.

Unsettling views at the shores of the inland Salton Sea and the desiccated remains of abandoned vineyards remind viewers of both the potential and the fragility of this powerful environment. At the same time, within the cycle of building and destruction, deSoto finds moments of pure beauty. The absence of people within these images focuses our attention on the impact of humankind.

— Kathleen Ash-Milby

OPPOSITE:
Detail of *Whitewater I*, June 10, 2013
Detail of *Highway 18 I*, June 11, 2013
Grand Terrace I, January 12, 2014

Aaron Dysart

b. 1975 in Minneapolis, U.S.A.; lives in Minneapolis

With his wry sculptural work, Aaron Dysart critiques society's obsession with fixing and "improving" the natural environment. He finds it amusing, if not disturbing, that modern civilization treats the natural world with distance, as something foreign that needs to be tamed or softened. As he puts it, "Humans are, of course, natural, but we like to think we are different."

Dysart often uses trees to talk about this societal obsession. With *Preserve 1*, 2014, the artist has set about fixing a portion of a tree limb by sanding down its rough edges and filling in, with pink and gray auto body filler, any dents or cracks that develop from the natural drying process. The result is a bizarrely patchy yet smooth and seamless log. For the counterpart, *Preserve 2*, 2015, the artist eliminates altogether the problem of surface imperfections in the wood grain by completely covering the limb in aluminum foil, a protective material that further removes the wood from its normal state. While the "fixing" of these organic objects seems absurd, in a larger context the desire to constantly improve or fight against the natural order often makes a problem worse. The artificial suppression of wildfires, for example, increases the fire hazards in many rural Western communities.

The lesson one takes from Dysart's interventions and playful absurdities—such as a boat constructed of soap whose purpose is to clean a river, or underwear designed to cover tree branch crotches—is that nature is not concerned with our desires. Trees themselves are living creatures that seek to grow and thrive regardless of the obstacles they encounter. Slow-moving though they may be, their roots stealthily penetrate our plumbing and subtly heave our sidewalks. *Second Growth*, a live ponderosa tree, underscores this essential drive as it bursts through the wall and reaches for the skylight above, oblivious to the sanctity of the pristine gallery space. Responsible environmental stewardship may require less intervention and more thoughtful understanding of our place in the world, lest we become the victims of our own doing.

— Kathleen Ash-Milby

OPPOSITE:
Second Growth (prototype with birch), 2016

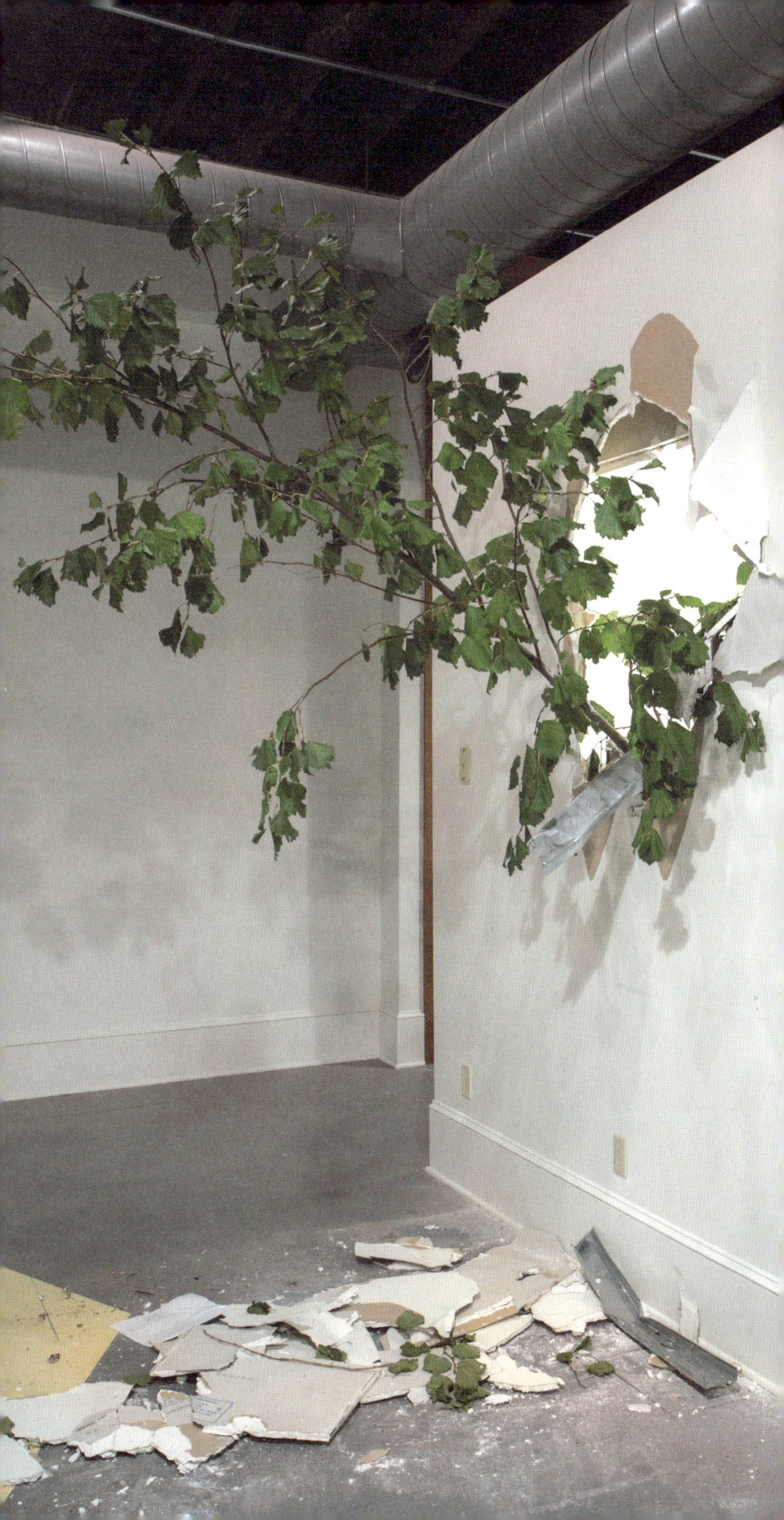

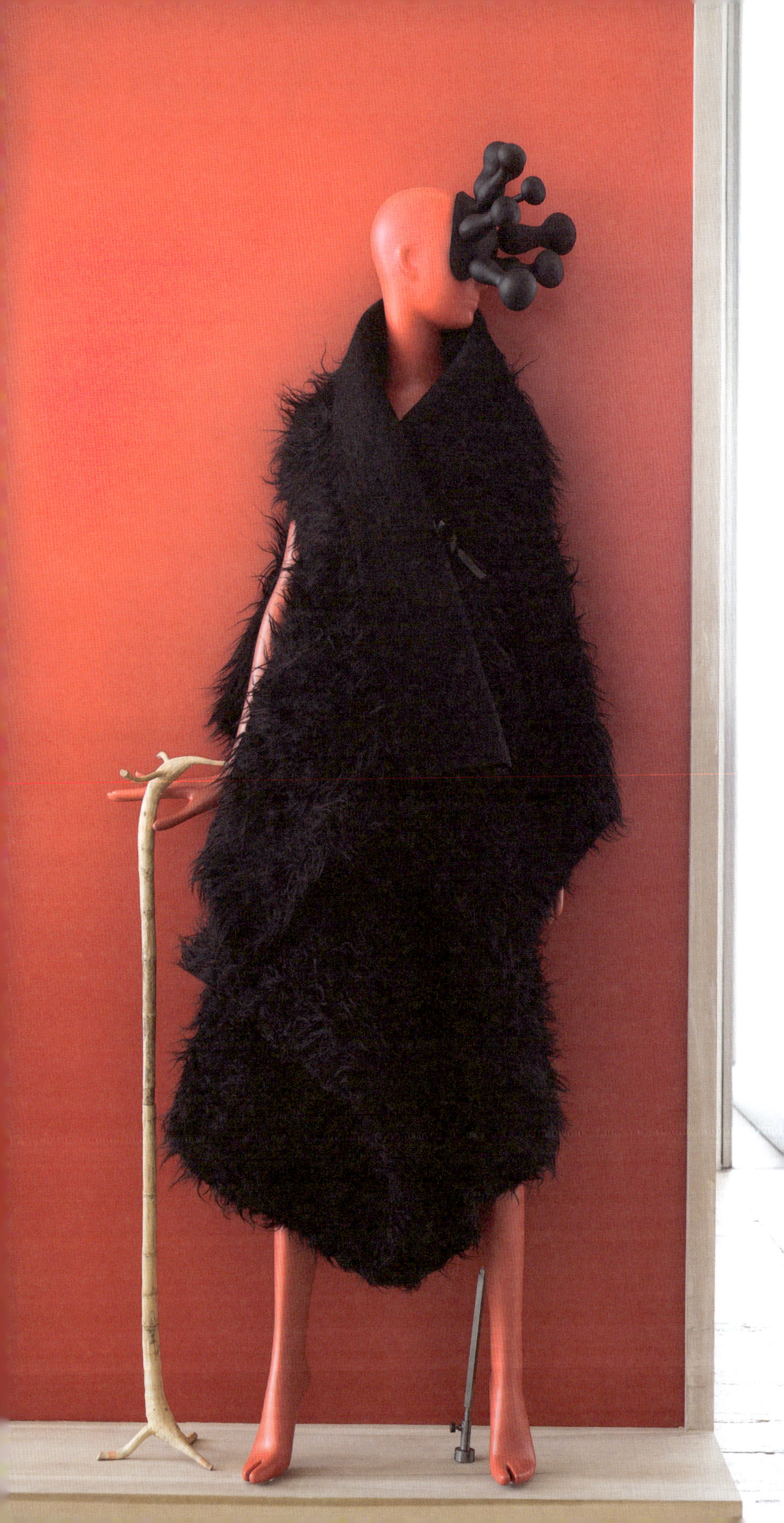

Carla Fernández

b. 1973 in Saltillo, Mexico; lives in Mexico City

Carla Fernández is a fashion designer and historian who for the past twenty years has studied, preserved, and revitalized the textile heritage of Mexico's Indigenous communities. She is the founder of Taller Flora (Flora Workshop), a studio that includes a fashion label as well as mobile design workshops. Traveling throughout Mexico, Fernández visits hand-spinners, weavers, embroiderers, and garment makers to document their traditional techniques, which include backstrap-loom weaving, natural dyeing, embroidering, as well as geometric structuring, pleating, and folding. Working with the local communities, Taller Flora adapts and transforms some of these practices to produce new models that generate income for the producers, while recognizing their contribution. This is especially significant in Mexico, where 90 percent of the artisans are women, most of them family bread-winners living below the poverty line.

Fernández's book *The Barefoot Designer: A Handbook* (2014) is a detailed archive of Mexico's rich Indigenous and *mestizo* textile traditions and her related work. The title pays homage to *The Barefoot Architect: A Handbook for Green Building* (2007) by Johan van Lengen, who traveled all over Mexico to learn how people constructed local vernacular architecture. Fernández's work is also inspired by and builds on the legacy of a previous generation of women who researched and defended Mexican Indigenous traditions, including Diana Kennedy on Mexican cooking and Mariana Yampolsky on Mexican vernacular housing.

For *much wider than a line*, Fernández collaborates with Mexican Indigenous communities to create ponchos, or *quechquemitls,* that exhibition visitors can wear. The *quechquemitl*—in Nahuatl, *quechtli* means "neck" and *tlaquemitl* means "garment"—is clothing made from two squares folded to form triangles that cover each side of the torso. The corners of the *quechquemitl* can be worn at the front and back, or to the sides, sloping down along the arms. In the production of each garment, Fernández collaborated with different communities of artisan weavers with whom she has long-term working relationships, including the Tzotziles from San Juan Chamula; Otomis from San Pablito, Pahuatlán Puebla, and El Nanthe, Hidalgo; Amuzgos from Xochsitlahuaca, Guerrero; Nahuatls from Hueyapan, Puebla; and Zapotecos from Teotitlán del Valle, Oaxaca.

— Pablo León de la Barra

OPPOSITE:
San Juan Chamula Wool Coat, 2014

Miguel Gandert

b. 1956 in Española, New Mexico, U.S.A.; lives in Albuquerque

Miguel Gandert's most common subject is the daily life of rural Hispanos living in the Rio Grande Valley, which stretches from Mexico to southern Colorado. He has also focused on the urban lives of Hispano families in cities such as Albuquerque and smaller towns in northern New Mexico. Photographing for four decades, he has produced a multifaceted portrait of life along the U.S.-Mexico border and in the crossings of Spanish colonial and Indigenous Mesoamerican traditions. His insider status as a native New Mexican of mixed Indo-Hispano heritage helps him approach a variety of contexts, people, and situations.

In the early 1980s, the New Mexico Museum of Art in Santa Fe commissioned twelve New Mexico photographers to document their state for a book funded in part by the National Endowment for the Arts. Earlier surveys undertaken by major nineteenth- and twentieth-century photographers for the United States Geological Survey and the Farm Security Administration, respectively, were points of reference. Focused on the people of urban New Mexico, Gandert's contributions show quiet domestic moments in the historically working-class neighborhoods of Albuquerque, demonstrations of youthful prowess, and bodies and faces marked by the strains of daily life. In one image, the brutalist architecture of the Civic Plaza in downtown Albuquerque, built in 1974, is a backdrop for a water fountain that in the 1980s served as a makeshift pool for local residents. Designed in the shape of the Zia Indian sun symbol that appears on the New Mexico state flag, the fountain was, ironically, a source of relief from the intense heat of the sun for Albuquerque youth. The variety of subjects seen in the artist's works emphasizes his commitment to acknowledging and recording the diversity of the populations of New Mexico.

— Rocío Aranda-Alvarado

OPPOSITE:
Melissa Armijo, Eloy Montoya, and Richard "el Wino" Madrid, Albuquerque, 1983
Bathers, First Plaza, Albuquerque, 1982

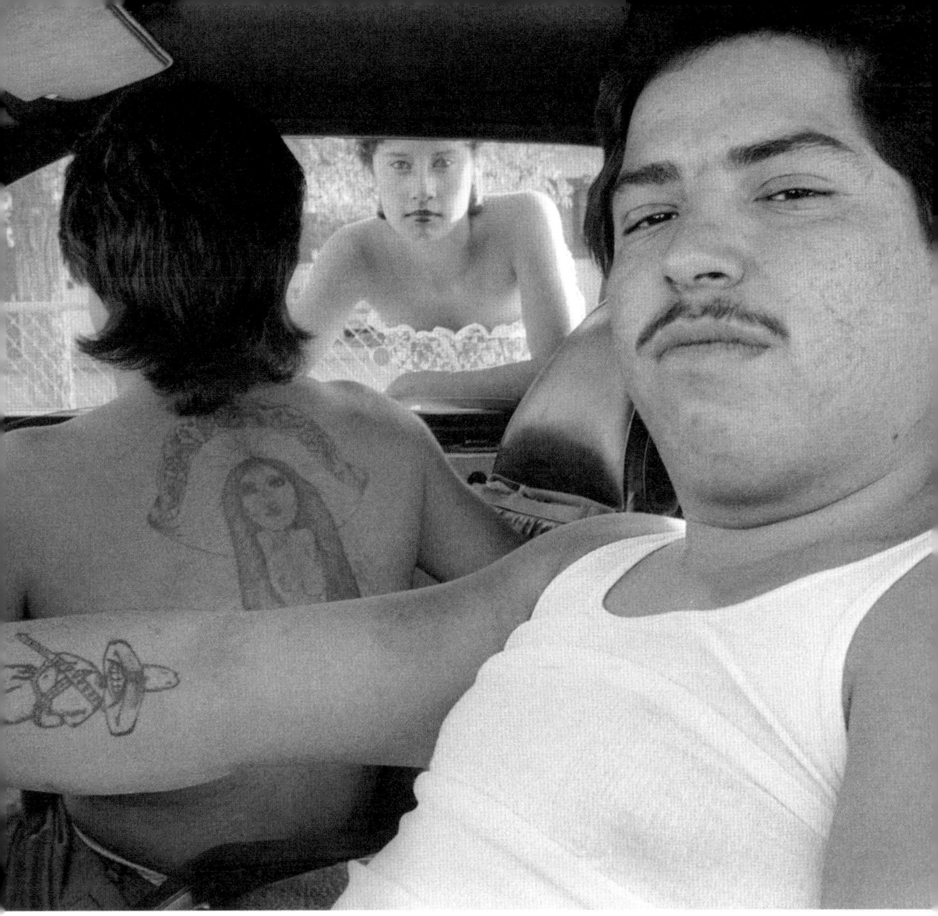

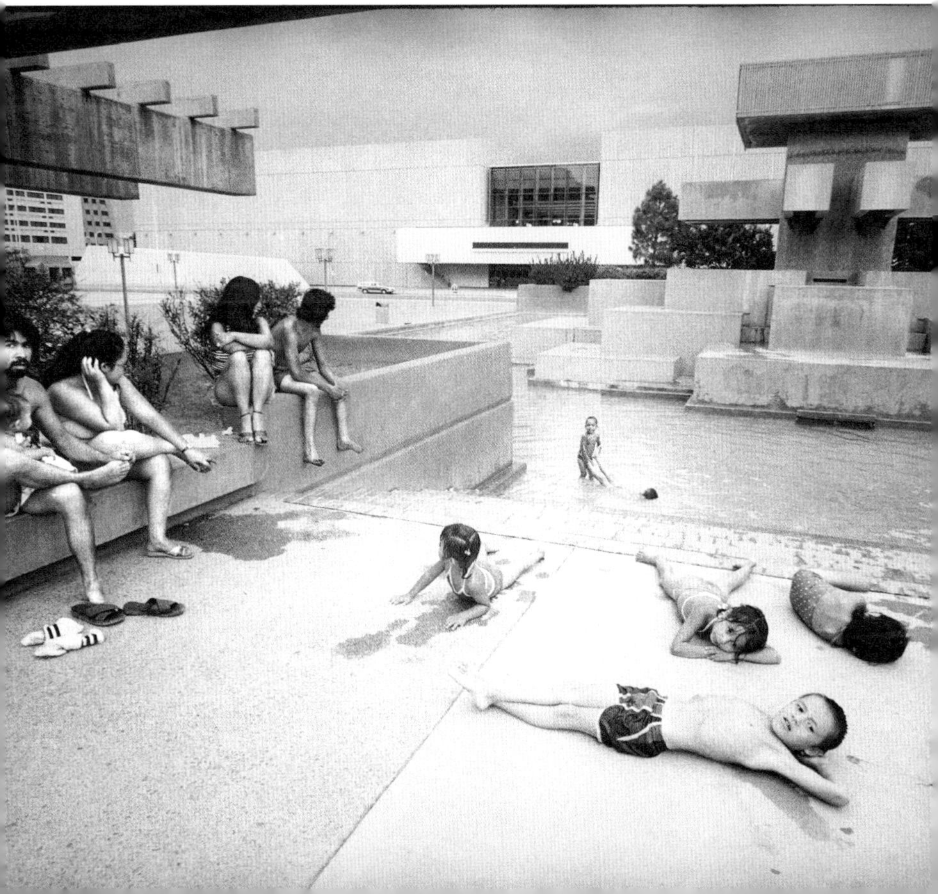

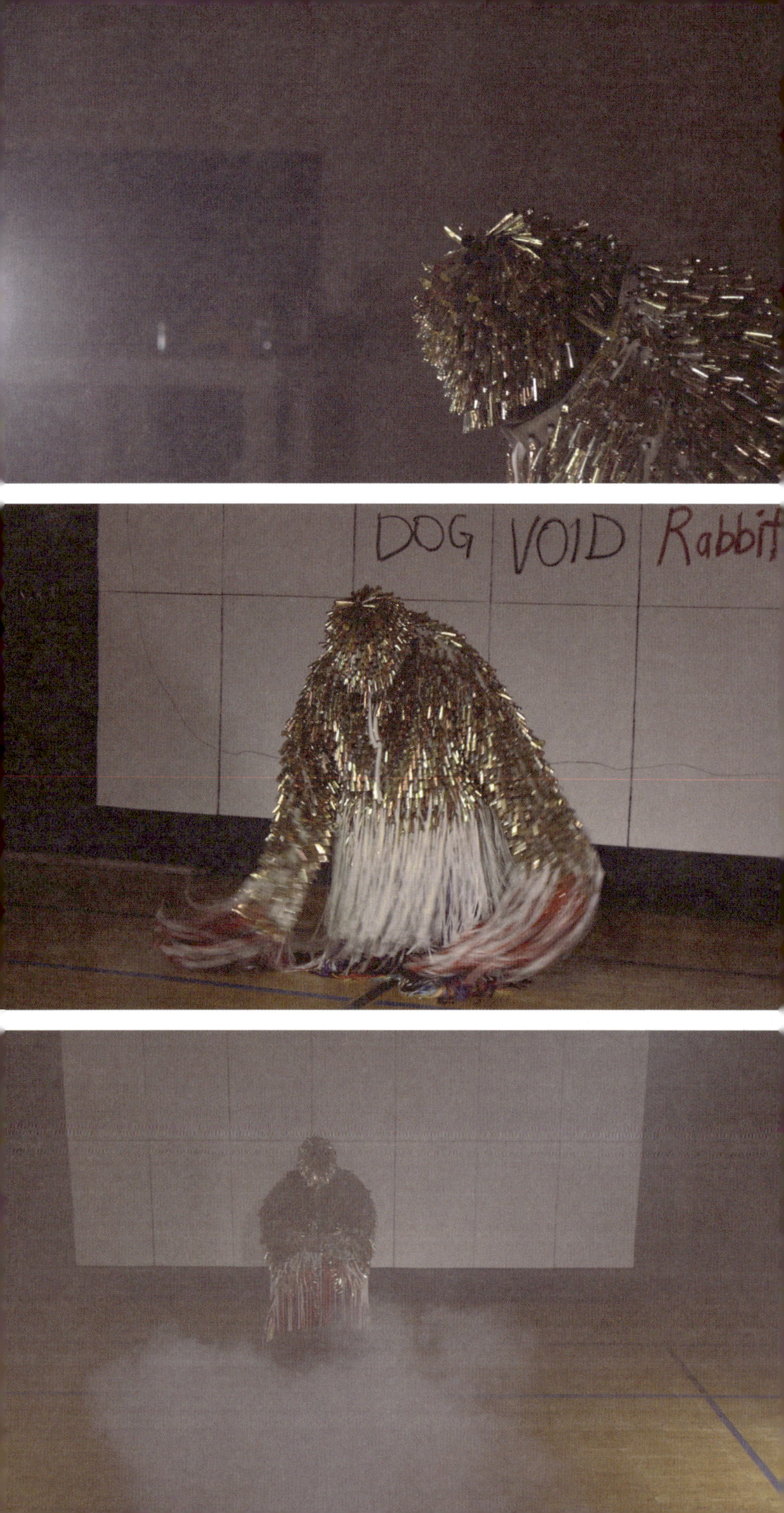
DOG VOID Rabbit

Jeffrey Gibson

b. 1972 in Colorado Springs, Colorado, U.S.A.; lives in Hudson, New York

Jeffrey Gibson uses a wide range of media to create conceptually complex, visually vibrant works. Starting his career as a painter, he pushed the boundaries of the medium, building up layers of pigmented acrylic that fought to escape the surface. His sculptural work ranges from organic forms created with the most inorganic materials to layered constructions of repurposed and found objects. He draws from various cultural influences—club culture, song lyrics, minimalism, and fashion—and employs materials as diverse as oil paint and fluorescent light tubes, a mix that reflects his equally complex identity. His dialogue with traditionally Native-American materials, such as hide and beadwork, confronts and challenges perceptions and expectations.

LIKE A HAMMER, an installation and performance, is an amalgam of many of these disparate sources. Like the title's source, the Civil Rights-era folk song "If I Had a Hammer," the work is both hopeful and defiant. At first glance, the work appears to draw on traditional Native forms, such as hide robes, the sound of the drum, and metal jingles. Despite the outward appearance of the performance as Native cultural practice—an easy presumption, since the artist is Choctaw and of Cherokee heritage—this work is far more nuanced than it seems.

The robe as an element has multiple references: robes have adorned royalty as well as boxers and iconic pop stars such as James Brown, Freddy Mercury, and David Bowie. Certainly, the work references historical Native cultural objects, but it also subtly defies the gendered use of jingles on women's items. Jingles were once made from the turned lids of tobacco tins but are now mass-produced in Taiwan, as is the nylon fringe. The artist's drumming and dancing throughout the recorded performance, the first of many that will continue until the drum is broken, represents his process of learning through sound and movement, as well as paying homage to his teachers. *LIKE A HAMMER* decontextualizes the robe, layering a mix of cultural references and personal experiences within a repeating performative work that tests the limits of the artist's endurance.

— Kathleen Ash-Milby

OPPOSITE:
Video stills from *LIKE A HAMMER*, 2016

Jorge González

b. 1981 in San Juan, Puerto Rico; lives in San Juan

Jorge González focuses on recovering the craft knowledge of Puerto Rico, where, because of the colonial condition of the island, almost all goods are imported from the U.S. mainland. Central to his research has been the Casa Klumb, a 1947 modernist house in San Juan, now in disrepair, that German-American architect Henry Klumb designed in response to the island's culture and climate. González was inspired by Klumb's collaboration with craft workers to found the Escuela de Oficios (Trade School), which functions as a symbolic space that honors Klumb's ideals about learning. Knowledge—ranging from ancestral techniques to collective practices—is shared in meetings. These meetings are mobile, occurring throughout Puerto Rico, so participants can learn from local artisans and engage in conversation, workshops, and exhibitions.

González developed the *Banquetas Chéveres* (*Chéveres Stools*) through these encounters, beginning with conversations with Eustaquio Alers, a weaver from Aguadilla who works with hammock-weaving techniques. González adapted his technique to create stool seats for wooden stools he designed with artisan Joe Hernández from Ciales. With the participation of Escuela de Oficios members, the first four stools were made. In 2015, in New York, González inserted the stools, without authorization, in the Arts of Africa, Oceania, and the Americas galleries at The Metropolitan Museum of Art and in the exhibition *Latin America in Construction: Architecture 1955–1980* at the Museum of Modern Art. Easy to fold and carry, the stools embody the nomadic and flexible nature of the Escuela de Oficios.

For SITElines, González has made new stools, which can be moved throughout the exhibition spaces. González collaborated on their construction with MAOF, a wood-salvaging research and design studio in San Juan, and the seats were woven in workshops guided by Alers. In the Caribbean, the word *chévere* means "more than cool." In one of González's research trips in Puerto Rico, he met the Chévere family, potters who live in the caves of Las Cabachuelas de Morovis and descend from the Taino Indians, thought to have been eradicated during the Spanish conquest. González dedicates the name of the stools to the survival of Indigenous knowledge and people like the Chéveres.

— Pablo León de la Barra

OPPOSITE:
Banquetas Chéveres, 2015–16

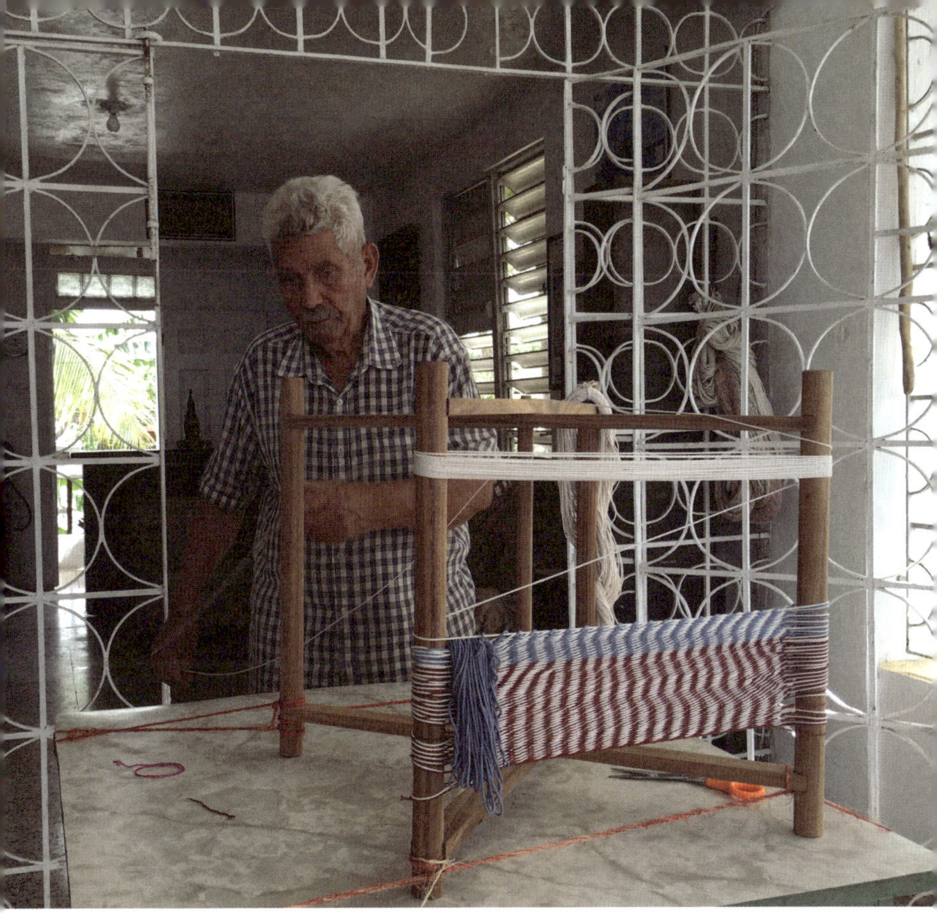

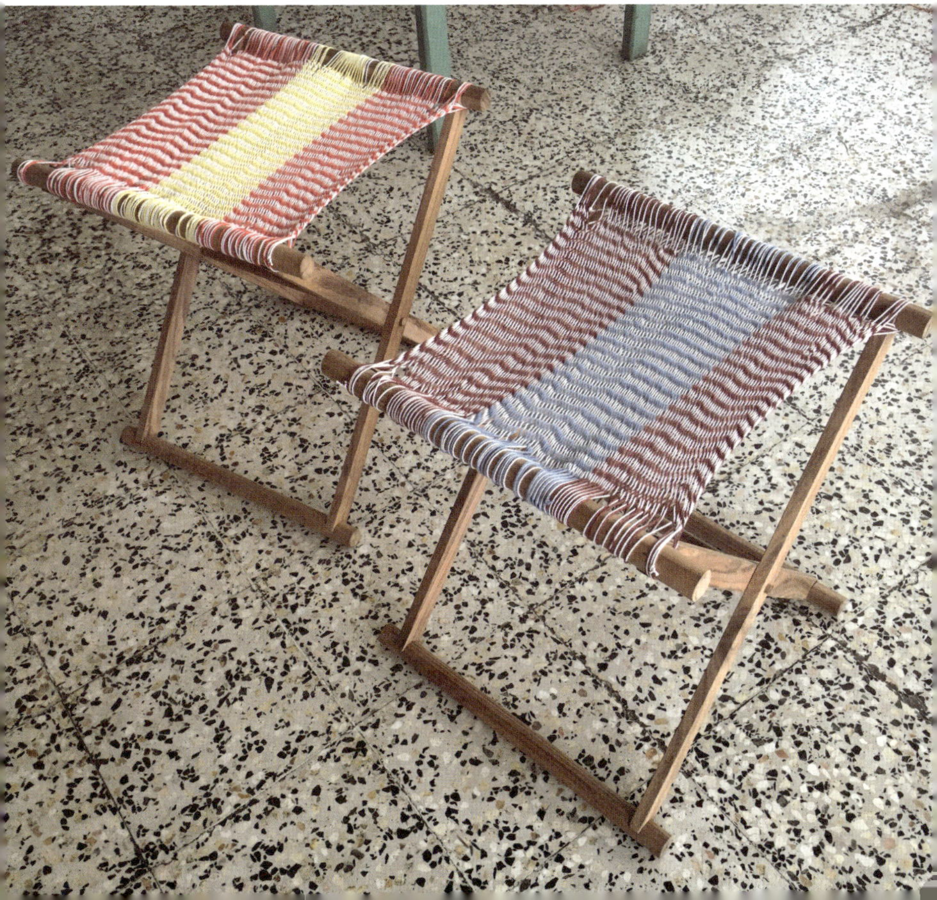

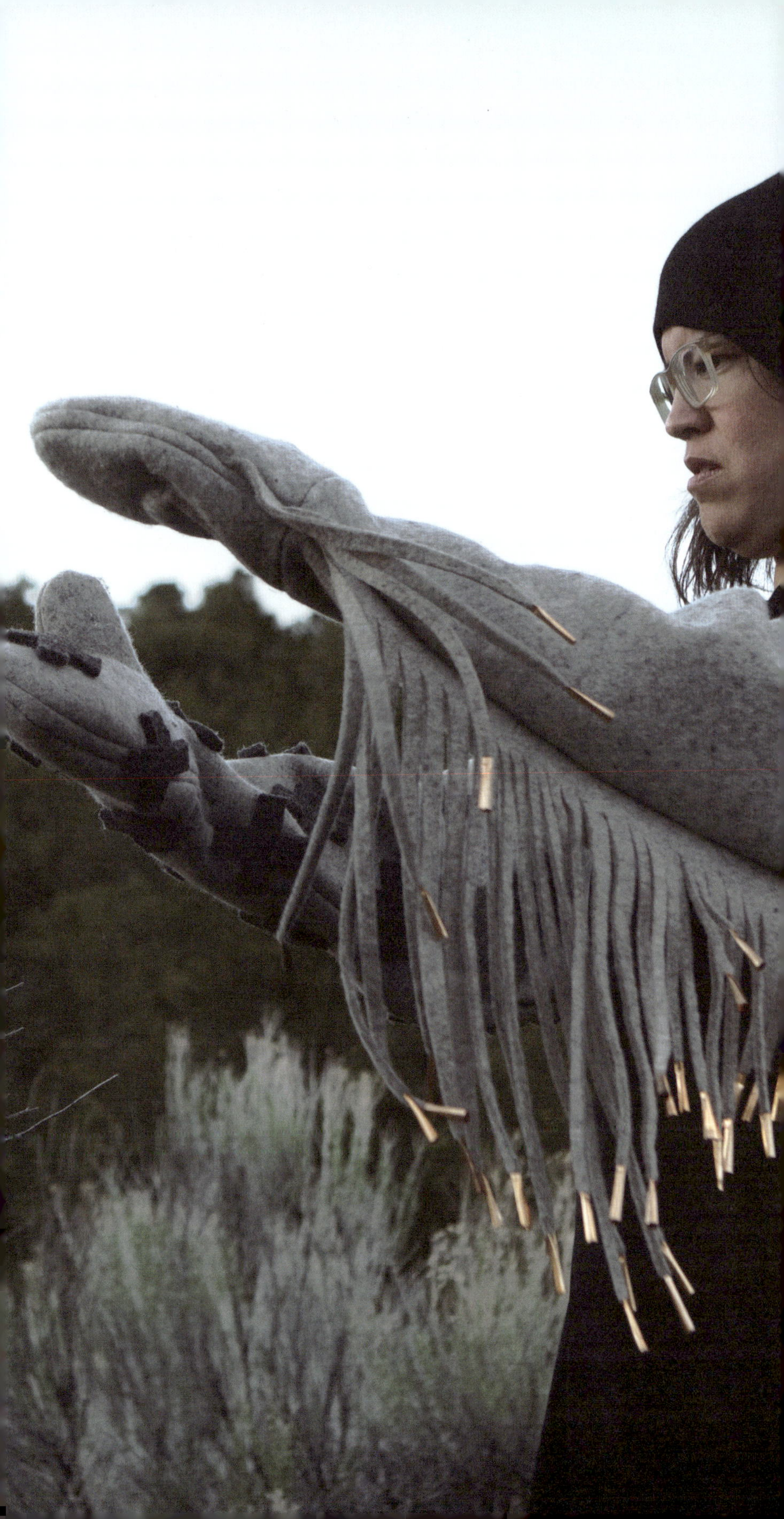

Maria Hupfield

b. 1975 in Parry Sound, Canada; lives in New York, U.S.A.

Living, doing, taking action, "a way of being": all of these things are part of my process. I aspire to be productive, to contribute, and to make beautiful things that reflect this way of living, which is connected to mino-bimaadziwin, *the Anishinaabe phrase often interpreted to mean a way in which we are "living well" or "living a good life."*[33]

— Maria Hupfield

Maria Hupfield's practice centers on presence and performance. Her early work—photography and unconventional sculpture—is often focused on the idea of movement and action. Her recent sculptural forms are tactile objects constructed of thick, gray, industrial-grade felt and crinkly, reflective silver Mylar sheets. Though these material choices have origins in industry and manufacturing, Hupfield's forms and patterns are inextricably tied to Anishinaabe material culture. The corporeal elements in Hupfield's work reflect the Indigenous practice of using the body as a canvas. Objects such as the boots and mittens in *It Is Never Just about Sustenance or Pleasure*, are made to contain a human figure in motion. She has also constructed large, amorphous felt pouches into which she herself can crawl and move about. These hand-sewn objects function as physical and conceptual tools for performance and interaction with her audience.

In her installation and performance *It Is Never Just about Sustenance or Pleasure*, Hupfield places objects made for wetlands within a desert environment. Worn by the artist in performances, the felt mittens and boots are cartoonishly large and awkward, suggesting a dissonance between the wearer and reality. Within the installation, these items, displayed on plain two-by-four lumber boards in a spare corner of the gallery, are further estranged from their function as protection from cold air and water. Native cultures are known for their adaptability and integration within distinctive locales throughout the Americas. Hupfield, a member of the Wasauksing First Nation, mines her own Indigenous cultural references to create a provocation that questions our adaptability in the face of rapid environmental change.

— Kathleen Ash-Milby

OPPOSITE:
Video still from *It Is Never Just about Sustenance or Pleasure*, 2016

Graciela Iturbide

b. 1942 in Mexico City, Mexico; lives in Mexico City

In 1978, photographer Graciela Iturbide was invited by the Archivo Etnográfico Audiovisual of the Instituto Nacional Indigenista in Mexico City to participate in an initiative in which photographers, musicians, and cinematographers documented the cultural aspects of Mexico's various Indigenous groups. Iturbide chose to photograph the Seri (autoethnonym Comcáac), who live on the desert coast of the northern state of Sonora. The photographs were published in 1981 in the book *Los que viven en la arena* (*Those Who Live in the Sand*).

Under constant threat of extermination, the Seri resisted three hundred years of Spanish colonization as well as later subjugation by the Mexican State. They constitute a highly distinctive group in Mexico. Once nomadic, at the time of Iturbide's visit they remained so to a degree. They lived from fishing, although this was changing, as they had started to produce carved wooden handcrafts. And, at the time, their population was so small that they were considered to be on the verge of extinction; today they currently number about one thousand.

In her portraits, Iturbide captures the Seris' way of living, the effect of the desert and sea landscape on their culture, and the tension between their traditional lifestyle and their adaptation to modernization. In particular, Iturbide photographed the act of female face-painting, once part of everyday life but by then done almost exclusively for ceremonies. While documenting this practice, Iturbide had her own face painted (as shown in the self-portrait opposite), which symbolizes both her acceptance by the women of the group and her own process of transformation through this contact.

— Pablo León de la Barra

OPPOSITE:
Self-Portrait with the Seri, Sonora Desert, Mexico, from the series *Those Who Live in the Sand*, 1979

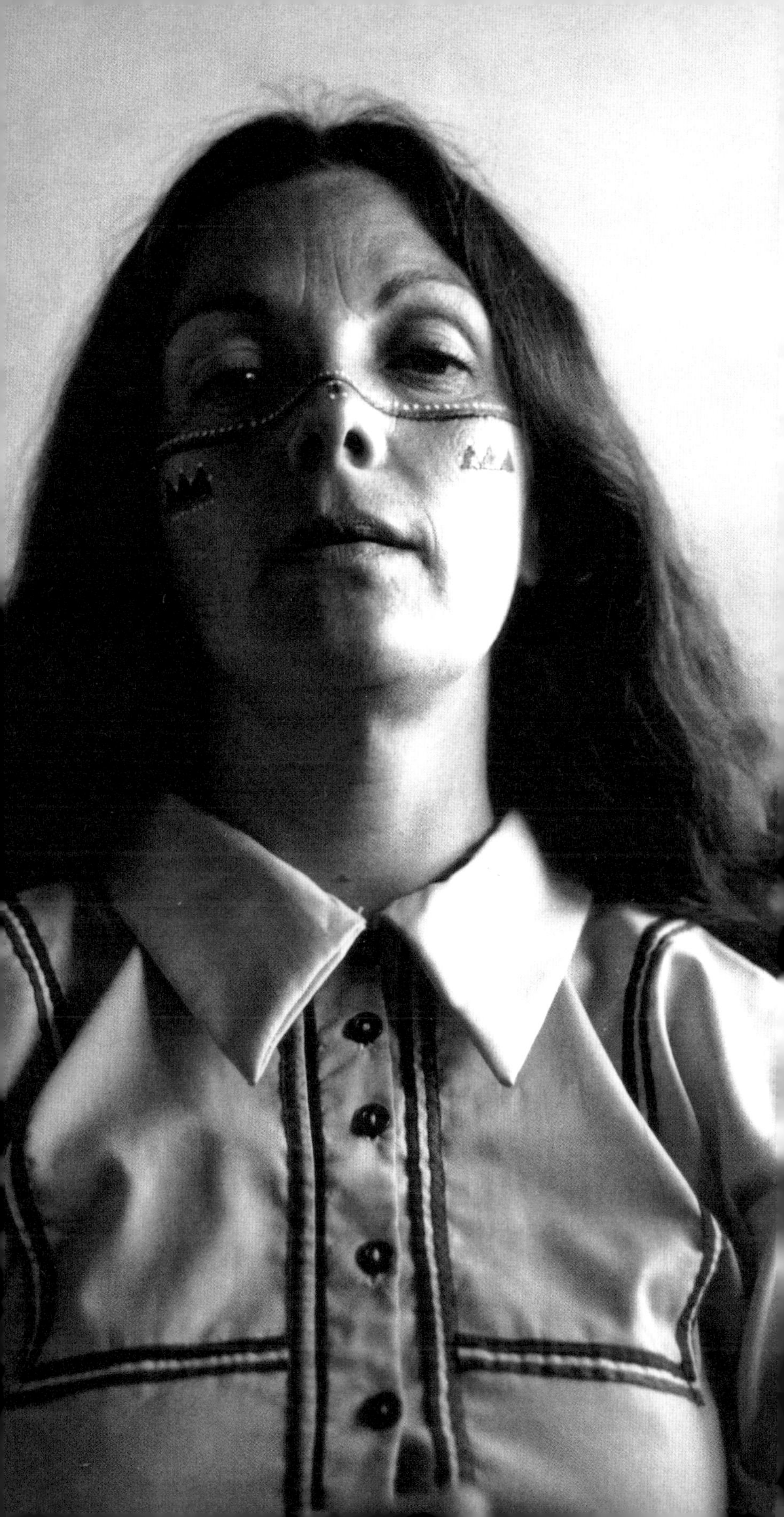

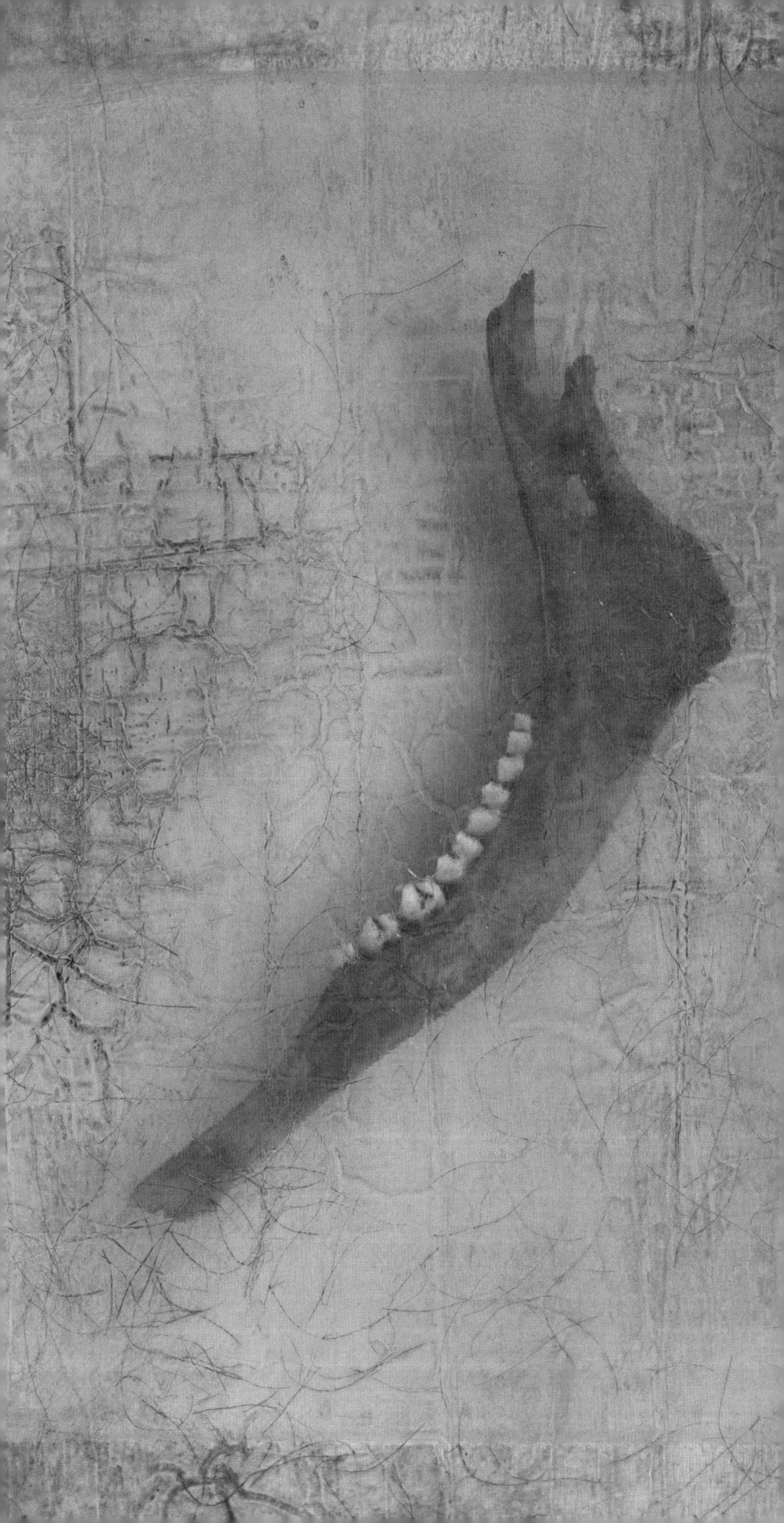

Sonya Kelliher-Combs

b. 1969 in Bethel, Alaska, U.S.A.; lives in Anchorage

Sonya Kelliher-Combs was taught from a young age about the interdependence of humanity and the environment. Indigenous teachings emphasize restraint in the consumption of natural resources—taking only what you need and appreciating the fruits of the harvest and hunt as a gift. As an artist, she has infused these teachings into her practice, which, like the material culture of the Iñupiaq and Athabaskan peoples themselves, are multimedia works combining natural and synthetic materials. Her sculptural works rely heavily on sheep and reindeer rawhide, as well as marine animal gut, while her two-dimensional works are luminous constructions of acrylic medium in which disparate materials, from human hair to sewing thread, are imbedded.

Remnant is a site-specific installation that comments on the threatened state of the natural environment of Alaska, a location where the folly of our human-centric approach to industry is achingly clear. As the artist asks, "What has gone so wrong that our shores are filling with the waste of others, the debris of twenty-first century mass consumption? The irony of technology intended to make our lives easier, more comfortable, is choking the water, land and air—causing irreparable harm."

Within the installation, the viewer is surrounded by fragments and scraps of the natural world of the North: bits and pieces of animal hide, hair, and other detritus submerged in synthetic media like so many specimens from a way of life that no longer exists. These relics are reminders of the precariousness and fragility of life in this unforgiving terrain. They are treated simultaneously as precious, preserved vestiges and carelessly discarded garbage. Kelliher-Combs pulls together materials that are captivating but sometimes disturbing in their raw vulnerability. *Remnant* invites the viewer into a dialogue that exposes the tenuousness of our own existence. In the end, is it really humankind that will be reduced to a mere remnant?

— Kathleen Ash-Milby

OPPOSITE:
Detail of *Remnant*, 2016, showing *Remnant: Moose Jaw Bone*

Zacharias Kunuk

b. 1957 in Kapuivik, Canada; lives in Igloolik, Canada

Made entirely in the North, *Atanarjuat: The Fast Runner*, 2001, is the first feature film written, directed, and acted in the Inuit language, Inuktitut. Inuk director Zacharias Kunuk has referred to the trilogy it belongs to as reflecting "four thousand years of oral history silenced by fifty years of priests, schools, and cable TV."[34] Paying tribute to the power of historical Inuit legends, in *Atanarjuat* Kunuk explores the themes of love and community through the story of a shaman's curse that results in betrayal, rivalry, and revenge. Today, the film is screened in the context of current resistance movements across the North, of a burgeoning politics of self-determination, and of the controversies around the denigrating depictions of Inuit cultures and peoples that persist within dominant settler rhetoric.

In order to achieve historical accuracy about Inuit cultural practices suppressed by colonial authorities, elders were extensively consulted throughout the making of the film. The situated knowledges gained in the process led to an intricate interweaving of narratives, voices, and elements of the spirit world in an almost-anthropological testament to ancient lifeways. Kunuk's forensic attention to detail allows the film to operate powerfully within the rich storytelling traditions of the Inuit. The filmmaker also lodges the cautionary tale of Atanarjuat squarely within contemporary discourse about global warming, making the film and the knowledges it depicts directly pertinent to the urgent worldwide task of reestablishing natural balance on the planet.

Atanarjuat is a powerful interruption to dominant narratives and widespread misconceptions about the cultures and traditional practices of the North.

— Pip Day

OPPOSITE:
Film stills from *Atanarguat: The Fast Runner*, 2001

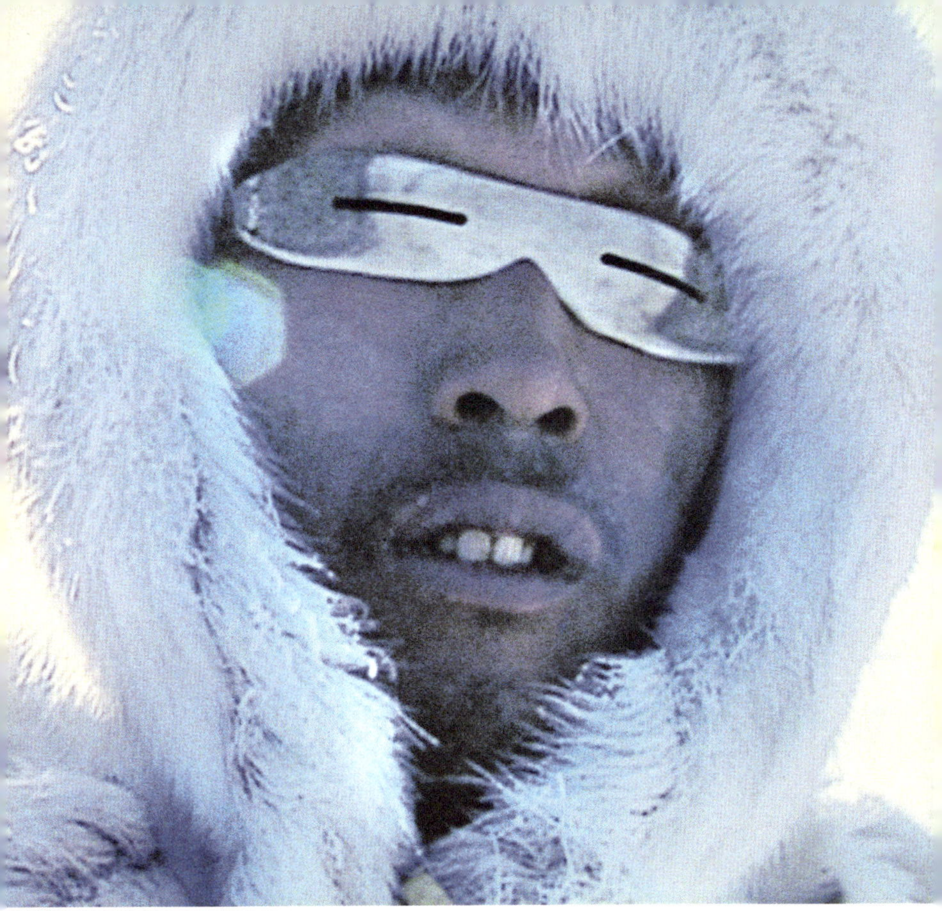

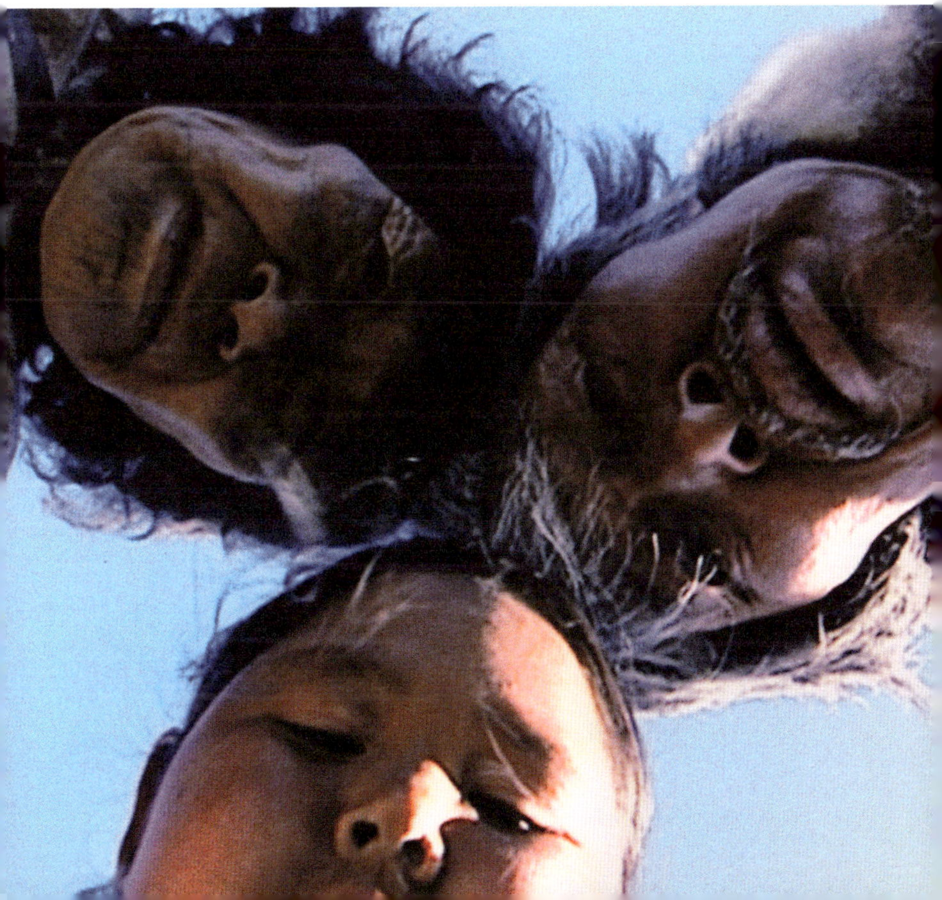

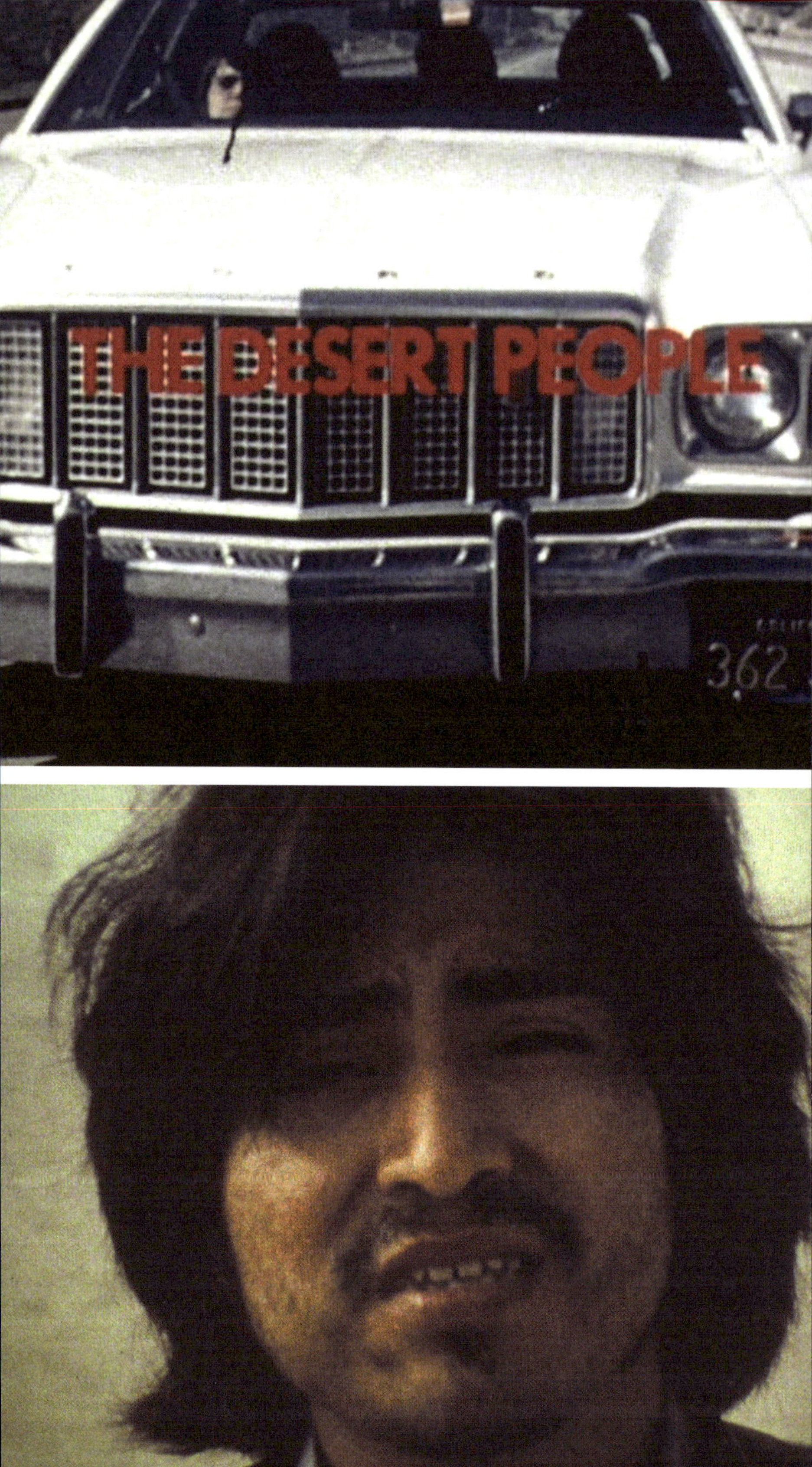
THE DESERT PEOPLE

David Lamelas

b. 1946 in Buenos Aires, Argentina; lives in Los Angeles, U.S.A./Buenos Aires

Argentinian-born David Lamelas made *The Desert People* in 1974 in Los Angeles, a city that immediately influenced his work and where he soon moved. Previously, in Buenos Aires and London, his conceptual durational work had addressed the issues of space and time. L.A. generated a new subject for him through the confrontation with U.S. culture, film, and television.

Shifting in genre between fictional road movie and ethnographic documentary, *The Desert People* subverts the Hollywood film. Through its characters, it offers multiple perspectives on the Tohono O'odham, a Native-American group who reside in the Sonoran Desert of eastern Arizona and northwestern Mexico. Tohono O'odham is the autoethnonym of the group, and means "desert people"; at the time, they were known as the Papago.

In the film, a white Ford Gran Torino drives through a U.S. landscape colonized by cars and highways. In their respective scenes, five passengers describe their experience on the Papago Indian reservation. The first four are white U.S. Americans: John, an anthropologist; Carol, a hippie student; Chris, a New York journalist writing an article on Papago women; and Michael, who observes his fellow-travelers as outsiders. The last passenger, Manny, is of Tohono O'odham origin. In the desert landscape, he testifies to the cultural extinction of his people. He starts speaking in English, shifts to Spanish (once the second language of his group), and finally speaks in the Tohono O'odham language, impossible for most viewers to understand. We never see an image of the Tohono O'odham who live on the reservation or the place itself—our images of the group are constructed only through the characters' narrations.

The film makes manifest the cultural misinterpretations born of the travelers' Western perspective, while mourning the disappearance of the language through which Tohono O'odham cultural knowledge could be transmitted. The impossibility of communication in the pseudo-documentary is underscored by the ending, when the Ford falls off a cliff and crashes into the sea.

— Pablo León de la Barra

OPPOSITE:
Film stills from *The Desert People*, 1974

Cildo Meireles

b. 1948 in Rio de Janeiro, Brazil; lives in Rio de Janeiro

In the late 1960s, Cildo Meireles began his prolific career—which now spans over four decades—with drawing, later expanding his practice to include an extraordinarily diverse range of mediums. Part of a generation that emerged immediately following the rise of the Neoconcrete artists in the early 1960s in Brazil, Meireles produces work that is informed by the group's poetic and social dimensions, while also reflecting the conceptualist trend that was beginning to gain ground during the same period in various parts of the globe. Meireles's fundamental concerns are the investigation of representational systems in relation to the concepts of territory, value, and scale, and the shifting interaction between mental construct and sensory experience.

Measuring only 9 mm, *Cruzeiro do Sul* (*The Southern Cross*) is a tiny cube made of soft pine and hard oak, installed on the floor of a vast and empty gallery. Pine and oak are sacred trees in the cosmogony of the Tupi Indians: by rubbing pieces of their woods together, one can produce fire, which evokes the presence of an Indigenous divinity. The mythic narrative embedded in this work shifts the focus from its "objecthood" and confers on it an immense amount of energy, which has the effect of monumentalizing its minute proportions. According to Meireles, "*Southern Cross* was initially conceived as a way of drawing attention, through the issue of scale, to a very important problem, the over-simplification imposed by proselytizing missionaries—essentially the Jesuits—on the cosmogony of the Tupi Indians. The 'white' culture reduced an indigenous divinity to the god of thunder, when in reality their system of belief was a much more complex, poetic, and concrete matter, emerging through the mediation of their sacred trees, oak and pine."[35]

Fire can be a metaphor for both creation and destruction, and, forty years on, *The Southern Cross* continues to be a powerful reminder of the plight of Native peoples in Brazil.

— Kiki Mazzucchelli

OPPOSITE:
The Southern Cross, 1969–70 (shown on artist's finger to indicate scale)

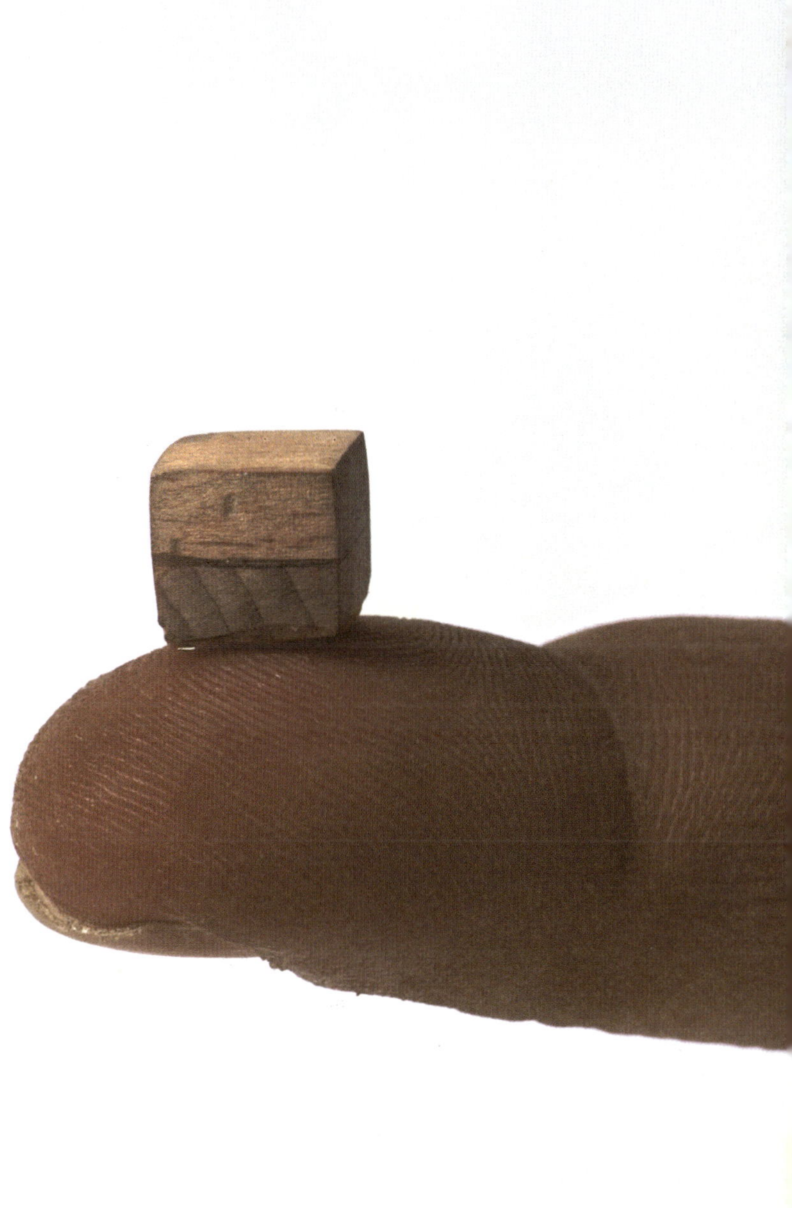

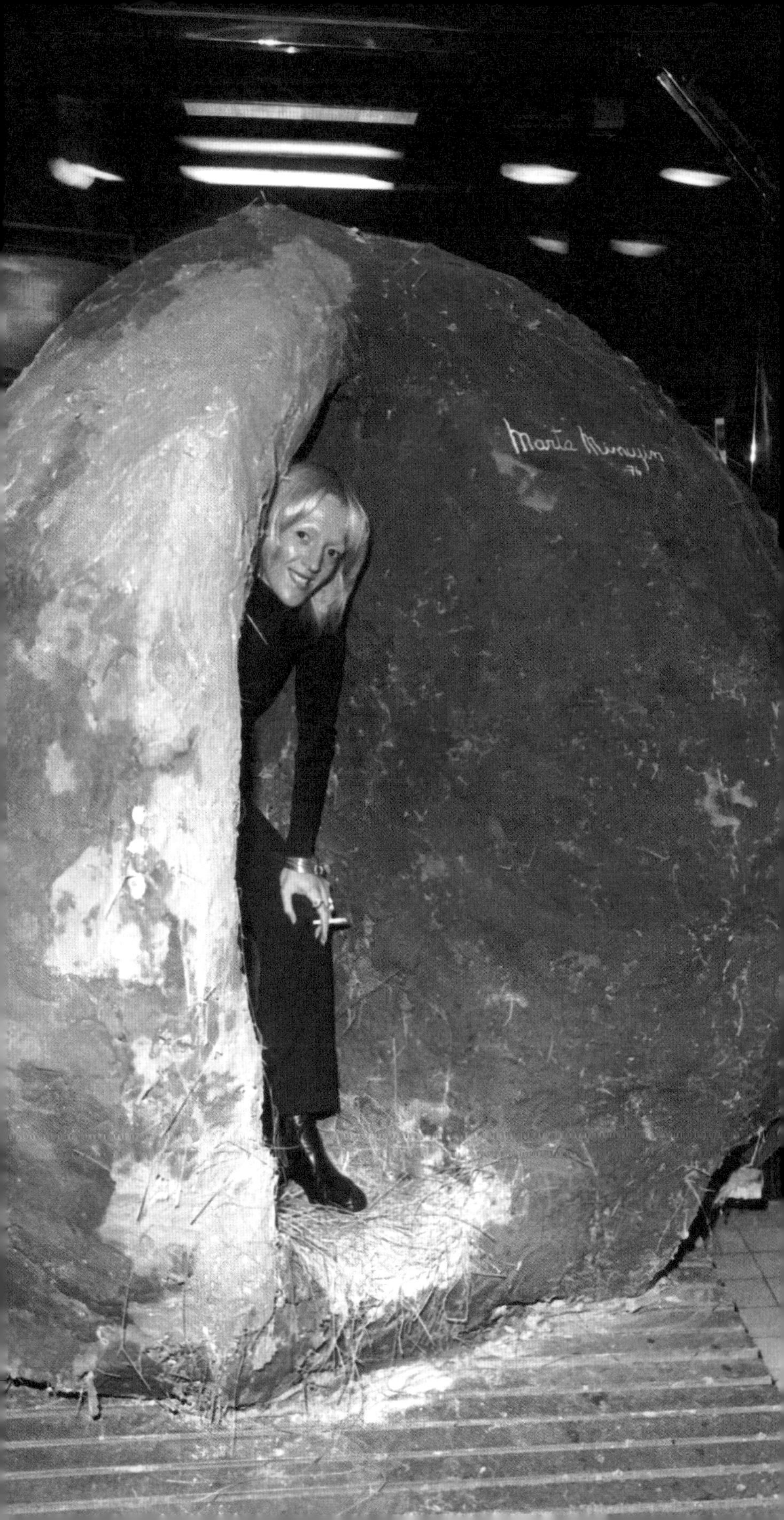
Marta Minujin
76

Marta Minujín

b. 1943 in Buenos Aires, Argentina; lives in Buenos Aires

Comunicando con tierra began in 1971 with Marta Minujín's visit to the historic Inca site of Machu Picchu in Peru. With the permission of the site's administration, she dug up thirty kilos of earth from various locations at Machu Picchu, which exuded a powerful energy for her, and had it taken to Buenos Aires for her exhibition at the Centro de Arte y Comunicación (CAYC). In the gallery, she combined five kilos of the earth with local soil and moistened it to create the nest of an ovenbird—a small songbird native to the Americas, closely related to warblers and sparrows—which resembles a clay oven. The remaining twenty-five kilos of Machu Picchu earth were displayed in plastic bags; at the end of the exhibition, Minujín mailed the bags of soil to twenty-five artists throughout the Americas, asking them to mix in earth from their own locations and return the mixture to her.

Again at Machu Picchu in 1976, Minujín organized a "ceremony of restitution," replacing the soil she had removed with the mixed earth the artists had sent her from across the continent. Through this simple gesture, the powerful physicality of soil makes a symbolic connection across time and space. Documentation of the work includes a hand-drawn map indicating where the Machu Picchu earth traveled and videos showing the artist at work with the mud. While creating the ovenbird nest, she wears masks that evoke the historical past of the continent and the prevalence of pre-Hispanic influences. The videos are shown on a monitor located inside a monumental version of the nest. Minujín's work suggests the importance of communication, cross-reference, and exchange in the creation of continental avant-garde art networks and movements.

— Rocío Aranda-Alvarado and Pablo León de la Barra

OPPOSITE:
Comunicando con tierra, 1976

Paulo Nazareth

b. 1977 in Governador Valadares, Brazil; lives in the favela of Palmital Santa Luzia outside Belo Horizonte, Brazil

Paulo Nazareth's open-ended practice emerges from his improvisational wanderings through various countries for extended periods of time. These journeys can be described as durational performances, in which he draws on his mixed African, Caucasian, and Indigenous heritage to establish personal bonds with local communities—particularly in Africa and Latin America—who are affected by the legacy of a colonial past, and whose culture and history has often been suppressed or erased by hegemonic discourses. Playing with his own *mestizo* background and the shifting way his racial identity is perceived depending on the context, Nazareth alternately presents himself as an "exotic other" and as a member of whatever group he associates himself with during his perambulations. He chronicles and organizes his experiences in works that include the elements of ephemera, photographs, drawings, videos, and texts; much of this material is made available online in the blogs he maintains while traveling. In one of his best-known projects, *Notícias de América* (*News from America*), Nazareth, wearing flip-flops, walked from his home in the outskirts of Belo Horizonte across several countries to the United States, a journey that lasted more than six months. As a symbolic ritual at the end of his trip, he rinsed the dust of all the countries he had visited off his feet into the Hudson River in New York. This project was followed by *Cadernos de África* (*Africa Notebooks*), 2013, another walk of epic proportions, this time from Cape Town north across the African continent, in search of "what there is of Africa in my home country," as he blogged.[36] In the investigation of his own identity, Nazareth has explored vast territories, guided by lived experience and intense social exchange, producing a politically charged yet delicate and humorous body of work that traces unsuspected correspondences between communities linked by shared histories.

— Kiki Mazzucchelli

OPPOSITE:
Untitled, from the series *Noticias de America* (*News from the Americas*), 2011-12

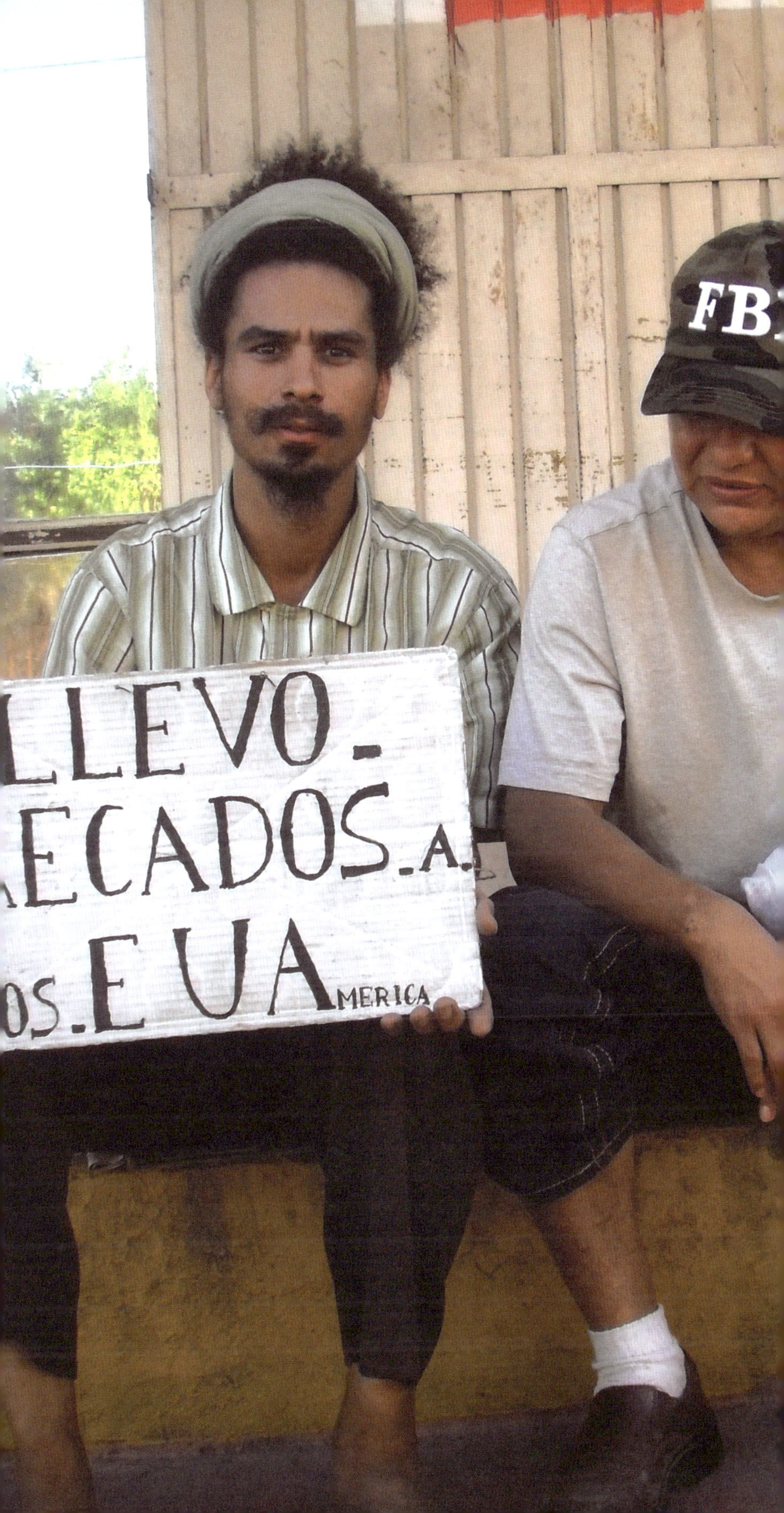
LLEVO-
ECADOS-A-
OS.E UA MERICA
FB

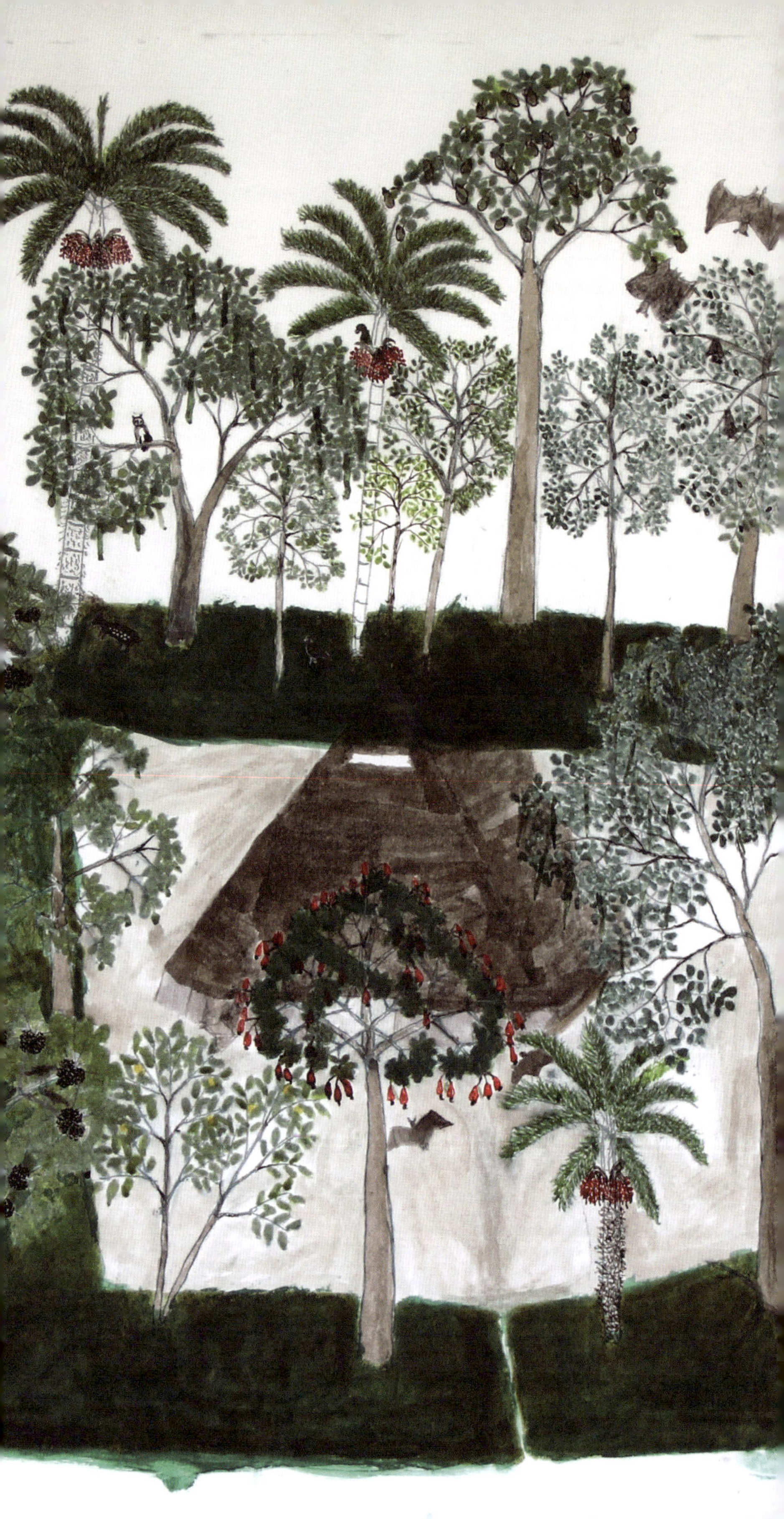

Abel Rodríguez

b. 1941 in La Chorrera, Colombia; lives in Bogotá

I learned about the forest the hard way: I had to be awake for long hours at night, I had to lend my ears to the elders and make special diets. Our learning was a spiritual process; that is why we consider knowledge as very valuable.

— Abel Rodríguez

A Nonuya elder, Abel Rodríguez is from La Chorrera, on the Amazon's Igaraparaná River. This place continues to inspire his practice, which is based on translating customary knowledge of plants and trees into drawing and writing. In collaboration with Tropenbos, an international NGO with an office in Bogotá, Rodríguez first worked as a guide in the 1980s for Dutch scientists, sharing his knowledge of the ecology of Amazonian plant life and the classification of species. Forced off his land by armed militia, Rodríguez relocated to the outskirts of Bogotá, where he began drawing in the 1990s to communicate his knowledge of the plants of his homeland, their growth cycles, their names in the Nonuya language, and their medicinal properties and uses.

Rodríguez's practice is informed by displacement and by the imposition of Western education. He began to study shamanism, learning "how to understand the cycles of time and the ecological and cultural relationships in our world, but I did not get to learn how to heal." This early education, he explains, was cut short when he was sent to boarding school. His drawings of growth in the forests along the river are divided not by conventional seasons but by the time when certain species flower in a given year, when seeds and fruits are ready for harvest, and how water levels affect growth. Others center on the specific qualities and traditional uses of the trees native to the region, or on food-based species, charting the diversity of cassava, piña, and other edible plants. Rodríguez's series *The Cycle of the Maloca Plants* documents the relation of the ancestral longhouse, used domestically and for ceremonies, to the seasonally changing flora around it. Recently, his practice has moved from documentation of nature to representing cosmologies. His drawing of the Tree of Life "narrates the origin of food for the indigenous people of the Mid River Caquetá."[37]

— Pip Day

OPPOSITE:
From the series *The Cycle of the Maloca Plants*, 2009

Rometti Costales

Julia Rometti: b. 1975 in Nice, France; lives in Mexico City, Mexico
Victor Costales b. 1974 in Minsk, Belarus; lives in Mexico City, Mexico

French-born Julia Rometti and Víctor Costales, of Belarusian-Ecuadorian origins, have been working together since 2007 on a practice that has taken them to France, Brazil, Ecuador, Morocco, Palestine, and Mexico, where they now live. Taking the form of drawings, rubbings, photographs, slide shows, films, publications, and site-specific installations, their work challenges Western rationalism. To scientific ethno-botanical and geological methodology they bring an animistic, shamanic recognition of invisible forces and alternate forms of knowledge. Their work decolonizes the dominant fields of geography, biology, and politics, opening them up to forms of measuring, mapping, and quantifying that go beyond their capability.

The installations of Rometti Costales include rocks, vegetation, and seeds, in addition to handcrafted and found objects. The duo's research on plants and minerals forms part of a larger investigation into the relationship of nature and culture that is in part informed by the writings of Brazilian anthropologist Eduardo Viveiros de Castro, specifically his concept of perspectivism: "The world is inhabited by different sorts of subjects or persons, human and non-human, which apprehend reality from distinct points of view [and provide] not a plurality of visions of the same and only world but a single vision of different worlds."[38]

The installation *Estrategias Suculentas / Succulent Strategies*, versions of which were presented in 2014 in a solo exhibition at Kunsthalle Basel and at the Cuenca Biennial in Ecuador, consists of concrete posts and rebar structures leaning against the wall, alternating with upright San Pedro cacti. Each element indicates a different way to demarcate boundaries: the manmade structures refer to modernity, colonial occupation, and the capitalist understanding of land as a place to be exploited; in contrast, the cactus refers not only to Amerindian ways of marking borders, but denotes access to other kinds of territory. The psychoactive San Pedro cactus has, historically, been consumed by Amerindian groups in entheogenic rituals for the visions and higher forms of perception and consciousness it produces. Although *Succulent Strategies* concerns at one level the ability of succulents to survive in the desert landscape, its meaning extends to the persistence of Indigenous rituals and forms of knowledge that provide alternate, multiperspectival understandings of the world.

— Pablo León de la Barra

OPPOSITE:
Detail of *Estrategias Suculentas / Succulent Strategies*, 2014

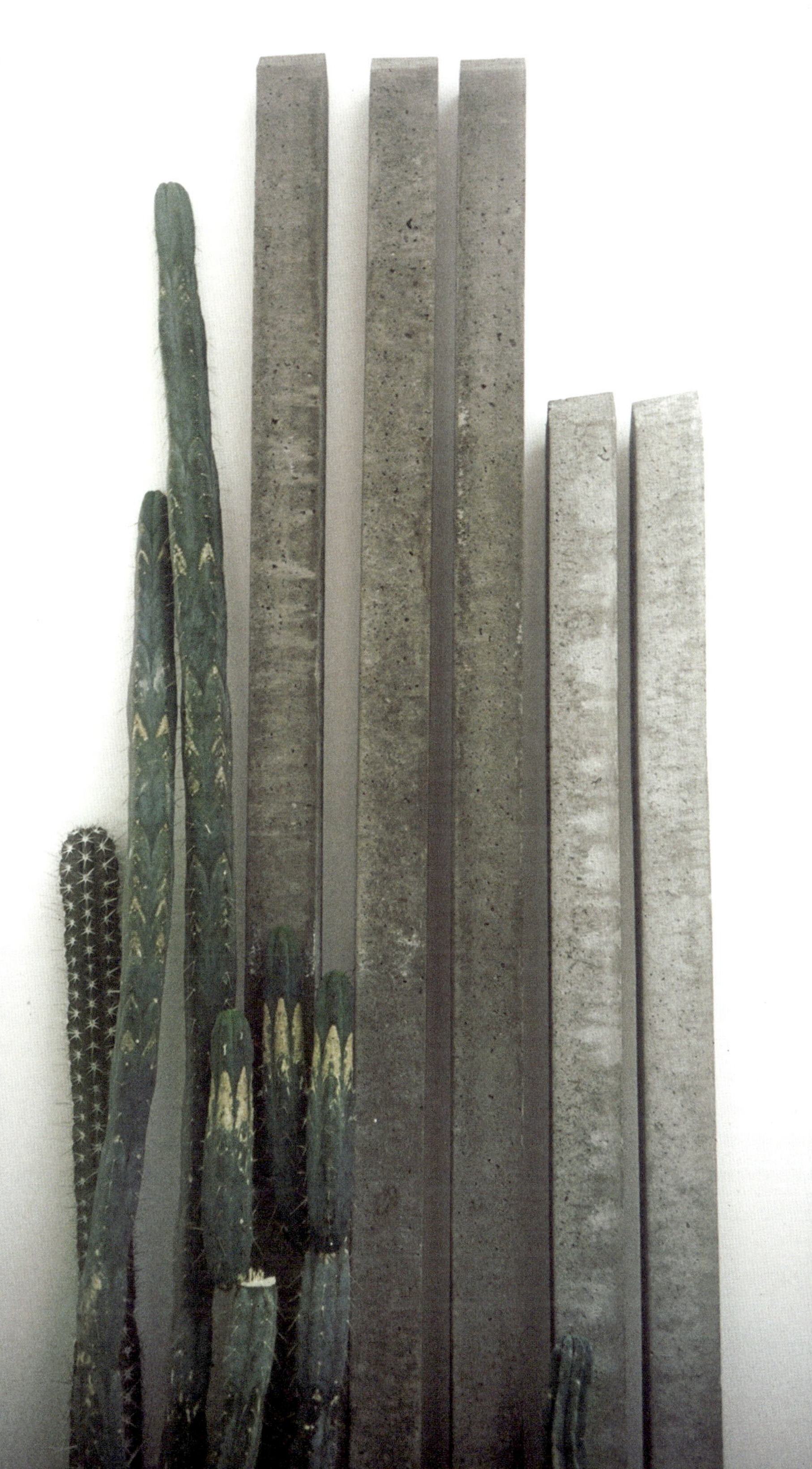

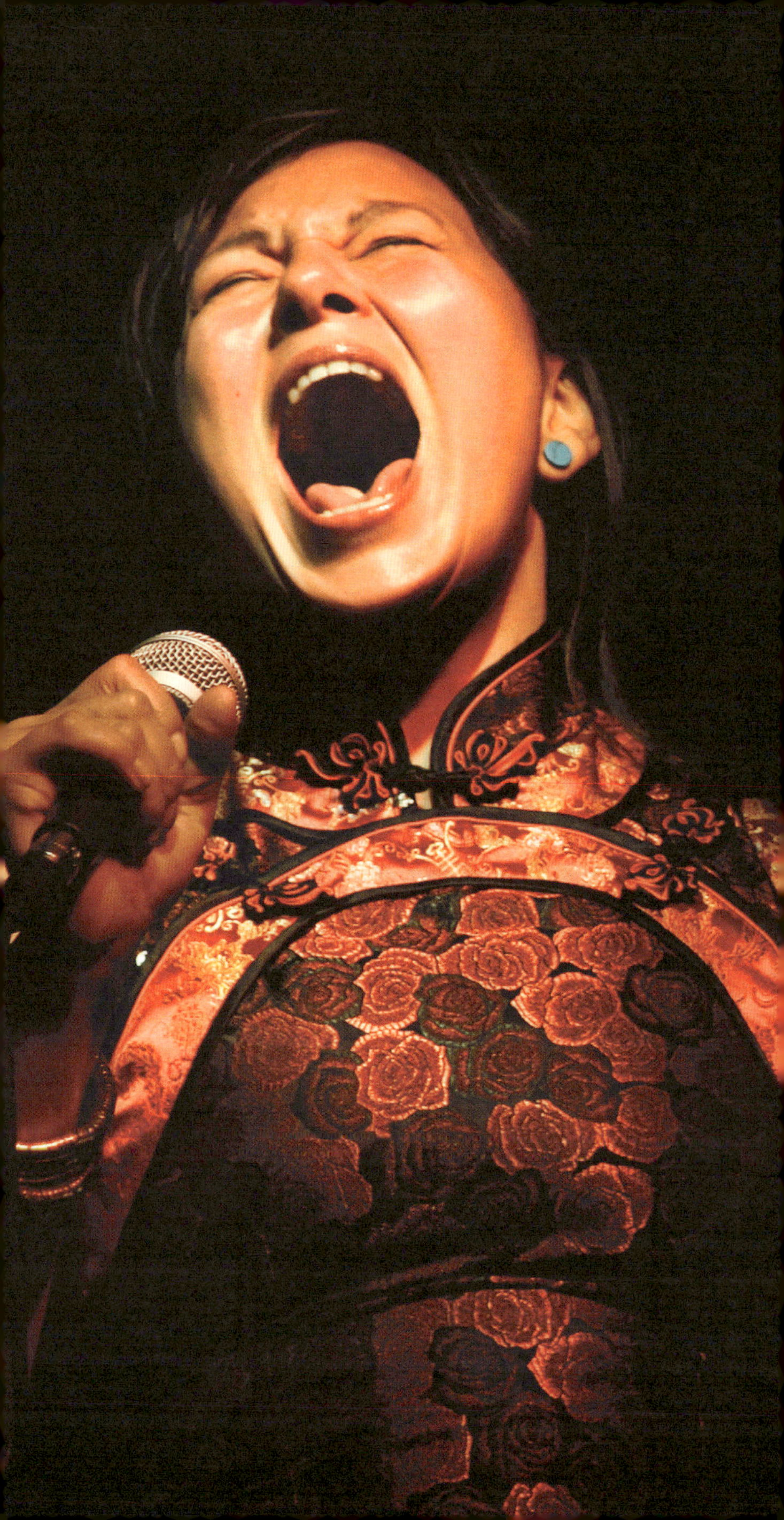

Tanya Tagaq

b. 1977 in Cambridge Bay, Canada; lives in Brandon, Manitoba

Tanya Tagaq takes the stage and begins to speak softly to the audience, giving something of an introduction to the coming evening's performance. She describes throat singing as a traditional Inuit pastime. She speaks about Robert Flaherty's 1922 silent film *Nanook of the North* almost fondly, acknowledging the respect that the director had for the Inuit he filmed. She does this while also pointing out the film's significant fault lines, the stereotypes that it produced and perpetuated. She interrupts her narrative to ask the audience not to take photographs or record the evening's performance, and invites them to simply be in the space together, in the moment, "just for us" and not for social media.

A traditional game in Inuit culture, throat singing was always an intimate affair. Usually sung between women in the home or another domestic setting—sometimes as a form of lullaby—this pastime, like many other Aboriginal cultural traditions, was suppressed by the church and by state powers for generations.

Tagaq revives this tradition of sound-making and works with it to generate a new practice, a new mode of employment of old customs. And this resurgent knowledge is put to new political use. By layering her powerful voice over the silent film *Nanook of the North*, she literally embodies and harnesses the power of her ancestors, replacing dominant stereotypes with incontrovertible agency, domination with acts of self-determination, and defeat with acts of resistance, crafted with great care and generosity.

As her first performance in the U.S. Southwest, Tagaq performs *Nanook of the North* at Santa Fe's Lensic Theater as part of SITElines.

— Pip Day

OPPOSITE:
Tanya Tagaq performing

Javier Téllez

b. 1969 in Valencia, Venezuela; lives in New York, U.S.A.

To Have Done with the Judgment of God is Téllez's second of a planned trilogy of films inspired by the French surrealist writer and avant-garde dramatist Antonin Artaud. Téllez collaborated on the first film, *La Conquista de México*, 2012, with outpatients of the Fray Bernardino Psychiatric Hospital in Mexico City, with whom he wrote the script and acted out the drama by Artaud about Hernán Cortés's conquest of Mexico.

To Have Done with the Judgment of God is based on the 1947 *A Voyage to the Land of the Tarahumara,* which Artaud wrote while interned in a French mental sanatorium. In the book, Artaud describes the trip he made in 1936 to the Sierra Tarahumara in the state of Chihuahua, Mexico, to meet the Tarahumara (today called by their autoethnonym, Rarámuri) and practice *Tutúguri*, the ritual in which peyote is ingested to heighten consciousness.

The title *To Have Done with the Judgment of God* comes from the radio play *Pour en finir avec le jugement de Dieu*, written by Artaud in the sanatorium and recorded in November 1947 for broadcasting on French Radio on February 2, 1948. Transmission was censored by the station's director, Vladimir Porché, who considered the piece immoral, despite its defense by prominent French intellectuals. Long after Artaud's psychonautic journey, Téllez retraced the dramatist's original route and filmed the rituals described. He commissioned a Rarámuri-language translation of Artaud's radio play and, with the collaboration of local radio station Radio Xetar, had it broadcast on December 5, 2015. The film shows the transmission of the play on the radio while contemporary Rarámuris pursue their everyday lives. In between these scenes, it highlights the anthropomorphic rock formations at the Valle de los Monjes to which Artaud dedicated his 1936 essay "The Mountain of Signs," together with the soundtrack of Artaud's censored play.[39] The film ends with the ceremony of *Tutúguri*. Téllez's film bring us closer to Artaud's Theater of Cruelty, a theatrical form intended to speak directly to the senses, without dialogue, in the manner of ritual.

— Pip Day and Pablo León de la Barra

OPPOSITE:
Video stills from *To Have Done with the Judgment of God*, 2016

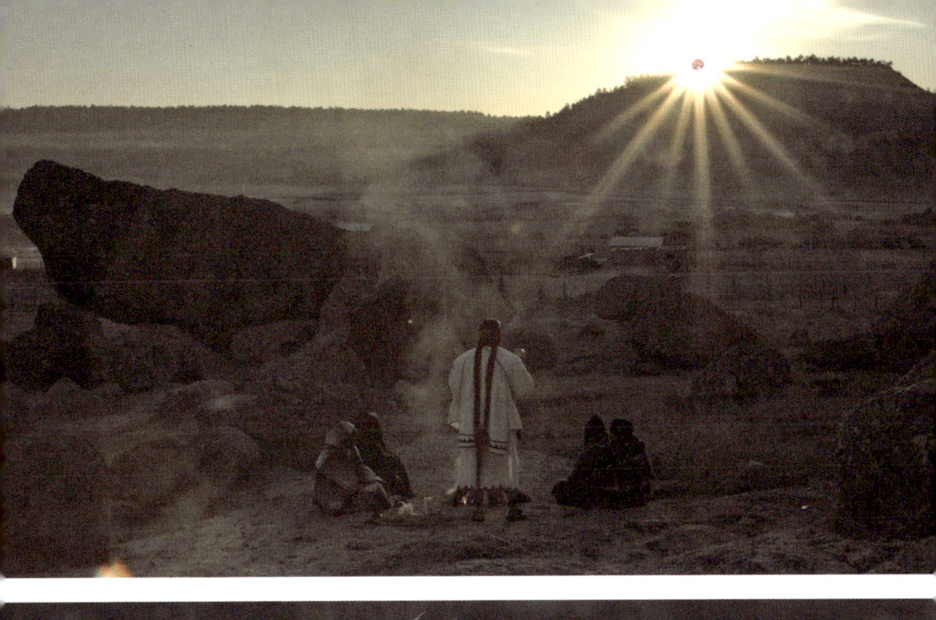

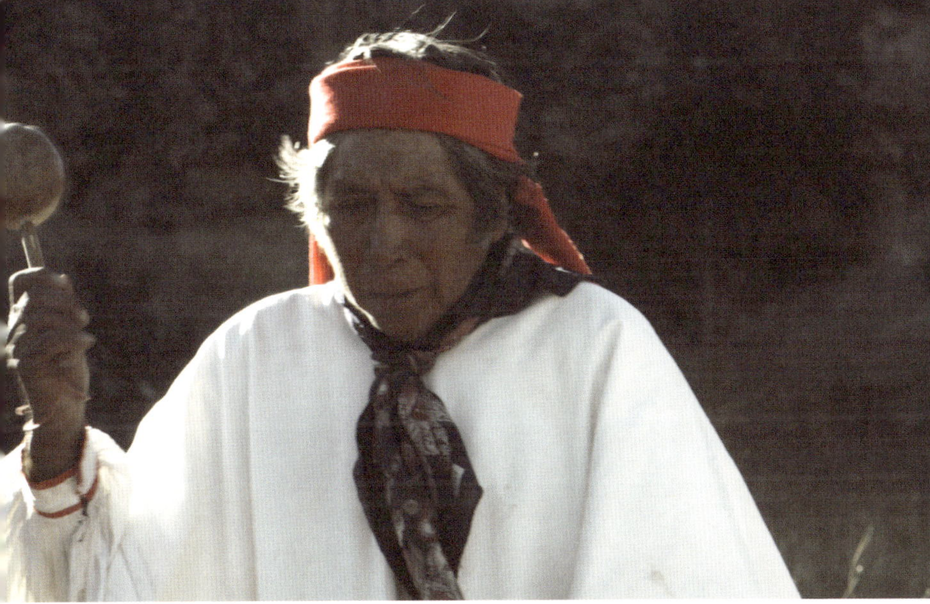

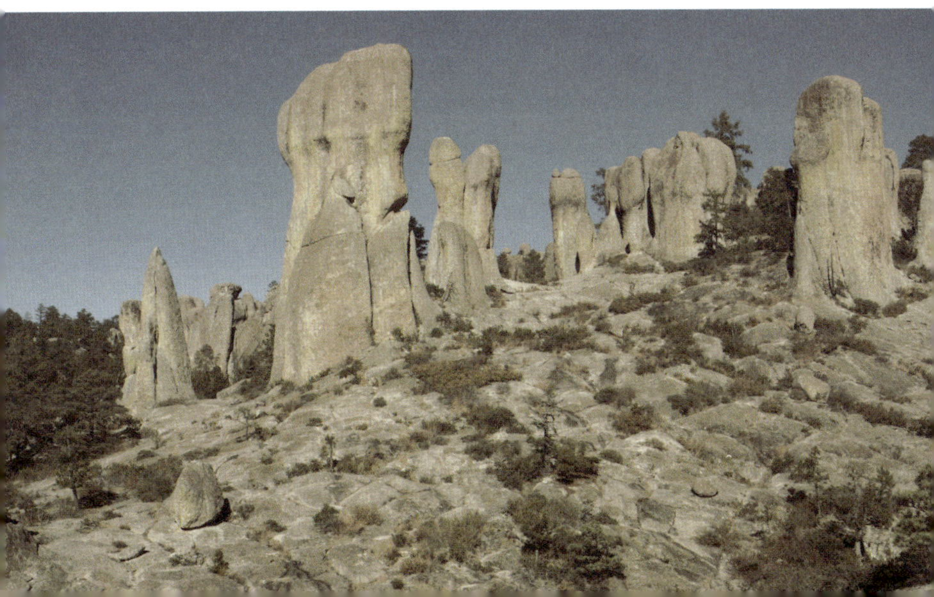

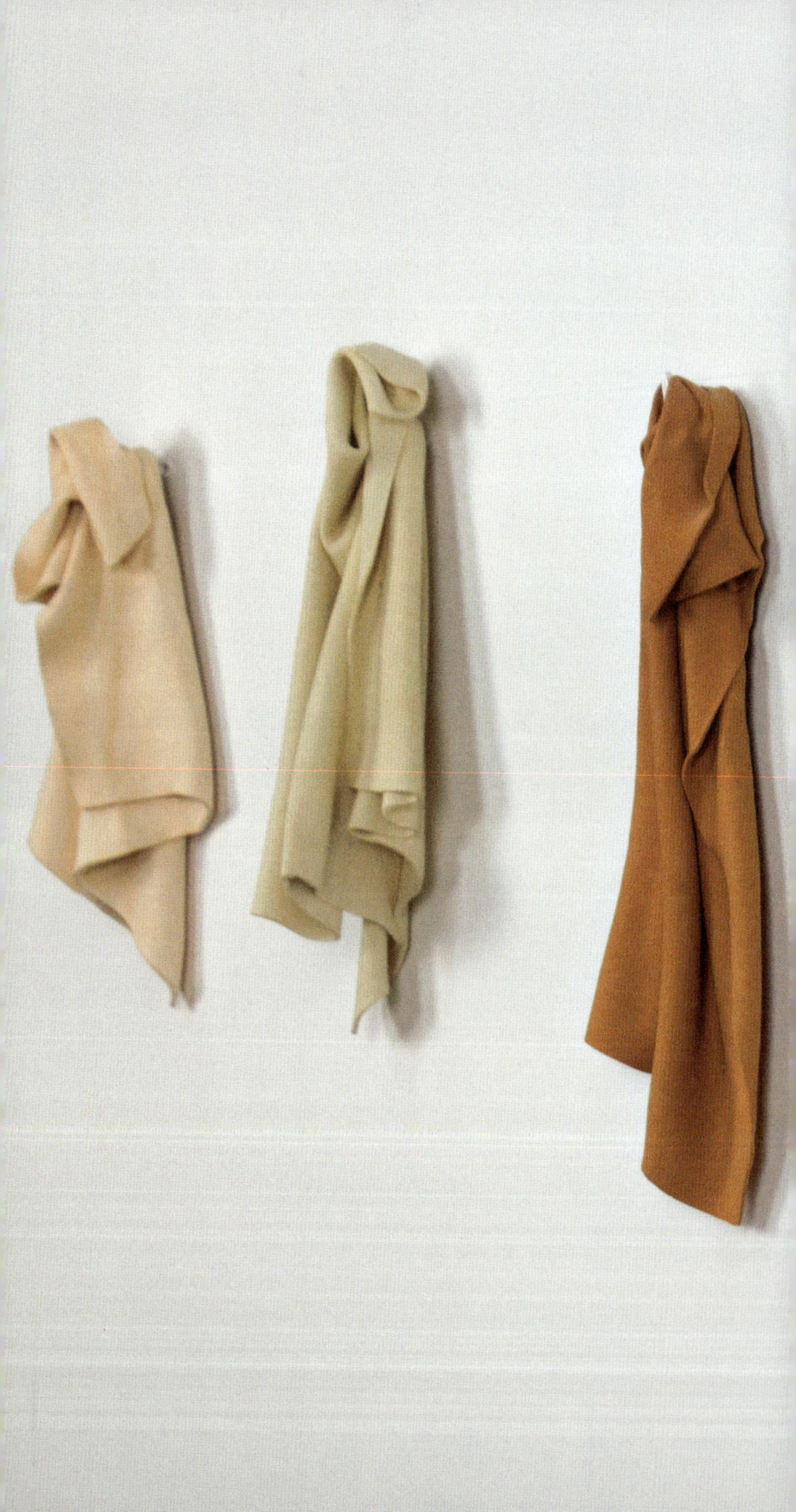

Juana Valdes

b. 1963 in Cabañas, Cuba; lives in Miami/New York, U.S.A.

Juana Valdes's ceramics, sculptures, site-specific installations, and works on paper reflect her concern with racial conditions in the Americas, including the United States. Through residencies at the Experimental Intermedia Huis in Ghent, Belgium, in 1996, and the Europees Keramisch Werk Centrum in Den Bosch, Netherlands, in 2002, she began working with materials from specific places of origin, such as porcelain. Though in the Netherlands porcelain is typically white or gray—with colored decoration added—Valdes invented a unique process that infuses the especially white porcelain called bone china with color. In recent work, she has used this technique to cast cleaning rags in flesh colors ranging from pale pink to dark brown. The firing burns away the fabric and solidifies its form in porcelain.

Colored China Rags alludes to labor, class, race, and gender. Cleaning rags, used by women immigrants to maintain homes and businesses, are something easily discarded. The work's original title, *La botaron como un trapo viejo* (*They Threw Her Away Like an Old Rag*), stresses the perceived disposability and negligibility of women. Studying the spectrum of colors associated with the rags, we see the range of immigrant and slave labor that has supported the economy of the American hemisphere throughout history.

In *Pulling at Me—a Thread*, 2015, the first panel in a set of nine prints presents the statement "It's about hanging by a nail, by a thread, by the skin of your teeth." With each additional print, words gradually disappear until the only ones remaining are "It's your skin." This simple linguistic gesture moves the message from colloquial expressions about the challenge of surviving a difficult situation to mental (in)stability to the impossibility of life under certain circumstances. The final, explanatory phrase critiques the prevalence of racial inequalities in social interaction and the power of phenotype to determine one's place in society.

— Rocío Aranda-Alvarado

OPPOSITE:
Detail of *Colored China Rags*, 2012

Pierre Verger

b. 1902 in Paris, France; d. 1996 in Salvador, Brazil

Pierre Verger was a photographer, ethnographer, anthropologist, historian, botanist, and one of the pioneering researchers of Afro-Brazilian religion and culture. In 1946, prior to settling permanently in Salvador, Verger traveled extensively across Africa, the Americas, and Southeast Asia, working as a freelance photojournalist for several magazines and newspapers. On arriving in Bahia, he devoted himself to an investigation of the ties between African and African-American culture, and quickly established a wide circle of friends—writers, artists, anthropologists, artisans, *capoeira* masters, and participants in *candomblé* rituals. In 1948, Verger met Dona Senhora, a senior priestess of the Yoruba Oshun cult, who made him an emissary to Africa. In 1953, in Ketou, Dahomey (now Benin), Verger was fully initiated into the Yoruba religion and received the name Fatumbí. His first study on Yoruba cults, *Dieux d'Afrique (African Gods,* 1954), featured photographs and texts that trace parallels between ceremonies in West Africa and Brazil. Though lacking academic training, in 1966 Verger received a doctorate in African Studies from the Sorbonne in Paris for his research on the slave trade and commercial relations between the Gulf of Benin and Bahia. Indeed, the intimacy and spontaneity of his photographs, as well as the affectionate and often erotic tone in his depictions of his subjects, reflect his lifelong commitment to African and African-American culture and his relinquishment of European roots. Although he had originally started to write as a requirement of the Institut Français d'Afrique Noire (French Institute for Black Africa, or IFAN), which awarded him several scholarships, Verger "believed that encouraging a reflection on Yoruba religion might help to inspire a less prejudiced vision of African religions and ultimately lead to a more enlightened encounter and exchange between cultures."[40] By the late 1970s, though Verger had abandoned photography, he continued to make research trips to Africa while leading a modest life in the outskirts of Salvador.

— Kiki Mazzucchelli

OPPOSITE:
Candomblé Opo Afonja, Salvador, Brazil, 1950

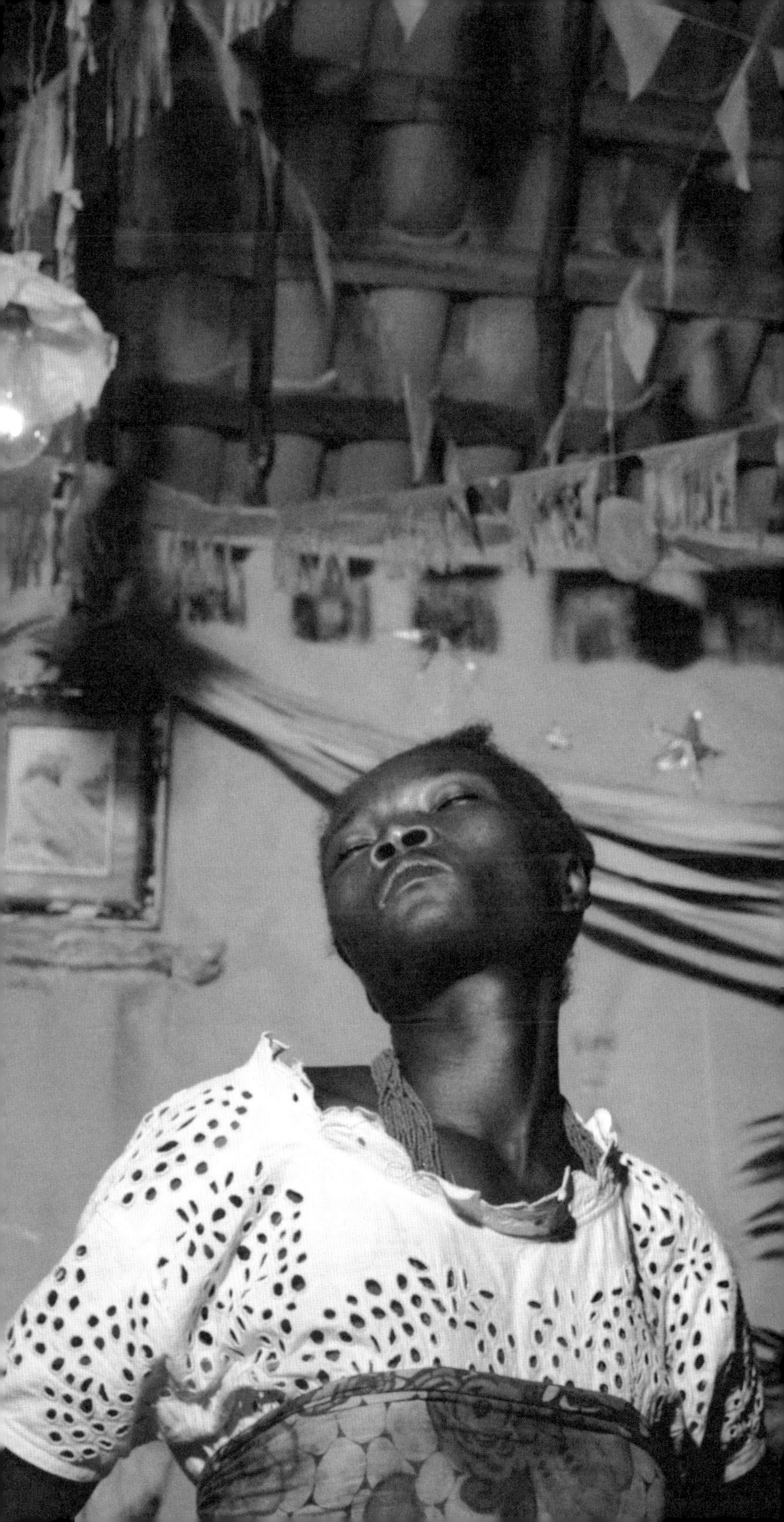

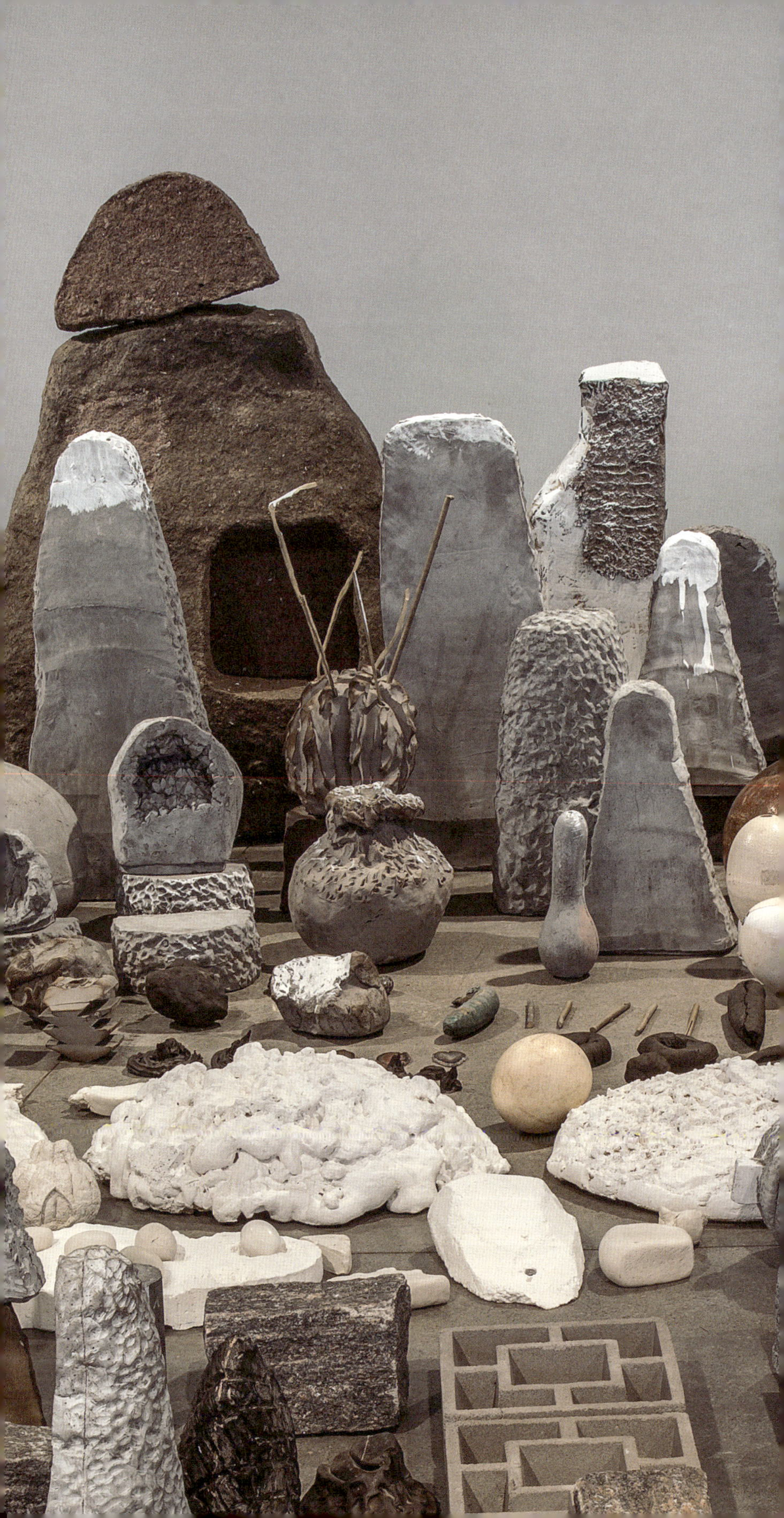

Erika Verzutti

b. 1971 in São Paulo, Brazil; lives in São Paulo

Over the past decade, Erika Verzutti has drawn from different sources to create a vast yet very particular taxonomy of forms, which she constantly expands on and recombines in her sculptures. Whether through the appropriation of natural readymades, such as tropical fruits, vegetables, and minerals, or through explicit reference to historical art by well-known artists, from Tarsila do Amaral to Jasper Johns and Pablo Picasso, Verzutti creates an enchainment of meanings that takes shape in visually appealing compositions. Eminently profane, the works testify to the artist's equal estimation of all the objects she selects as raw material for her structures, whether a makeup case spotted in an in-flight magazine or an iconic sculpture by a modernist master. *Star*, 2010, is a column made of stacked star fruits and pomegranates cast in bronze that alludes to Brancusi's *Infinite Column*. In a later iteration of the star fruit-column motif, a trickle of white paint runs across the humorously titled *Porn Star*, 2011. Many of Verzutti's works are titled to insinuate—and sometimes to spell out in a characteristically deadpan manner—associations that go beyond the meaning usually ascribed to their constituent parts. *Missionary*, 2011, is a bronze formed by an upturned half of a papaya perched atop an off-kilter butternut squash, while *Battle*, 2010, is a collection of olive-green watermelons cast in concrete and laid out on the floor like the helmets of a defeated battalion. Over the past few years, Verzutti has produced a series of floor works she has nicknamed "cemeteries," in which sculptures she sees as failures are organized like findings from an archaeological excavation. Sex and death, recurring themes in Verzutti's practice, are brought together in the cemeteries, monuments to ruin and sites of rebirth.

— Kiki Mazzucchelli

OPPOSITE:
Detail of *Cemitério com Neve*, 2015

FOLLOWING SPREAD:
Francisca Benitez, *As you lean on me and I lean on you, we move forward*, 2015
High Line performance, New York, 2015

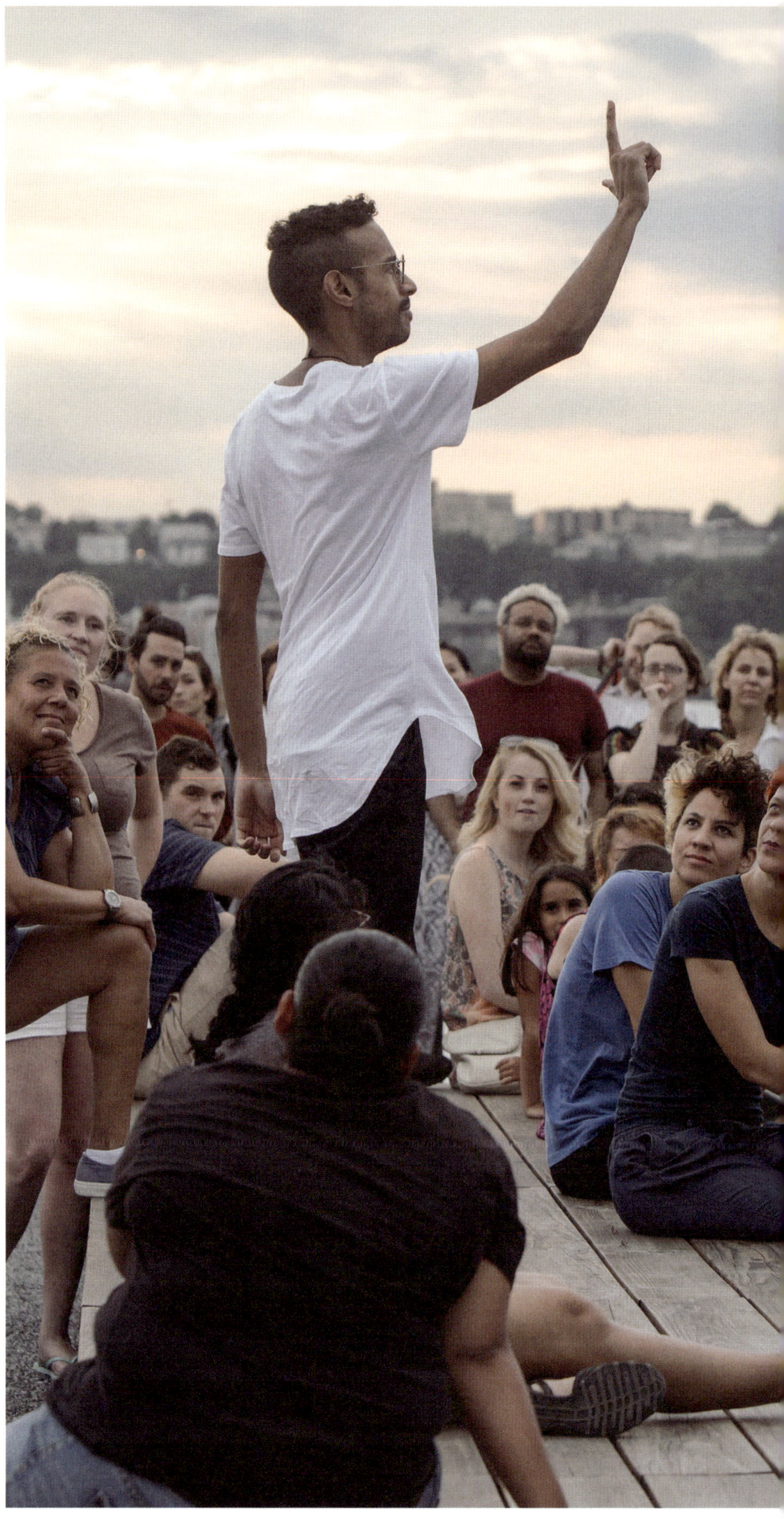

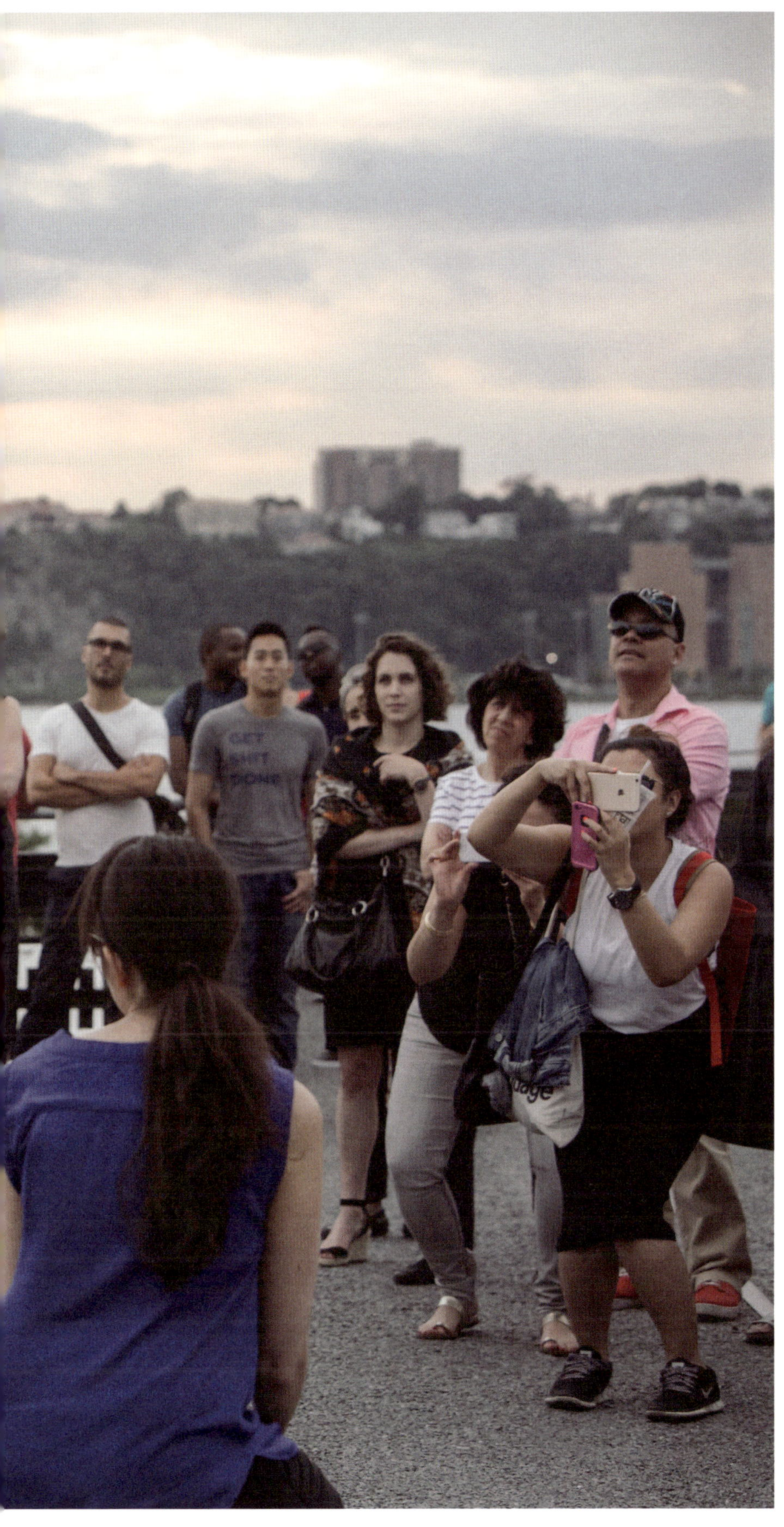

Out of SITE Center

Joanne Lefrak

Pursuing a deeper and more consistent engagement with audiences and artists, in 2013 SITE Santa Fe established SITE Center as a research and programming hub. Now a vital part of SITE's education and outreach activities, the Center provides a platform for the constructive critique of the traditional biennial model that offers no continuity between exhibitions and often little connection to community or place. SITE Center programming before, during, and after each SITElines exhibition builds public dialogue and contributes to expanded cultural competencies. Programming picks up on the themes of SITElines exhibitions to generate awareness of and responsiveness to the cultural and geographic complexities of our region.

While these public activities visibly support an ongoing relationship with our audiences, behind the scenes SITE Center works with select artists on long-term community-based or site-responsive projects. This vital function of SITE Center averts the pitfall of having biennial artists remotely conceive well-intended community gestures that too often misfire—at best producing surface readings of a place, and at worst insulting the very community they seek to engage. With the traditionally frenetic pace of biennial-making and short lead times given to artists who are charged with producing site-responsive works, it is no wonder that these projects are hampered from the outset. Within SITE Center, residencies are established for long-term research-based and community-centered projects, and are given the necessary infrastructure and support, along with elastic timelines.

The exhibition *much wider than a line* includes SITE Center projects by artists Francisca Benitez, Raven Chacon, and Pablo Helguera. In addition, SITE continues to work with artist Jamison Chas Banks, whose *Retour des Cendres Vol. 1 (Return of the Ashes Vol. 1)*, 2014, was presented in *Unsettled Landscapes*. In that project, Banks used the metaphor of baseball to look at complex issues related to "stealing home" through a game played by teams called the Purchasers and the Exiles. For the next phase, Banks will invite local Native students to explore their family histories through the lens of sports and printmaking.

Francisca Benitez breaks down barriers between the Deaf and hearing communities in Santa Fe by making a durable connection between SITE and the New Mexico School for the Deaf and developing related public programming. Raven Chacon introduces Pueblo students to the art of musical composition, often for the first time. Because the students have no previous formal training, there is no need to free them from Western classical conventions: their compositions are unique expressions that reference personal biography and social practices of Pueblo culture. Pablo Helguera engages historians and local residents to examine hidden histories and cultural conflicts in New Mexico and presents an installation that shares these stories with museum visitors. Connecting artists like Banks, Benitez, Chacon, and Helguera to the region at a deep level allows for meaningful interactions between artists and the community and the forging of sustainable collaborations with diverse populations. SITE is committed to supporting these artists with ample time, resources, and access to the community so that creativity can be generated outside the building's walls, reaching a broad audience through authentic and transformative engagement.

Francisca Benitez

b. 1974 in Santiago, Chile; lives in New York, U.S.A.

Chilean-born, New York-based artist Francisca Benitez engages directly with the public, creating programming and presentations based on interaction. For her community-engaged artwork at SITE Santa Fe, Benitez connected the Deaf community of Santa Fe with the contemporary art world. Her work generates a sustainable relationship between the Deaf community and SITE, which in turn helps to integrate the hearing and the Deaf within the city of Santa Fe. While not hard of hearing herself, Benitez has spent a lifetime learning about and understanding Deaf culture. In honor of her father, who was Deaf, Benitez uses her personal experience to break down barriers within Santa Fe.

At the New Mexico School for the Deaf, the oldest educational institution in Santa Fe, the Kenneth E. Brasel Centennial Museum houses one of the most comprehensive collections of documents and memorabilia related to American Deaf educational history. Benitez has begun her project by organizing a walk between the two institutions, just half a mile apart. The simple act of walking together creates a viscerally felt connection. The walk brings SITE's public to the museum, where students from the school give presentations on the history of Deaf education and the items in the collection. The mode of presentation is left up to each individual—it may be poetic, composed of sound effects, communicated through bodily movement like dance, or oral, translated by an interpreter. Some of the objects and presentations have a physical presence in SITElines so that gallery visitors can be exposed to this little-known history.

In another component of the project, the Deaf community walks to SITE for an ASL poetry slam. Using her connections in the Deaf community, Benitez has been able to identify ASL poetry educators and invite them to Santa Fe. The slam occurs in the SITE galleries and responds to the work on view. The hearing audience members who don't know ASL can engage with the poetry slam in the manner of a dance performance, experiencing sign language in new ways within the exhibition space. With this multidimensional work, Benitez creates meaningful connections that endure beyond the run of the exhibition.

— Joanne Lefrak

OPPOSITE:
Son en Señas, 2015, in collaboration with the Asociación Nacional de Sordos de Cuba (ANSOC), Bienal de La Habana, Havana, Cuba, 2015
Vintage postcard issued by the Albertype Company, Brooklyn, showing New Mexico School for the Deaf, Santa Fe, date unkown

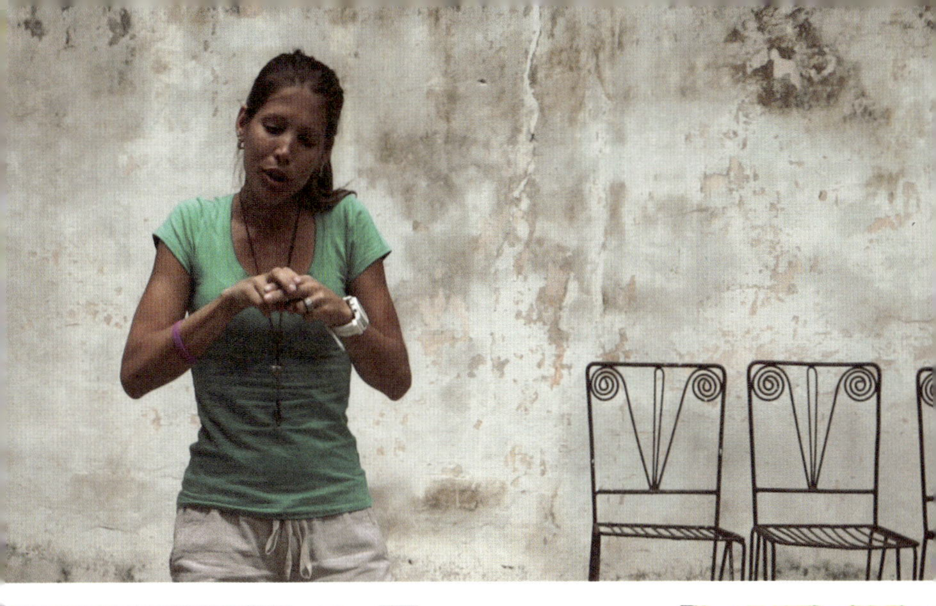

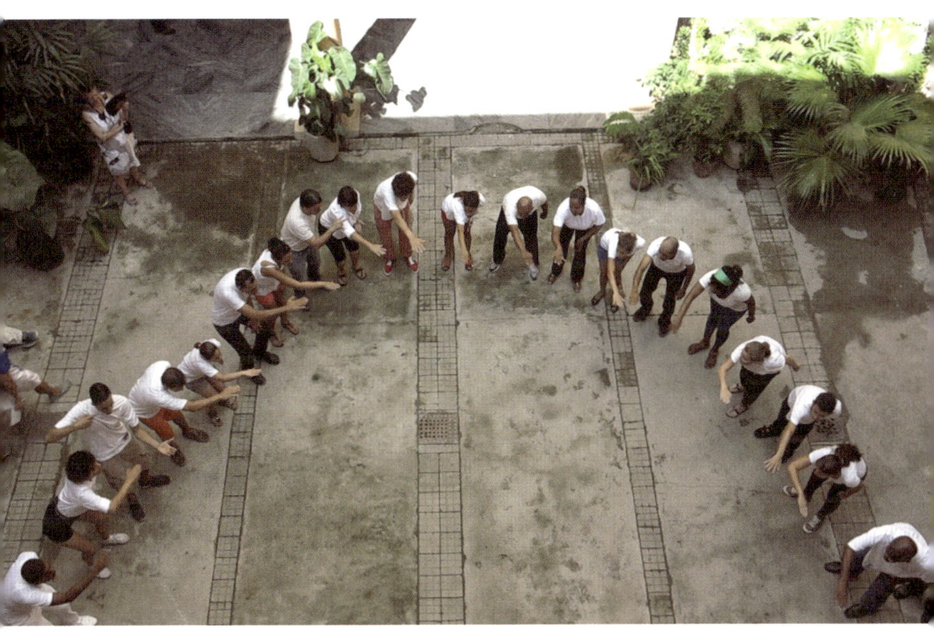

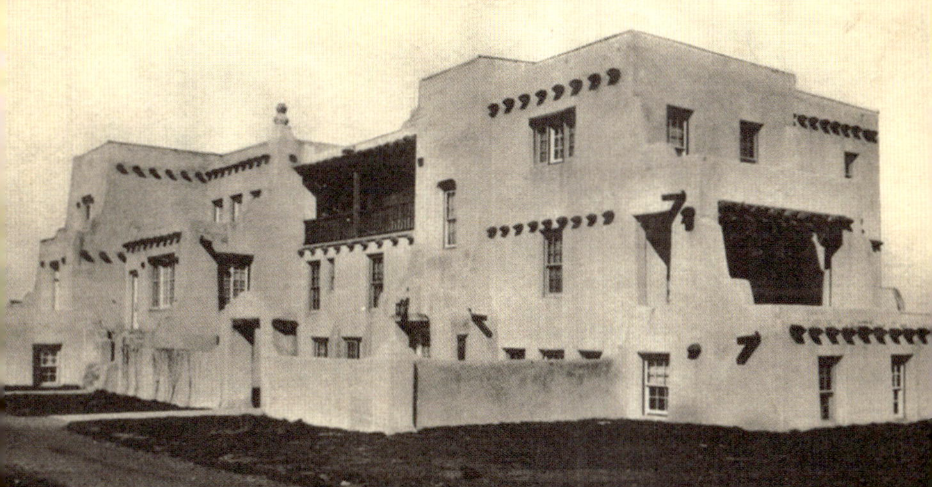
Mexico School for the Deaf. Santa Fe.

17

m.17-20 as slow as you want

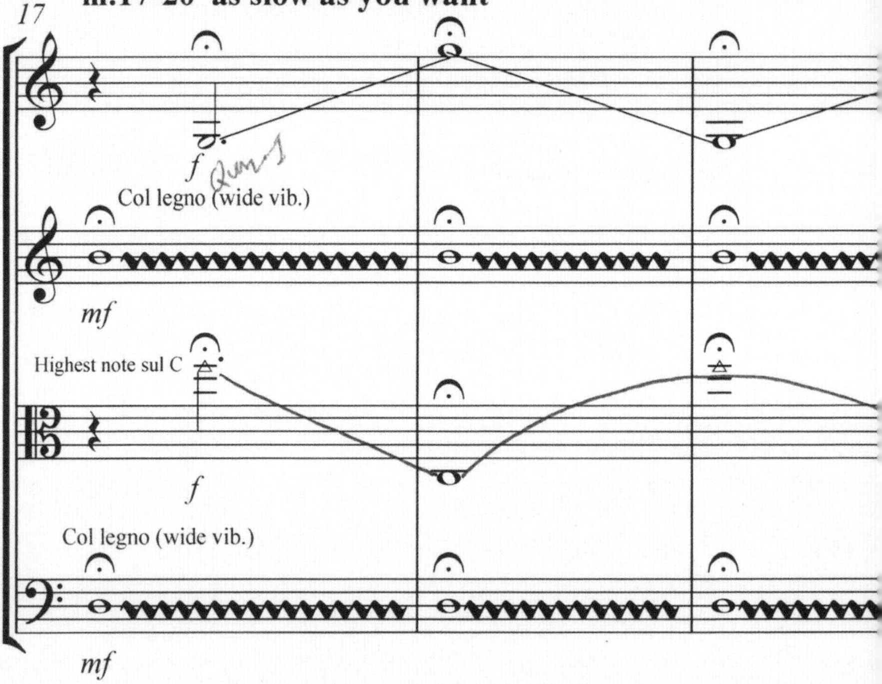

f

Col legno (wide vib.)

mf

Highest note sul C

f

Col legno (wide vib.)

mf

Sound fast! Yay, we're all done. Fast!

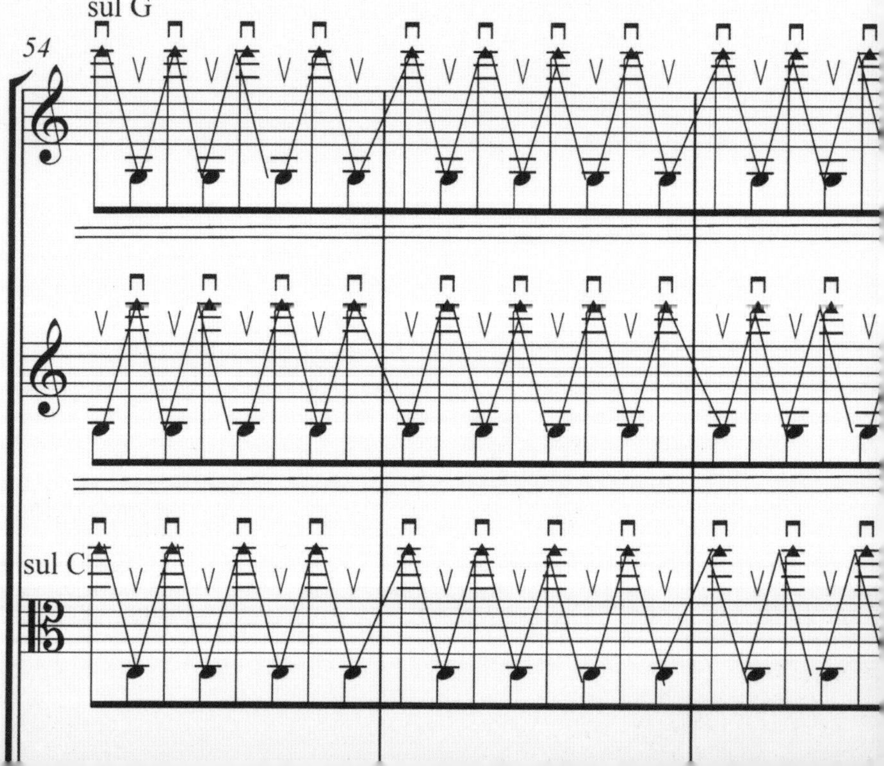

sul G

54

sul C

Raven Chacon

b. 1977 in Fort Defiance, Arizona, U.S.A.; lives in Albuquerque, New Mexico

Raven Chacon is a sound artist who creates unique chamber music, experimental noise music, and large-scale sound installations. Using digitization, masterful feedback loops, and handmade instruments, he transforms analog sounds into fantastically eerie soundscapes. In 2012, his installation *Singing toward the Wind Now / Singing toward the Sun Now* created music from natural elements and forces. Installed in Canyon De Chelly in the Navajo Nation, Chacon's "instrument" took the form of four 5-foot-high metal sculptures designed to resemble both electrical utility towers and geometric Navajo weaving designs. The strings of two of the towers were activated by the wind and sand to produce a quiet singing drone, and the other two towers were solar-powered oscillators, yielding a subtle electronic beat.

In addition to his practice as an experimental musician and installation artist, Chacon has been a longtime composer-in-residence with the Native-American Composers Apprenticeship Project, an outreach program based in Arizona that teaches concert music composition to young Native Americans. Chacon's SITE Center project for *much wider than a line* brings the spirit of this work to a new program for Native youth in the northern New Mexico region in which he works with four Native students, ranging in age from thirteen to seventeen. He gives the participants the assignment of writing a two-to-three-minute-long musical composition for a string quartet—though some may not ever have had access to musical instruments, school music programs, or, in many cases, support systems at home. The students are given an extensive orientation on how each of the string instruments—violin, viola, and cello—is played, the names of its parts, how it might function in a composition for a quartet, and what its normal, as well as "unnatural," sounds are. Encouraged to make any type of music they want, the students create work that is an amalgam of their influences, which might include tribal music, traditional music, popular music, heavy metal, sounds of nature—perhaps from the desert and its animals—sci-fi, horror movie and video game soundtracks, and any other sounds that might find their way into a contemporary Indigenous young person's ears. The culmination of the project is a concert series in which world-class professional musicians perform the students' compositions.

— Joanne Lefrak

OPPOSITE:
Score excerpt of Celeste Lansing (b. 1995), *Pink Thunder*, 2009

Pablo Helguera

b. 1971 in Mexico City, Mexico; lives in New York, U.S.A.

Pablo Helguera completes his SITE Center residency with a presentation in *much wider than a line*. For *Unsettled Landscapes*, he examined the brief historical period when New Mexico was part of Mexico. That first phase of research resulted in *Nuevo romancero nuevomejicano*, 2014, which consisted of a performance and an interactive installation rooted in the legacy of the musical form of the medieval Spanish *romance* that has been preserved in New Mexico.

In the second phase of his project, Helguera addresses the history of conflict in New Mexico and its constructed image as a tourist haven. He writes: "As someone born and raised in Mexico, New Mexico and Santa Fe in particular offer an attractive urban landscape that evokes a sweet image of old Mexico; yet this image strikes one as a staged representation of reality, a nostalgic illustration of a place that never quite existed. I am interested in delving deeply into the core of the history of New Mexico that has led to the construction, and the performance, of these mythical stories."[41]

For this final phase of the project, Helguera has created a theatrical prop shop at SITE Santa Fe where visitors can purchase items pertinent to a fictional play titled *The Hermit Battalion*. Each object in the store is catalogued in a way that connects it to a larger story. As in *Nuevo romancero nuevomejicano*, which interweaves multiple events from New Mexico's past, *The Hermit Battalion* references multiple stories, including the creation of the Fiestas de Santa Fe and the reconquest of New Mexico; the history of St. Patrick's Battalion, a unit of Irish immigrants who defected from the United States to fight with the Mexican Army during the Mexican-American War; and the tale of John Augustiani, an Italian immigrant and religious recluse who became a legend in Las Vegas, New Mexico, and gave the nearby Hermit Peak its name. Helguera meets with local historians to dig more deeply into these narratives, and the store is staffed with storytellers who expound on the histories and legends presented in the installation. This chapter of Helguera's project again presents a multifaceted narrative in a kaleidoscopic way.

— Joanne Lefrak

OPPOSITE:

Study images and store sign for *The Hermit Battalion*, 2016

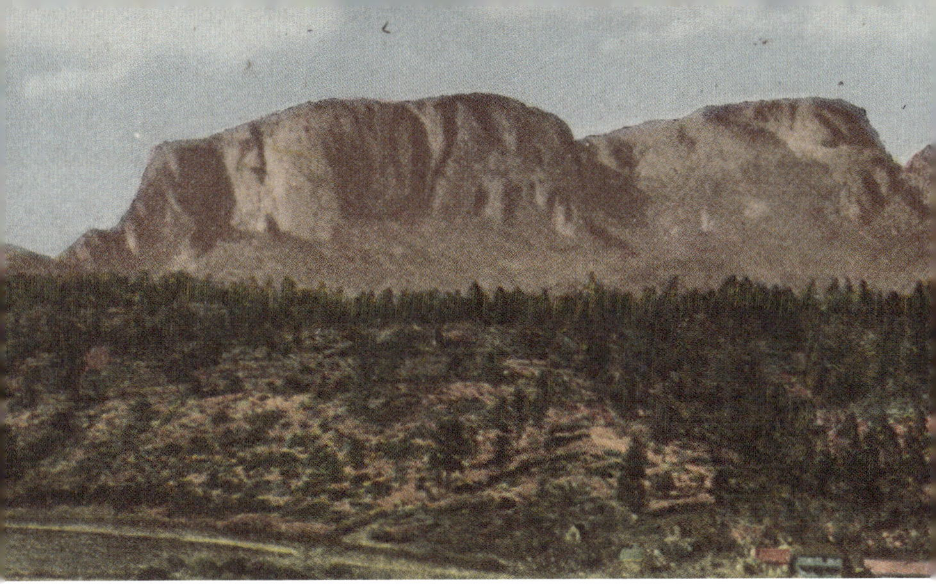

The Hermit Battalion

Theatrical Goods

&

Prop Shop

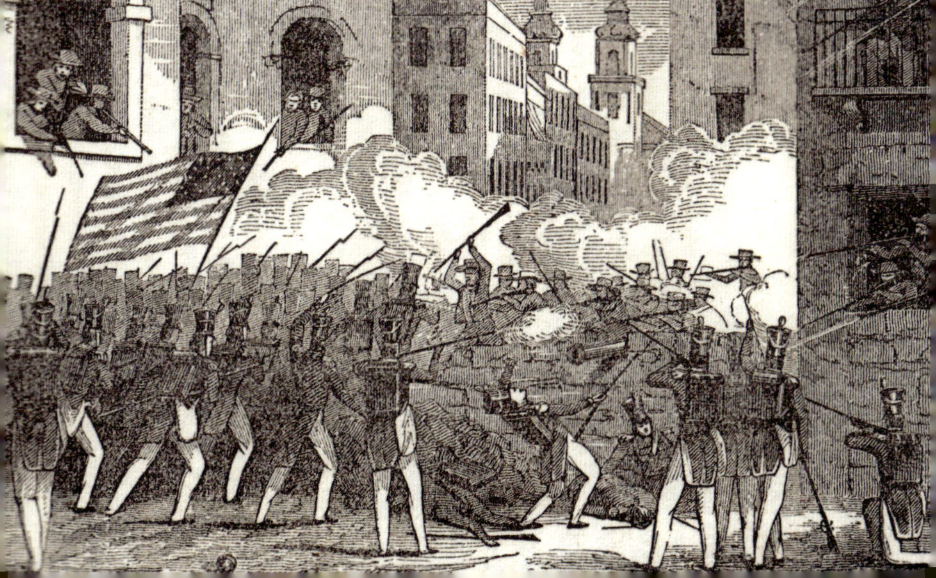

Notes

1. Leanne Simpson, *Dancing on Our Turtle's Back: Stories of Nishnaabeg Re-Creation, Resurgence, and a New Emergence* (Winnipeg: Arbeiter Ring Publishing, 2011).

2. Earth building is a construction technique that has endured since prehistory in which soil—mud bricks and rammed earth—is the primary building material.

3. Simpson, *Dancing on Our Turtle's Back.*

4. La construcción en tierra es una técnica constructiva que ha perdurado desde la prehistoria, en la cual el suelo -lodo, ladrillos y tierra apisonada- es el principal material de construcción.

5. Simpson, *Dancing on Our Turtle's Back.*

6. L'architecture en terre est une technique de construction qui perdure depuis la préhistoire. La terre - briques de boue et pisé - est le principal matériau de construction.

7. Simpson, *Dancing on Our Turtle's Back.*

8. Construção em adobe é uma técnica que existe desde a pré-história, na qual tijolos de barro e terra prensada são o principal material de construção.

9. Kristin Barendsen, "Miguel Gandert," in Thomas Barrow et al., *Photography: New Mexico* (Albuquerque: Fresno Fine Art Publications, 2008), 81.

10. Simpson, *Dancing on Our Turtle's Back*, 89.

11. This project concerns an Ecuadorian anti-mining court case in which the forest was treated as a legal entity unto itself, with rights within a court of law. See Ursula Biemann and Paulo Tavares, *Forest Law—Selva Jurídica* (East Lansing, Mich.: Eli and Edythe Broad Art Museum, Michigan State University, 2014).

12. Hu Fang, "Why We Look at Plants in a Corrupted World," trans. Andre Maerkle, *e-flux journal*, 56th Venice Biennale website, posted June 15, 2015.

13. Rebecca Solnit, *Hope in the Dark: Untold Histories, Wild Possibilities* (2004; Chicago: Haymarket Books, 2016).

14. Achille Mbembe, *Decolonizing Knowledge and the Question of the Archive*, Atavist e-book, May 11, 2015, Africa Is a Country website, accessed May 14, 2016.

15. Irmgard Emmelhainz, embedded electronic comment, March 25, 2016.

16. Donna J. Haraway, *When Species Meet* (Minneapolis: University of Minnesota Press, 2008), 3.

17. Eve Tuck and K. Wayne Yang, "Decolonization is not a metaphor," introduction to *Decolonization: Indigeneity, Education, and Society* 1, no. 1 (2012), 1-40.

18. Mbembe, *Decolonizing Knowledge and the Question of the Archive.*

19. Lina Bo Bardi, "Por que o Nordeste?," in *Tempos de grossura: o design no impasse*, ed. Marcelo Suzuki (São Paulo: Instituto Lina Bo e P. M. Bardi, 1994), 20.

20. The lecture was published posthumously, without Warburg's prior authorization, as "A Lecture on Serpent Ritual," *Journal of the Warburg Institute* 2, no. 4 (April 1939): 277-92.

21. Ibid., 292.

22. Daystar/Rosalie Jones, "Inventing Native Modern Dance: A Tough Trip through Paradise," in *Native American Performance and Representation*, ed. S. E. Wilmer (Tucson: University of Arizona Press, 2009), chap. 1.

23. Lloyd Kiva New, "In Pursuit of Indian Education: The Role of the Institute of American Indian Arts," submitted to the Special Sub-committee on Indian Education, United States Senate Committee on Labor and Public Welfare, February 1969.

24. Rolland Meinholtz, conversation with the author, 2011.

25. Doug Lee, conservation with the author, October 28, 2010.

26. Daystar/Jones, "Inventing Native Modern Dance," 27.

27. Meinholtz, conversation.

28. See Santa Fe Indian School website, accessed May 23, 2016.

29. See Kent R. Brown, "Opening on the American Scene: A Native American Theater Ensemble," *Journal of American Indian Education* 13, no. 1 (October 1973).

30. Dan Gibson, "Paolo Solari's Innovative Design Puts Amphitheater on Center Stage," *New Mexico Magazine*, June 1993, 58.

31. See Chavajay's commentary in the Q&A "Chavajay (Guatemala)," 2013, Cisneros Fontanals Art Foundation (CIFO) website, accessed February 15, 2016.

32. Lewis deSoto, *Empire* (Berkeley, Calif.: Heyday, 2016), xv.

33. Maria Hupfield, e-mail to the author, January 29, 2016.

34. The second and third films in the trilogy are *The Journals of Knud Rasmussen*, 2006, and *Before Tomorrow*, 2009.

35. Cildo Meireles, "Cruzeiro do Sul, 1969–70", in *Cildo Meireles*, ed. Guy Brett (London: Tate Publishing, 2008), 58.

36. Paulo Nazareth Arte Contemporânea, Cuadernos de Africa blog, accessed April 26, 2016.

37. "Abel Rodriguez, Local Researcher, Receives 2014 Principal Prince Claus Laureate Award," Tropenbos International website, September 8, 2014, accessed May 9, 2016.

38. Eduardo Viveiros de Castro, "Cosmological Perspectivism in Amazonia and Elsewhere" (lecture delivered at the Department of Social Anthropology, University of Cambridge, February–March 1998), published in *Hau: Journal of Ethnographic Theory*, Masterclass Series 1 (2012): 77, available on the Hau website, accessed May 3, 2016; Viveiros de Castro, "Perspectival Anthropology and the Method of Controlled Equivocation," in *Tipití: Journal of the Society for the Anthropology of Lowland South America* 2, no. 1 (2004), available on the Digital Commons website of Trinity University, accessed May 3, 2016.

39. Antonin Artaud, "La Montaña de los Signos" (1937), *México y Viaje al país de los Tarahumaras* (1975; Mexico City: Fondo de Cultura Económica, 1984), 273.

40. Angela Lühning, "Pierre Fatumbí Verger: A View from Bahia," Revues MSH-Paris website, accessed May 9, 2016.

41. Pablo Helguera, e-mails to the author, March 14–18, 2016.

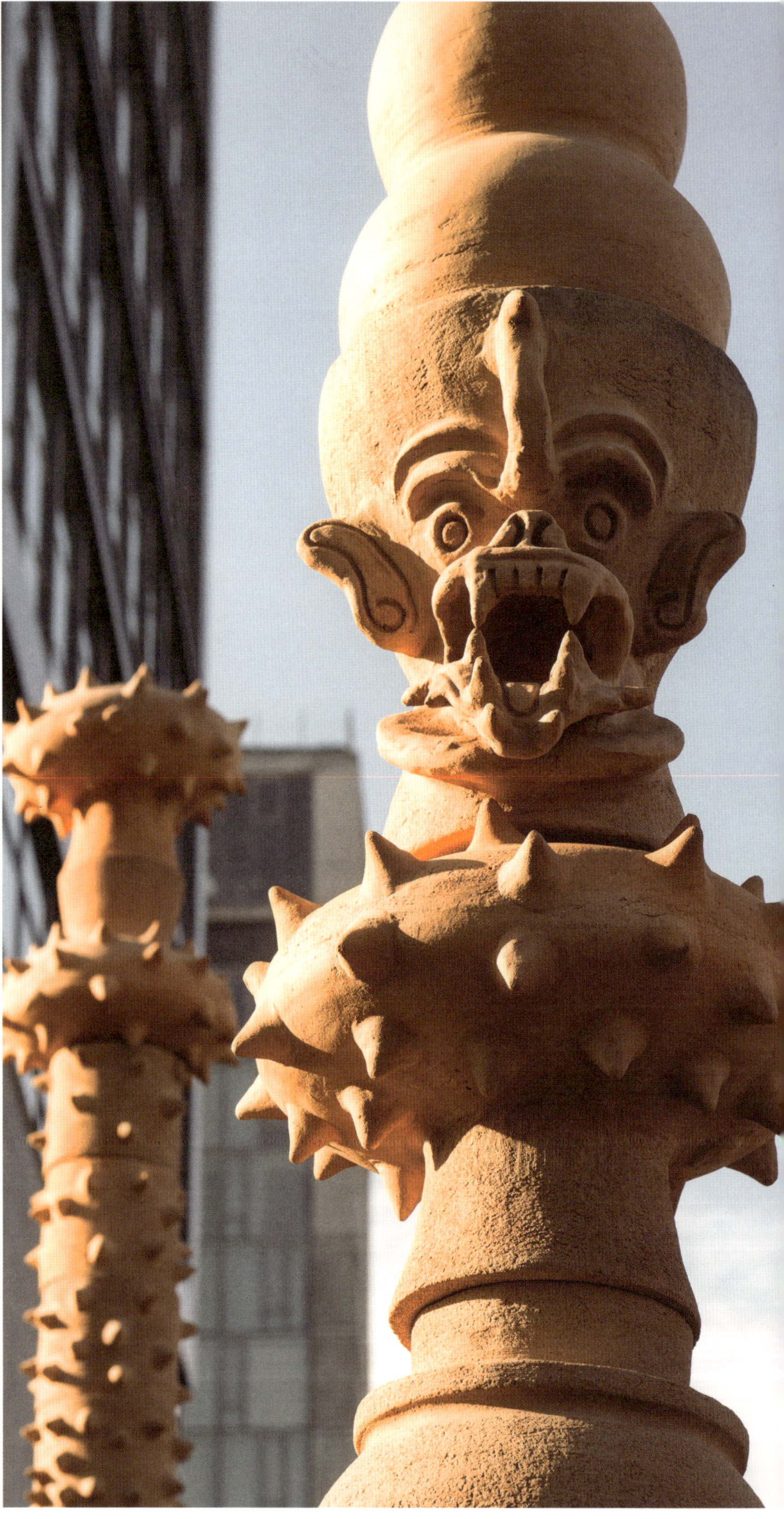

Works in the Exhibition

Unless otherwise indicated, all artworks and images are courtesy of the artists. Where relevant, artists have acknowledged their production collaborators.

Xenobia Bailey

Sistah Paradise's Revival Tent,
1999–present
Cotton and acrylic yarn, metal frame, electrical tape, shells, acrylic wall mural
120 x 60 x 60 inches
(304.8 x 152.4 x 152.4 cm)

Lina Bo Bardi

Beira de Estrada (Roadside Chair), 2016
Wood
Dimensions variable
Courtesy of the artist and Instituto Lina Bo e P. M. Bardi, São Paulo
Exhibition copy

Anna Boghiguian

Woven Wind, 2016
Mixed media installation
Dimensions variable
Courtesy of the artist and Galerie Sfeir-Semler, Hamburg and Beirut
† SITE Santa Fe commission

Margarita Cabrera with Candelaria Cabrera

Space in Between-Nopal, 2010–12
Border patrol uniform fabric, copper wire, thread, terra-cotta pot
36 x 26 x 28 inches
(91.4 x 66 x 71.1 cm)

Margarita Cabrera with Maria Lopez

Space in Between—Saguaro, 2010–12
Border patrol uniform fabric, copper wire, thread, terra-cotta pot
52 x 25 x 24 inches
(132.1 x 63.5 x 60.9 cm)

Mariana Castillo Deball with Taller Coatlicue, Atzompa, Oaxaca

¿Quién medirá el espacio, quién me dirá el momento? (Who would measure the space, who would tell me the moment?), 2014–15
Ceramics (mud from Atzompa, Oaxaca), metal structure
Three parts, height 168 1/2 inches (428 cm); 152 3/4 inches (388 cm); 169 1/4 inches (430 cm)
Courtesy of the artist and kurimanzutto, Mexico City

Benvenuto Chavajay

Doroteo Guamuch, 2013
Digital print
24 x 36 inches (60.9 x 91.4 cm)

OPPOSITE:
Maria Castillo Deball, *Who will measure the space, who will tell me the time?*, 2014–15, part of *Panorama*, a High Line commission, on view on the High Line, New York, April 2015–March 2016

En Guatemala hay pueblos tan pequeños que caben en la mira de un fusil (In Guatemala There Are Villages So Small That They Fit within the Crosshairs of a Gun), 2014
From the series *Congelación*
Baked clay
Dimensions variable

William Cordova

yawar mallku: sculpting in time, 2016
Mixed media installation
Dimensions variable
† SITE Santa Fe commission

Jonathas de Andrade

A Study of Race and Class: Bahia >< Santa Fe, 2016
Photographic installation with text
Dimensions variable
† SITE Santa Fe commission

Lewis deSoto

San Bernardino 25, West Rialto Avenue, February 10, 2013
Epson K3 inks on archival paper
13 x 20 inches (33 x 50.8 cm)
Courtesy of Chandra Cerrito Contemporary, Oakland, California

Palm Springs 15, South La Verne Way, June 10, 2013
Epson K3 inks on archival paper
13 x 20 inches (33 x 50.8 cm)
Courtesy of Chandra Cerrito Contemporary, Oakland, California

Whitewater I, June 10, 2013
Epson K3 inks on archival paper mounted and laminated on Dibond
20 x 139 inches (50.8 x 353 cm)
Courtesy of Chandra Cerrito Contemporary, Oakland, California

Highway 18 I, June 11, 2013
Epson K3 inks on archival paper, mounted and laminated on Dibond
20 x 75 inches (50.8 x 190.5 cm)
Courtesy of Chandra Cerrito Contemporary, Oakland, California

Grand Terrace I, January 12, 2014
Epson K3 inks on archival paper, mounted and laminated on Dibond
20 x 94 inches (50.8 x 238.8)
Courtesy of Chandra Cerrito Contemporary, Oakland, California

Ontario I, January 12, 2014
Epson K3 inks on archival paper, mounted and laminated on Dibond
20 x 83 inches (50.8 x 210.8 cm)
Courtesy of Chandra Cerrito Contemporary, Oakland, California

Bombay Beach I, January 15, 2014
Epson K3 inks on archival paper
13 x 20 inches (33 x 50.8 cm)
Courtesy of Chandra Cerrito Contemporary, Oakland, California

Salton Sea Beach, Coachella Avenue, January 15, 2014
Epson K3 inks on archival paper
13 x 20 inches (33 x 50.8 cm)
Courtesy of Chandra Cerrito Contemporary, Oakland, California

Aaron Dysart

Preserve 1, 2014
31 x 14 1/2 x 9 inches
(78.7 x 36.8 x 22.9 cm)
Wood, auto body primer, filler

Preserve 2, 2015
Wood, aluminum foil
29 1/2 x 7 x 6 inches
(74.9 x 17.8 x 15.2 cm)

Second Growth, 2016
Ponderosa pine tree, drywall
Dimensions variable

Carla Fernández

Cotton and hand-woven woolen capes made with artisan collaborators, 2016
†SITE Santa Fe commission

San Pablito Spirits Cape, 2016
Artisans: Jorge Santos Rojas and Juan Santos Rojas from San Pablito, Pahuatlán, Puebla (hand-cut appliqué)

Hueyapan Poncho, 2016
Artisans: Manuela Salvado from Hueyapan, Puebla (pedal-weaving); Geovanna Olvera Guzmán from Mexico City (cochineal dyeing); Athziri Magaña from Mexico City (shibori dyeing); Guillermo Pascual from Hueyapan, Puebla (punto de cruz embroidery)

Poem Poncho, 2016
Artisans: Manuela Salvado from Hueyapan, Puebla (pedal-weaving); Geovanna Olvera Guzmán from Mexico City (cochineal dyeing); Athziri Magaña from Mexico City (shibori dyeing); Guillermo Pascual from Hueyapan, Puebla (punto de cruz embroidery)

Teotitlán del Valle Poncho, 2016
Artisan: Beto Ruiz from Teotitlán del Valle, Oaxaca (pedal-weaving)

Enndy López Rebozo, 2016
Artisans: Fermin Escobar from Tenancingo, State of Mexico (rebozo); Enndy López from Tenango de Doria, Hidalgo (pata de gallo embroidery)

San Juan Chamula Poncho, 2016
Artisan: Ana Santis from San Juan Chamula, Chiapas (waist-loom weaving and mud-dyeing)

Waterfall Tecuan Pancho, 2016
Artisan: Maria Antonia Vazquez Perez from Chenalho, Chiapas (waist-loom weaving and mud-dyeing)

Miguel Gandert

Bathers, First Plaza, Albuquerque, 1983
Archival digital print
17 x 22 inches (43.2 x 55.9 cm)

Brothers, Coal Avenue SE, Albuquerque, 1983
Archival digital print
17 x 22 inches (43.2 x 55.9 cm)

Priscilla, Paulette and Martha Stevens, South Broadway, Albuquerque, 1983
Archival digital print
17 x 22 inches (43.2 x 55.9 cm)

Melissa Armijo, Eloy Montoya, and Richard "el Wino" Madrid, Albuquerque, 1983
Archival digital print
17 x 22 inches (43.2 x 55.9 cm)

Adam and Eden King, Lomas Blvd NW, Albuquerque, 1983
Archival digital print
17 x 22 inches (43.2 x 55.9 cm)

Little Frankie Alderete, Albuquerque, 1986
Archival digital print
17 x 22 inches (43.2 x 55.9 cm)

'51 Chevy, David and Cheryl, Albuquerque, 1986
Archival digital print
17 x 22 inches (43.2 x 55.9cm)

Jeffrey Gibson

LIKE A HAMMER, 2016
Installation
Garment: Canvas, wool, artificial sinew, glass beads, tin and metal jingles, nylon fringe
72 x 90 x 12 inches
(182.9 x 228.6 x 30.5 cm)
Drum: Wood, rawhide, acrylic paint
24 x 34 x 34 inches
(60.9 x 76 x 76 cm)
Single-channel video, approximately 15 minutes
Courtesy of the artist and
MARC STRAUS, New York

Jump into the Void, 2016
Oil stick on paper
Seven parts, each 40 x 26 inches
(101.6 x 66 cm)
Courtesy of the artist and
MARC STRAUS, New York

Jorge González

Banquetas Chéveres
(*Chéveres Stools*), 2015–16
Handmade portable stools, designed in dialogue with artisan Eustaquio Alers, as part of the Artisanal Route of Escuela de Oficios among the following workshops in Puerto Rico: Familia Alers-Méndez from Aguadilla; Familia Chéveres-Chéveres from Morovis; Felix Cordero from San German; Joe Hernández from Ciales; Guadalupe Villalobos from Ciales; and MAOF from San Juan

Calophyllum brasiliense and
Tabebuia heterophylla
Wood, woven tainted cotton cord
15 parts, each 22 x 19 x 17 inches
(55.8 x 48.2 x 43.1 cm)
† SITE Santa Fe commission

Maria Hupfield

It Is Never Just about Sustenance or Pleasure, 2016
Industrial felt, polyester thread, copper jingles, 2 x 4 pine lumber, acrylic paint, digital video
Boots: approximately 12 x 12 x 48 inches
(30.5 x 30.5 x 121.9 cm) overall
Mitts: 12 x 6 x 48 inches (30.5 x 15.2 x 121.9 cm) overall
† SITE Santa Fe commission
Performance presented Thursday, July 14, 2016, at SITE Santa Fe

Graciela Iturbide

Selected works from the series
Los que viven en la arena
(*Those Who Live in the Sand*), 1979
Gelatin silver prints
Dimensions variable

Sonya Kelliher-Combs

Remnant: Moose Jaw Bone, Musk Ox Fur, Polar Bear Fur, Seal Intestine Stitched, Seal Intestine, Wolf Fur, Caribou Antler, Human Hair, 2016
Acrylic polymer (synthetic paint skin), moose bone, caribou and reindeer fur, caribou antler, musk ox fur, wolf fur, polar bear fur, beaver fur, seal skin, walrus stomach, seal intestine, walrus ivory, moose hide, porcupine quill, feathers, human hair, and nylon thread Dimensions variable
† SITE Santa Fe commission

Zacharias Kunuk

Atanarjuat: The Fast Runner, 2001
Digital video transferred from film
172:00 minutes

David Lamelas

The Desert People, 1974
16mm film (sound, color)

48:00 minutes
Hammer Museum, Los Angeles.
Purchased through the Board of
Overseers Acquisition Fund.

Cildo Meireles

The Southern Cross, 1969–70
Oak, pine
3/8-inch (9mm) square
Courtesy of the artist and Galeria Luisa Strina, São Paulo

Marta Minujín

Comunicando con Tierra, 1976
Installation: Documents, photographs, mud construction, video
Dimensions variable
Courtesy of the artist and Henrique Faria, New York and Buenos Aires

Paulo Nazareth

DESERT FLOWER, 2016
Dimensions variable
Courtesy of the artist and Mendes Wood DM, São Paulo
† SITE Santa Fe commission

Abel Rodríguez

Selected drawings from the series *The Cycle of the Maloca Plants; Studies of Principal Trees in the Forest; Trees with Legends; The Cultivated Plants of the Center People; Drawings of Pineapples; Drawings of Cassavas and Other Tubers*, ca. 2009–16
Ink on paper
Courtesy of Tropenbos International Colombia

Rometti Costales

Winter Stories during Springtime, 2016
Mixed media installation
Dimensions variable
† SITE Santa Fe commission

Tanya Tagaq

Nanook of the North, 2016
Performance
Courtesy of the artist and Bernstein Artists Inc., Brooklyn
Presented Monday, August 29, 2016, at Lensic Theater, Santa Fe

Javier Téllez

To Have Done with the Judgment of God, 2016
Digital video, 37:19 minutes
† SITE Santa Fe co-commission with Koenig & Clinton, New York

Juana Valdes

Sienna Colored China Rags, 2012
Porcelain bone china
Six parts, each approximately
13 x 8 x 4 inches (33 x 20.3 x 10.2 cm)

Pulling at Me—a Thread, 2015
Nine embossed prints on 250g Somerset paper
Each 15 x 11 inches (38.1 x 27.9 cm)

Pierre Verger

Candomblé Joãnozinho da Goméa, Salvador, Brazil, 1946
Gelatin silver print
12 x 12 inches (30 x 30 cm)
Courtesy of Fundação Pierre Verger, Salvador, Brazil

Candomblé Joãnozinho da Goméa, Salvador, Brazil, 1946
Gelatin silver print
12 x 12 inches (30 x 30 cm)
Courtesy of Fundação Pierre Verger, Salvador, Brazil

Candomblé Joãnozinho da Goméa, Salvador, Brazil, 1946
Gelatin silver print
12 x 12 inches (30 x 30 cm)
Courtesy of Fundação Pierre Verger, Salvador, Brazil

Tambor, Belém, Brazil, 1948
Gelatin silver print
12 x 12 inches (30 x 30 cm)
Courtesy of Fundação Pierre Verger, Salvador, Brazil

Tambor, Belém, Brazil, 1948
Gelatin silver print
12 x 12 inches (30 x 30 cm)
Courtesy of Fundação Pierre Verger, Salvador, Brazil

Tambor, Belém, Brazil, 1948
Gelatin silver print
12 x 12 inches (30 x 30 cm)
Courtesy of Fundação Pierre Verger, Salvador, Brazil

Tambor, Belém, Brazil, 1948
Gelatin silver print
12 x 12 inches (30 x 30 cm)
Courtesy of Fundação Pierre Verger, Salvador, Brazil

Candomblé Opo Afonja, Salvador, Brazil, 1950
Gelatin silver print
12 x 12 inches (30 x 30 cm)
Courtesy of Fundação Pierre Verger, Salvador, Brazil

Pilon Oxala, Candomblé Opo Aganju, Salvador, Brazil, 1973
Gelatin silver print
12 x 12 inches (30 x 30 cm)
Courtesy of Fundação Pierre Verger, Salvador, Brazil

Labas, Candomblé Opo Aganju, Salvador, Brazil, 1974
Gelatin silver print
12 x 12 inches (30 x 30 cm)
Courtesy of Fundação Pierre Verger, Salvador, Brazil

Erika Verzutti

Cemetery with Snow, 2015
Concrete, clay, bronze, polyurethane, polystyrene, found objects
40 1/2 x 118 x 106 1/4 inches
(102.9 x 299.9 x 269.9 cm)
Courtesy of the artist and Lumber Room, Portland

SITE CENTER ARTISTS-IN-RESIDENCE PROJECTS

Francisca Benitez

Möbius Path, 2016
† SITE Santa Fe commission in collaboration with the New Mexico School for the Deaf

Raven Chacon

Native-American Composers Apprentice Project, 2004–present
Printed scores, speakers
† SITE Santa Fe commission

Pablo Helguera

The Hermit Battalion, 2016
Mixed media installation
† SITE Santa Fe commission

RESEARCH AND ARCHIVAL CONTRIBUTIONS

Margaret Randall

Installation of *El Corno Emplumado / The Plumed Horn*, issues 1–31 (1962–69)

Conrad Skinner

Paolo Soleri Amphitheater installation, with sculpted model by Eliza Naranjo Morse
With special thanks to the Institute of American Indian Arts Archives, Santa Fe, and the Soleri Archives at the Cosanti Foundation, Mayer, Arizona

IMAGE CREDITS

Cover: courtesy Institute of American Indian Arts Archives, Santa Fe, New Mexico; frontispiece: courtesy the artist and Galeria Luisa Strina, São Paulo; pages 4–5: courtesy Sprüth Magers and Jan Mot, Brussels; page 7: courtesy Museo Jumex; page 8: photograph by Paul Teeling; pages 34–35: courtesy the artist and Mendes Wood DM, São Paulo; page 36: photograph by Radius Books; pages 60–61: photograph by Studio Lux Photography, courtesy the artist and Galerie Sfeir-Semler, Hamburg and Beirut; page 62: photograph by Radius Books; pages 66–67: photograph by Kay V. Wiest, courtesy Institute of American Indian Arts Archives, Santa Fe, New Mexico; pages 70–71 courtesy Institute of American Indian Arts Archives, Santa Fe, New Mexico; pages 72–73: courtesy the artist and Mendes Wood DM, São Paulo; page 74: courtesy John Michael Kohler Arts Center; page 77: courtesy Instituto Lina Bo e P. M. Bardi; page 78: photograph by Studio Lux Photography, courtesy the artist and Galerie Sfeir-Semler, Hamburg and Beirut; page 81: photograph by Fredrik Nilsen; page 82: courtesy kurimanzutto, Mexico City; page 90: courtesy the artist and Chandra Cerrito Contemporary, Oakland, CA; page 94: courtesy Museo Jumex; page 98: photograph by Chris Arend, courtesy the artist and MARC STRAUS, NYC; page 102: photograph by Julie Nymann; page 109: courtesy Isuma Distribution International; page 110: courtesy Sprüth Magers and Jan Mot, Brussels; page 113: courtesy the artist and Galeria Luisa Strina, São Paulo; page 114: courtesy the artist and Henrique Faria, New York and Buenos Aires; page 117: courtesy the artist and Mendes Wood DM, São Paulo; page 118: courtesy Tropenbos International, Colombia; page 121: courtesy Galerie Jousse Entreprise, Paris; page 122: photograph by Nadya Kwandibens; page 125: courtesy Koenig & Clinton, New York; page 129: courtesy Fundação Pierre Verger, Salvador, Brazil; page 130: photograph by Rômulo Fialdin; pages 132–33: photograph by Liz Ligon; page 144: photograph by Timothy Schenck, courtesy Friends of the High Line; page 154: photograph by Kay V. Wiest, courtesy Institute of American Indian Arts Archives, Santa Fe, New Mexico

FOLLOWING SPREAD:
Miguel Gandert, *'51 Chevy, David and Cheryl, Albuquerque*, 1986

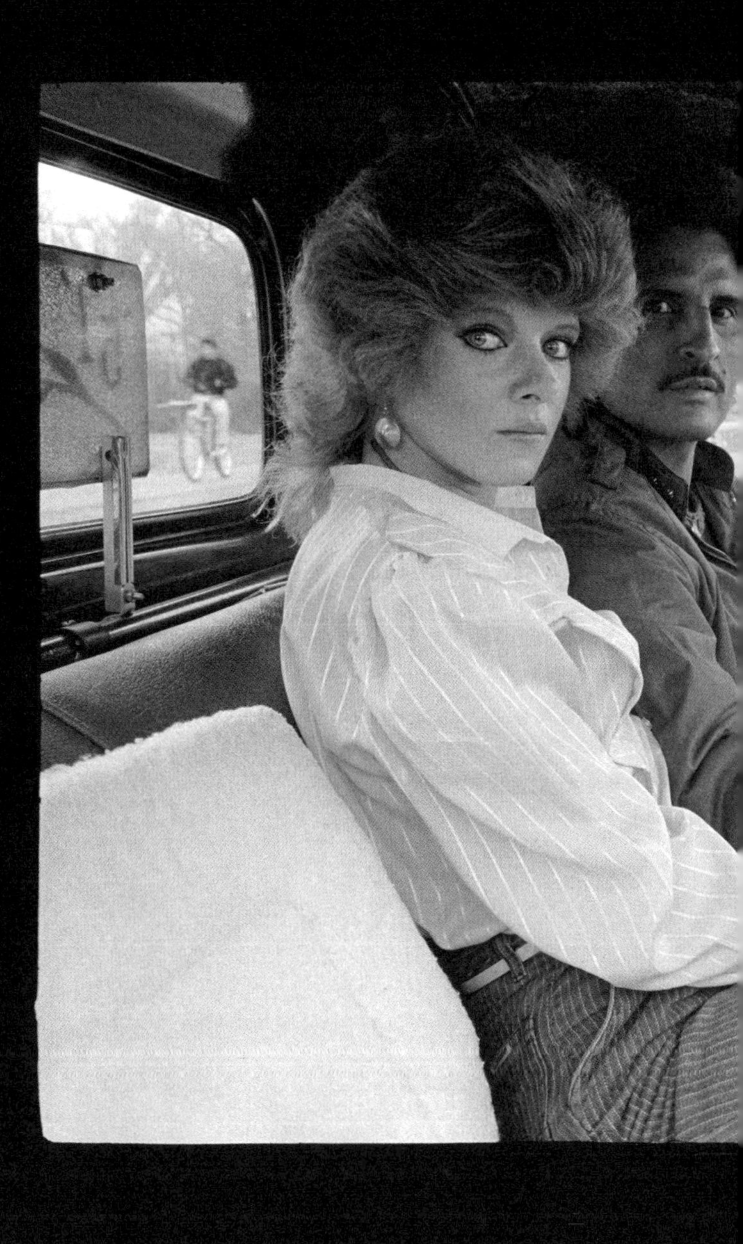

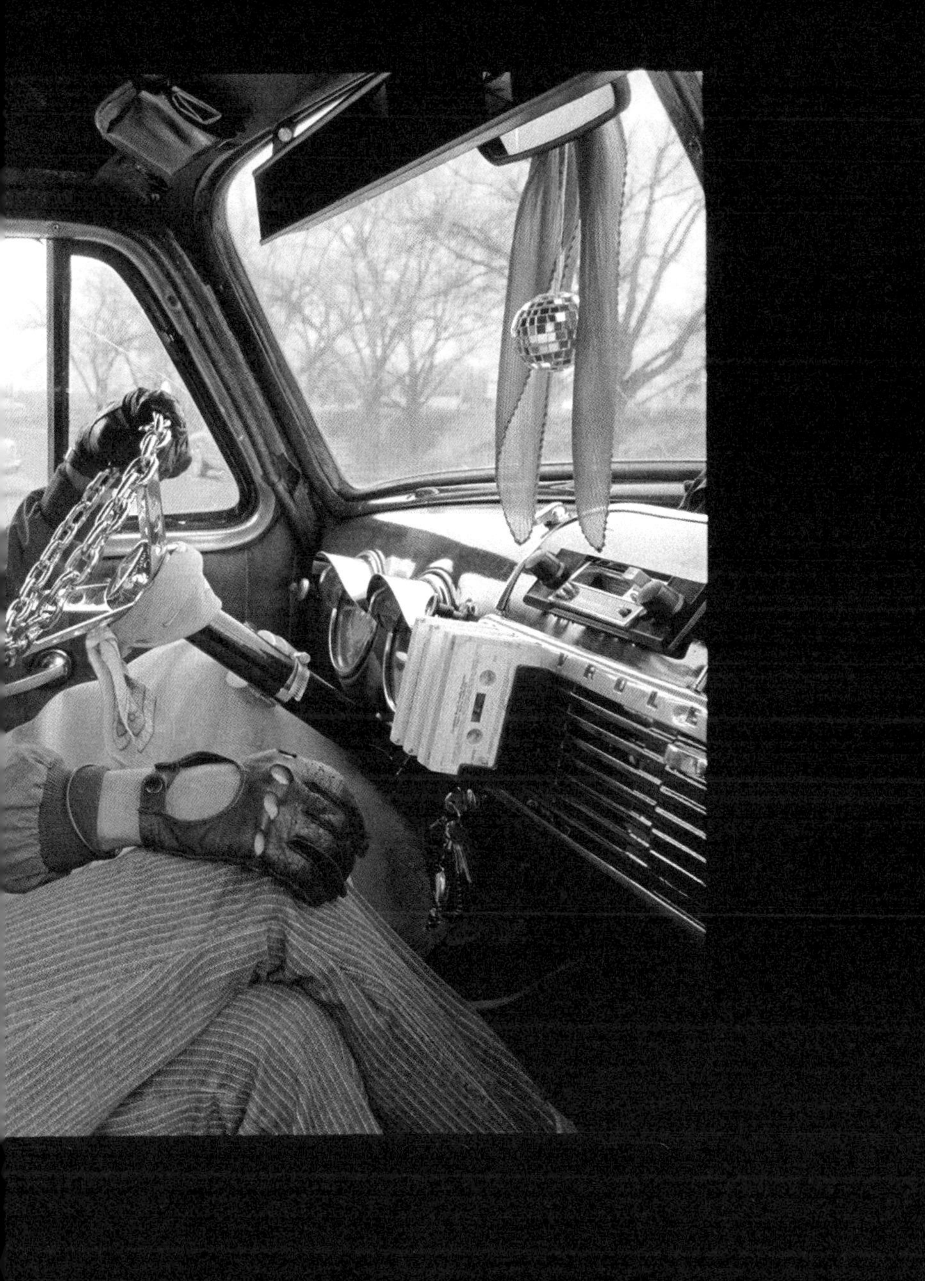

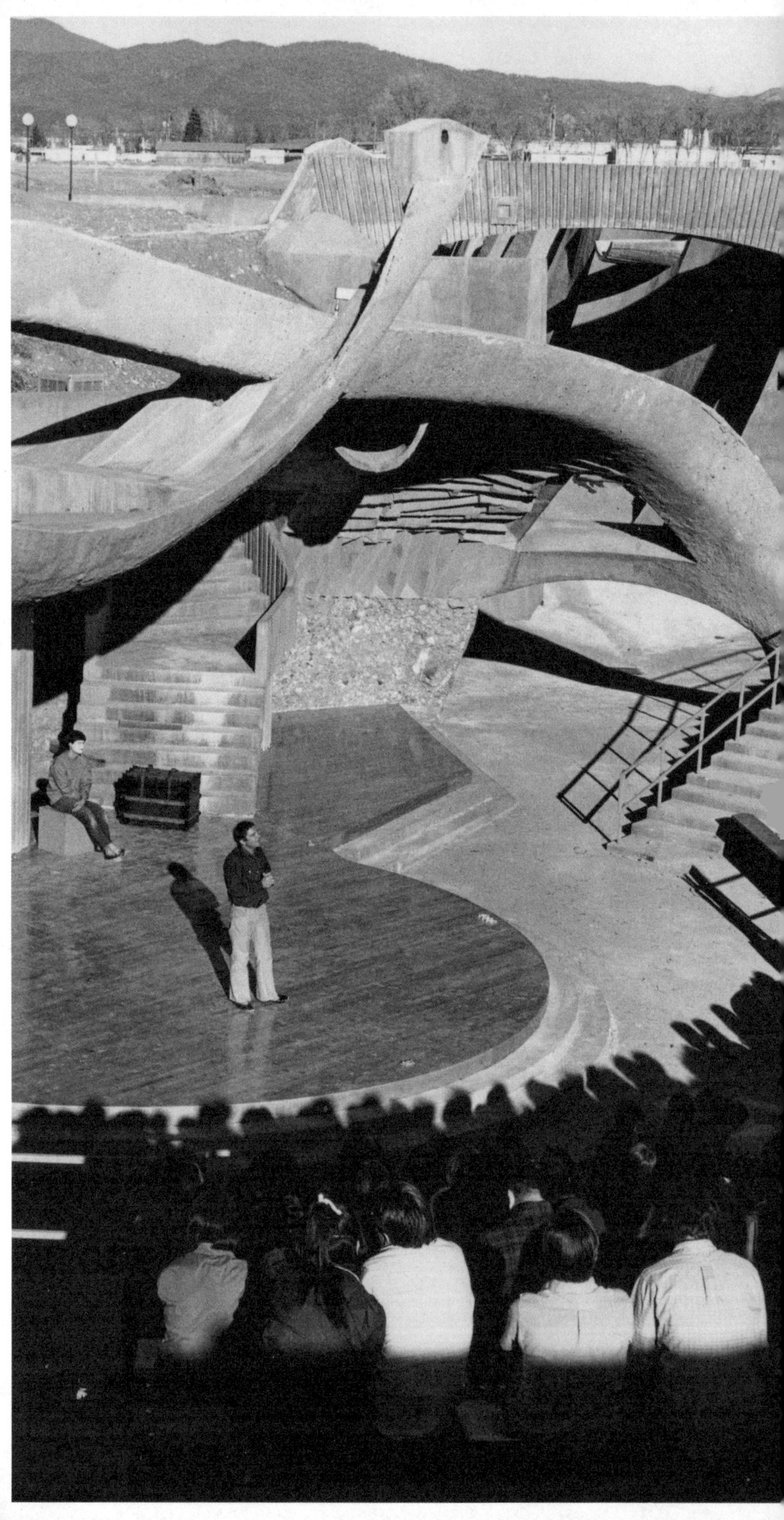

Acknowledgments

Realizing this ambitious and complex project would not have been possible without the commitment and hard work of so many. I am grateful to all who supported our efforts and dedicated themselves fully to this show.

My great admiration and gratitude go first to the talented, passionate team of curators who brought this exhibition together: Rocío Aranda-Alvarado, Kathleen Ash-Milby, Pip Day, Pablo León de la Barra, and Kiki Mazzucchelli. I am grateful for all that they contributed to our exhibition and institution over the past two years.

At SITE Santa Fe, a tireless team supported and collaborated with our curators. Co-curator of our inaugural SITElines exhibition in 2014, Candice Hopkins returned as Managing Curator to oversee the production and execution of *much wider than a line*. How lucky we are to have had Candice's intellect and sensibility back at SITE, providing invaluable continuity from one biennial exhibition to another. Working closely with Candice and me was Curatorial Assistant Brandee Caoba. On behalf of our entire team, I want to thank her for her many contributions to every aspect of this project and for her steadfast attention to detail all along the way. We owe huge thanks as well to Sage Sommer, Exhibitions Manager and Registrar, who coordinated the installation, kept a steady eye on planning, and managed every facet of the artworks' safe travel to SITE. Special thanks go to the outstanding installation team who, under the direction of John Cross, our immeasurably talented Lead Preparator, skillfully met the demands of this show. No mention of our exhibitions team would be complete without acknowledging the generative role of SITE's former Curator, Janet Dees, during the formative stages of this project. We thank Janet for all her important contributions.

Beyond our fine exhibitions team, there are many other staff members who helped make this show a reality. They have been essential to the success of this endeavor, and we are grateful for their talents. We express our appreciation to Joanne Lefrak, Director of Education and Outreach, who collaborated closely with the curatorial team. Joanne has established SITE Center as a hub for visionary SITElines programming, research, and long-term community-engaged artist projects that are expanding and deepening our connection to place and community. We would also like to acknowledge Winoka Begay, Indigenous Outreach Fellow, for her work connecting us with Native communities. We thank Anne Wrinkle, Director of External Affairs, who skillfully led our marketing and public

OPPOSITE:
Performance at the Paolo Soleri Amphitheater, Santa Fe, New Mexico, 1971

relations efforts and enhanced our work's visibility. We thank Cathy Putnam, Deputy Director and Chief Financial Officer, for supporting our work at every stage. We acknowledge the tireless efforts of SITE's Development Department, including Associate Director of Development Shelby Salmon; Individual Gifts and Membership Manager Paisley Mason; Events Manager Johanna Frenz; and Development Assistant Sophia Pushkin, who have focused their energies on fund-raising for the exhibition, and on conceiving and implementing extraordinary events to celebrate it. Our special thanks go to Amanda Gould, Executive Assistant, for juggling a vast number of details related to research, communications, and hospitality, and for so much more.

In the community, generous colleagues and collaborators facilitated our work. At the Institute of American Indian Arts, we thank Jamison Chas Banks, Adjunct Faculty in Printmaking; Ryan Flahive, Archivist; Robert Martin, President; and Lloyd Kiva New's widow, Ayshen New; at the New Mexico School for the Deaf, Shira Grabelsky and Keri-Lynn McBride; and at the Santa Fe Playhouse, Eliot Fisher, Vaughn Irving, and Andy Primm. We extend thanks also to historian Marcus Gottschalk; Rick Hendricks, State Historian; Frank Buffalo Hyde at Stephen's, A Consignment Gallery; Robert Martin, former Executive and Artistic Director of the Lensic Theater; Lois Rudnick, Professor Emerita of American Studies; and Chevo Serna at the Santa Fe Tree Farm.

There were many others farther afield whose counsel made an important contribution to the project. We wish to acknowledge these colleagues and friends, such as Adrienne Edwards at Performa, New York; Sue Kirsch, Jeff Stein, and Tomiaki Tamura at the Cosanti Foundation in Mayer, Arizona; José Roca at FLORA ars+natura in Bogotá; and Sally Talent and the Liverpool Biennial team. We are also grateful to former SITElines curator Lucía Sanromán, who offered invaluable support and advice over the course of the development of SITElines.2016.

Also crucial to the project was the support and kind assistance of the staff at many galleries and artists' studios, who include: Akiki Aoki at Galeria Vermelho, São Paulo; Sue Bernstein, Manager, Tanya Tagaq; Annie Bielski, Jeffrey Gibson Studio, Hudson, New York; Maggie Clinton, Peter Gynd, and Christopher Saunders at Koenig & Clinton, New York; Henrique Faria, Alexandra Schoolman, and Eugenia Sucre at Henrique Faria Fine Art, New York; Leticia Florence at Galpão Fortes Vilaça, São Paulo; Nidia Holguin, Studio Margarita Cabrera, El Paso; Jeanine Jablonski and The Lumber Room, Portland, Oregon; Julie Jensen, videographer for Maria Hupfield; José Kuri, Amalia Hinojosa, Martha Reta, and Julia Villaseñor at kurimanzutto, Mexico City; Diego Lacayo Jaén, assistant to Carla Fernández, Mexico City; Michy Marxuach at Beta Local, San Juan, Puerto Rico; Ernesto Oroza, assistant to William Cordova, Miami; Oswaldo Ruiz, Studio Graciela Iturbide, Mexico City; Renato Silva at Mendes Wood DM, São Paulo; Marc Straus and Ken Tan at MARC STRAUS Gallery, New York; Luisa Strina and Thamy Echigo at Luisa Strina Gallery, São Paulo; and Anna Szaflarski, Studio Castillo Deball, Berlin. For pulling together the works from these locations and elsewhere, we acknowledge the important role played by Bob Simon and his stellar logistics team at Transport Consultants International (TCI), Cranford, New Jersey.

We are grateful to the following public lenders and museum and foundation staff members for entrusting us with their works and assisting in the loan process: Archives of the Institute of American Indian Arts, Santa Fe; Catalina Vargas Tovar at FLORA ars+natura, Bogotá; Portland McCormick, Aram Moshayedi, and Michael Nock at the Hammer Museum, Los Angeles; Ashley Tickle at High Line Art, New York; Marcella Carvalho at Instituto Lina Bo e P. M. Bardi, São Paulo; Roberto Rodrigues at Fundação Pierre Verger, Salvador, Brazil; Carlos Rodríguez at Tropenbos International, Bogotá; and Vtape, Toronto.

Throughout the launch of our show, John Melick and the team at Blue Medium in New York guided our national PR efforts and propelled our work onto a larger stage. We thank them for their exceptional work.

For their unwavering belief in our project, we are grateful to SITE Santa Fe's Board of Directors. Under the steadfast leadership of Andrew Wallerstein, SITE's Board has contributed immeasurably to our work. We are grateful for their engagement and their commitment to SITElines and the bold new direction it represents. We are deeply appreciative of the leadership funding support of Karen and Steve Berkowitz, Jeanne and Mickey Klein, Jim Manning and Dana Pope Manning, John and Anne Marion, Marlene Meyerson, Marleen De Bode Olivié and Marc Olivié, Mary Sloane and Andrew Wallerstein, Courtney Finch Taylor and Scott Taylor, and Carl and Marilynn Thoma.

For championing our show early on with vital and generous support, we wish to acknowledge the leadership grant of The Andy Warhol Foundation for the Arts. Grants from the National Endowment for the Arts and the Millstream Fund also provided crucial support. We are grateful to the Davidoff Art Initiative for their support of the Caribbean artists in our show and to Avalon Trust for their support of our exhibition's public programming. The Canada Council for the Arts provided valuable support for the participation of Canadian artists in the exhibition.

For helping us to realize the ambition and vision of this project, we are indebted to David Chickey and Montana Currie of Skolkin + Chickey for their beautiful design of this publication. We thank Nora Dolan, Catalogue Manager, for expertly pulling together the many components of this book and looking after every detail. We are grateful once again to have worked with Lucy Flint, our talented editor, whose counsel and wisdom have produced another SITElines book we can be very proud of.

Finally, we express our deepest gratitude to the artists, whose exceptional works and probing aesthetic inquiries provided the inspiration for this exhibition.

— Irene Hofmann

Exhibition Curators

Rocío Aranda-Alvarado

(b. in Santiago, Chile; lives in New York, U.S.A.)

Rocío Aranda-Alvarado has been with El Museo del Barrio in New York since 2009. Her curatorial work and research is focused on modern and contemporary art of the Americas. She is currently working on *A Brief History of (Some) Things*, an exhibition exploring the persistence of pre-Hispanic imagery in contemporary art. She recently organized *PRESENTE! The Young Lords in New York*, *CUT N MIX: Contemporary Collage*, and *MUSEUM STARTER KIT: Open With Care*—celebrating the museum's forty-fifth anniversary—and several of El Museo's biennials of emerging artists. She was formerly Curator at the Jersey City Museum, where she organized retrospective exhibitions of the work of Chakaia Booker (2004) and Raphael Montañez Ortiz (2006), and group shows on various themes, including *Tropicalisms: Subversions of Paradise* (2006), *The Superfly Effect* (2004), and *The Feminine Mystique* (2007). Aranda-Alvarado holds degrees in Art History from the University of Maryland, Tulane University, and the Graduate Center of the City University of New York.

Kathleen Ash-Milby

(b. in Albuquerque, U.S.A.; lives in Maplewood, New Jersey)

Kathleen Ash-Milby is Associate Curator at the Smithsonian National Museum of the American Indian (NMAI) in New York. She has organized numerous contemporary art exhibitions at the museum, including *Kay WalkingStick: An American Artist* (co-organized with David Penney) (2015), *C. Maxx Stevens: House of Memory* (2012), *HIDE: Skin as Material and Metaphor* (2010), and *Off the Map: Landscape in the Native Imagination* (2007). She was the co-curator, with Truman Lowe, of *Edgar Heap of Birds: Most Serene Republics*, a public art installation and collateral project for the 2007 Venice Biennale. She was Curator and Co-director of the American Indian Community House Gallery in New York City from 2000 to 2005. A member of the Navajo Nation, Ash-Milby holds an M.A. in Native-American art history from the University of New Mexico.

Pip Day

(b. in Chelmsford, U.K.; lives in Montreal, Canada)

Since 2012, Pip Day has been Director/Curator of SBC Gallery of Contemporary Art in Montreal, where she developed the Focus Programs Sovereignty and Água Viva. Previously, Day was as an independent curator, writer, and educator in the arts, primarily in Mexico City, New York, and London. In 2003, she founded teratoma, the first graduate-level curatorial studies program in Latin America, and RIM, an international residency program for curators, artists, and critics in Mexico City. In

Mexico, she also established el instituto, which generated exhibitions and events such as *Spatial Practices in Revolution* and *Talk Show*. Day has published numerous texts on art and culture, has taught in curatorial graduate programs at Bard College and at Goldsmiths College, and has lectured widely in university and other cultural contexts. In the late 1990s, Day was Curator at Artists Space in New York. She holds a B.A. in Art History from the University of Toronto and an M.A. in Curatorial Studies from Bard College.

Pablo León de la Barra

(b. in Mexico City, Mexico; lives in Rio de Janeiro, Brazil)

Pablo León de la Barra is the Guggenheim UBS MAP Curator, Latin America, at the Solomon R. Guggenheim Museum. From 2014 to 2016 he served as Director of Casa França Brasil in Rio de Janeiro. His exhibitions include *To Be Political It Has to Look Nice* at Apexart and Art in General in New York (2003); *PR04 Biennale* (co-curator) in Puerto Rico (2004); *Incidents of Mirror Travel in Yucatan and Elsewhere* at the Museo Tamayo, Mexico City (2011); *Under the Same Sun: Art from Latin America Today* at the Guggenheim Museum in New York, Museo Jumex in Mexico City, and South London Gallery (2014–16); *Dominique Gonzalez-Foerster / Temporama* at the Museu de Arte Moderna, Rio de Janeiro (2015); and *United States of Latin America* at the Museum of Contemporary Art Detroit (2015). León de la Barra writes frequently, and is editor of the blog "Centre for the Aesthetic Revolution." He holds a Ph.D. in History and Theories from the Architectural Association in London.

Kiki Mazzucchelli

(b. in São Paulo, Brazil; lives in London, U.K./São Paulo)

Kiki Mazzucchelli is an independent curator and writer working in London and São Paulo. She organized the exhibitions *Tonico Lemos Auad / That Which Cannot Be Repaired* at Pivô, São Paulo (2015). Other recent curatorial projects include the two-part exhibition *Mythologies* and *Mythologies by Proxy* (co-curated) at the Cité Internationale des Arts, Paris, and the Museu de Arte Moderna de São Paulo (2011, 2013); *Beyond the Avant-Garde / Bienal Naïfs do Brasil*, at SESC Piracicaba in São Paulo (2012); and the radio program *OIDARADIO Conversations Developed for the 30th São Paulo Bienal with Mobile Radio and Resonance.fm* (2012). Recent publications include "The São Paulo Biennial and the Rise of Contemporary Brazilian Art," in *Contemporary Art Brazil*, ed. Hossein Amirsadeghi and Catherine Petitgas (2012) and a chapter on the São Paulo art scene in *Art Cities of the Future: 21st Century Avant-Gardes* (2013). Holding an M.A. in Visual Cultures from Goldsmiths College, she is a Ph.D. candidate at TrAIN (University of the Arts London).

Contributors

Irene Hofmann

(b. in New York, U.SA.; lives in Santa Fe, New Mexico)

Irene Hofmann is the Phillips Director and Chief Curator of SITE Santa Fe, a position she has held since 2011. In her role at SITE she is expanding the breadth and reach of SITE's exhibition program, which includes reimagining SITE's signature biennial exhibition as a new series of connected biennials with a focus on contemporary art from the Americas. Over the last two decades she has curated new commissions and solo exhibitions by artists including Enrique Martínez Celaya, Jason Dodge, Futurefarmers, Joseph Grigely, Fabrice Gygi, Fritz Haeg, Iñigo Manglano-Ovalle, Marjetica Potrc, Mary Temple, and Mungo Thomson. She has also held positions at the Contemporary Museum, Baltimore; the Orange County Museum of Art; Cranbrook Art Museum; the Art Institute of Chicago; the Walker Art Center; and the New Museum of Contemporary Art. She holds a B.A. in Art History from Washington University, and an M.A. in Modern Art History, Theory, and Criticism from The School of the Art Institute of Chicago.

Candice Hopkins

(b. in Whitehorse, Canada; lives in Albuquerque, New Mexico, U.S.A.)

Candice Hopkins is Managing Curator for SITElines.2016. She is a curatorial advisor for the upcoming documenta 14, and has held curatorial positions at the IAIA Museum of Contemporary Native Arts, National Gallery of Canada, Western Front, and Walter Phillips Gallery. Hopkins's writings on history, art, and vernacular architecture have been published by MIT Press, BlackDog Publishing, Revolver, New York University, Fillip Review, and the National Museum of the American Indian, among others. She has lectured widely, including a keynote presentation with Hetti Perkins on the "sovereign imagination" for dOCUMENTA (13). She is co-curator of the exhibitions *Close Encounters: The Next 500 Years*, at Plug In Institute of Contemporary Art, Winnipeg Art Gallery, and Urban Shaman Contemporary Aboriginal Art (2011); *Sakahàn International Indigenous Art*, at the National Gallery of Canada (2013); and the SITElines.2014 biennial *Unsettled Landscapes*, at SITE Santa Fe (2014). Hopkins has co-edited the books *Jimmie Durham: The Second Particle Wave Theory* (2005) and *Recipes for an Encounter* (2010).

Joanne Lefrak

(b. in Long Branch, New Jersey, U.S.A.; lives in Santa Fe, New Mexico)

Joanne Lefrak is Director of Education and Outreach at SITE Santa Fe. She is also a visual artist and a teacher. She has worked at SITE for over twelve years. Specializing in community outreach, Lefrak has developed, and leads, many innovative programs at SITE that engage students at the high-school, college, and graduate level, as well as adult visitors. She works on long-term community-engaged projects with artists and presents public programs with art-world luminaries. She also organizes a biennial retreat for museum educators in order to generate and maintain a high level of discourse around museum education. Joanne serves as Chair of the City of Santa Fe Children and Youth Commission, and was the recipient of the 2014 Mayor's Award for Excellence in the Arts in Santa Fe. She holds a B.S. in Studio Art, with a minor in Art History, from Skidmore College and an M.F.A. from Montclair State University.

Conrad Skinner

(b. in Boston, U.S.A.; lives in Santa Fe, New Mexico)

Conrad Skinner, AIA, is a practicing architect whose designs are largely inspired by the physical, visual, and auditory passage that runs all the way through the house that Adolf Loos designed for Tristan Tzara on Avenue Junot in Paris. Skinner worked as studio assistant to Dennis Oppenheim, and during the 1980s participated in events with the Colab group at ABC NoRio and other venues. He holds a B.A. from Reed College and an M.Arch. from the University of New Mexico. Beginning with Survival Research Laboratories' participation in the Santa Fe Institute Artificial Life Conference in 1990, Skinner has programmed multidisciplinary events. In 2014, he brought Vito Acconci to the American Institute of Architects Western Mountain Regional Conference. Conrad has written on Provoke Era Japanese photography, Pietro Belluschi's Equitable Building, dancers Eiko and Koma, Walter DeMaria's Lightning Field, and the work of Nic Nicosia. He is currently working on a history of the Paolo Soleri Amphitheater in Santa Fe.

SITE Santa Fe Board

SITE Santa Fe Staff

Brandee Caoba
Curatorial Assistant

Matthew Contos
School Programs Manager

John Cross
Lead Preparator

Caley Dennis
Public Programs Assistant

Johanna Frenz
Events Manager

Amanda Gould
Executive Assistant

Bill Hinsvark
Visitor Services & Publications Associate

Irene Hofmann
Phillips Director & Chief Curator

Amanda Lee
Education Coordinator

Joanne Lefrak
Director of Education & Outreach

Drew Lenihan
Digital Communications & Social Media Coordinator

Paisley Mason
Individual Giving Manager

Stanley Olivarez
Facility Manager

Sophia Pushkin
Development Assistant

Catherine Putnam
Deputy Director & Chief Financial Officer

Shelby Salmon
Associate Director of Development

Laura San Román
Design Assistant

Sage Sommer
Exhibitions Manager & Registrar

Don White
Accounting Associate

Anne Wrinkle
Director of External Affairs

Susan Young
Visitor Services Manager

SITE GUIDES

Ashley Blanton
John McKissick
Elizabeth Mesh
Ryan Miller
Deborah Morris
Valeria Neri
Laura San Román
Timothy Scott
Liana Woodward

INSTALLATION CREW

Johnny Bell
Damon Griffith
Sabrina Griffith
Maxwell Holmes
Drew Lenihan
Jebb Norton
Keith Ryan Riggs
John Simmons

This catalogue accompanies the exhibition

much wider than a line
SITElines.2016: New Perspectives on Art of the Americas
SITE Santa Fe
July 16, 2016 - January 8, 2017

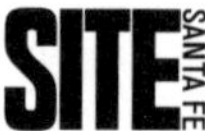

SITE Santa Fe nurtures innovation, discovery, and inspiration through the art of today.

SITE Santa Fe
1606 Paseo de Peralta, Santa Fe, NM 87501 USA
t: 505.989.1199 www.sitesantafe.org

Available through
D.A.P. / Distributed Art Publishers
155 Sixth Avenue, 2nd Floor, New York, NY 10013 USA
t: 212. 627.1999 www.artbook.com

ISBN: 978-0-9856602-3-9

Library of Congress Cataloguing-in-Publication Data available from the publisher upon request.

Printed by The Avery Group, Shapco Printing, Inc., Minneapolis

Catalogue Manager: Nora Kabat Dolan
Editor: Lucy Flint
Design: David Chickey, with Montana Currie
Translation Editors: Jen Hofer, Kiki Mazzucchelli, Julia Smith

Cover image: Paolo Soleri Amphitheater, Santa Fe, New Mexico, 1970

BACK ENDPAPERS:
Frontispiece of *El Corno Emplumado / The Plumed Horn*, no. 25 (January 1968)

el corno emplumado

número 25 • enero 1968

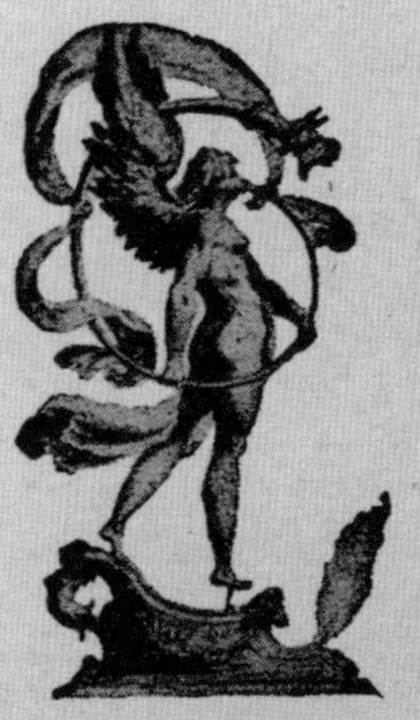

the plumed horn

number 25 • january 1968